Beneath the
Big Top

This book is dedicated to all my grandchildren, so that they too may tell the magical story of the circus to their grandchildren in the future.

The author clowning around in the show *Pellagrini*. (*Photograph courtesy of Yvonne Notzon*)

A SOCIAL HISTORY OF THE CIRCUS IN BRITAIN

Steve Ward

PEN & SWORD HISTORY

First published in Great Britain in 2014 by
Pen & Sword History
an imprint of
Pen & Sword Books Ltd
47 Church Street
Barnsley
South Yorkshire
S70 2AS

ISBN 978 1 78303 049 1

A CIP catalogue record for this book is available from the British
Library

Typeset in Ehrhardt by
Mac Style Ltd, Bridlington, East Yorkshire
Printed and bound in the UK by CPI Group (UK) Ltd, Croydon,
CRO 4YY

Pen & Sword Books Ltd incorporates the imprints of Pen & Sword
Archaeology, Atlas, Aviation, Battleground, Discovery, Family History,
History, Maritime, Military, Naval, Politics, Railways, Select,
Transport, True Crime, and Fiction, Frontline Books, Leo Cooper,
Praetorian Press, Seaforth Publishing and Wharncliffe.

For a complete list of Pen & Sword titles please contact
PEN & SWORD BOOKS LIMITED
47 Church Street, Barnsley, South Yorkshire, S70 2AS, England
E-mail: enquiries@pen-and-sword.co.uk
Website: www.pen-and-sword.co.uk

Contents

Acknowledgements   vi
Foreword   viii
Introduction   ix

Chapter 1   From Ancient Roots to the Restoration: The Circus
                 Survives   1

Chapter 2   Acrobats, Ale and Aristocrats: The Eighteenth Century
                 Age of Decadence   16

Chapter 3   Clowns, Competition and Conflagrations: The Circus
                 is Born!   33

Chapter 4   The Queen and the 'Lion King': The Rise of the
                 Nineteenth Century Menageries   51

Chapter 5   Spectacles, Disasters and Murder: The Victorian
                 Circus   72

Chapter 6   Railways and Rings: The Circus in Nineteenth
                 Century America   100

Chapter 7   Magic, Movies and Music Halls: Stiff Competition
                 for the Late Nineteenth Century British Circus   117

Chapter 8   The Circus Goes to War: 1900–1919   134

Chapter 9   Decades of Depression: The Circus Between the
                 Wars   151

Chapter 10   Fighting for Survival: The 1940s–1960s   173

Chapter 11   And So the Wheel Turns: The Circus from 1970 to
                 the Present   190

Select Bibliography   205
Sources on the British Circus Industry   207
Index   212

Acknowledgements

In compiling this book I have received help and support from many people. Although they are far too numerous to mention in full, I am grateful for the assistance they have given, but I would specifically like to thank the following:

The staff of the National Fairground Archive in Sheffield for their tireless help in my research; Jen Newby for her constant advice and support; Bob Bain of the Scottish Music Hall and Variety Theatre Society; Matt Buck of the Malt Cross Music Hall in Nottingham; Keith Wardell; T.W. Ward CNC Machinery Ltd Sheffield; David Jamieson of the Circus Friends Association; Kitty Ross, the Curator of Social History at Leeds Museums and Galleries Service; Edgar Pickles and the Kippax and District Historical Society; Jim Riley of Skylight Circus; Charlie Holland; Chuck Johnson of the American Youth Circus Organisation for their help and support; Martin Burton of Zippo's Circus; Circus San Pedro Piccolino; Gerry Cottle; Norman Barrett, Arthur Pedlar and the Rapide Brothers for their hospitality, interviews and help; Mrs Erica Parnell, Simon West, and all other unsuspecting members of the public at Heathrow airport for their interviews ... and finally my wife Linda, who has become a circus 'widow' throughout this project.

In memory of Mrs Erica Parnell, 1921–2013.

Foreword

'Circus is good for you. It is the only spectacle I know that while you watch it gives the quality of a truly happy dream.'
(Ernest Hemingway, The Circus, 1954)

I am a josser – a person who was not born into the circus world, although a couple of my distant ancestors were comedy acrobats. My journey into the circus has been a roundabout one: through theatre, *Commedia dell'Arte*, slapstick, clowning, performing, teaching and directing. Most of my circus work has been with young people, and the joy and wonder on their faces as they enter into the dream world of the circus has never ceased to amaze me.

This book reveals how that dream world evolved. It is a history book, yes, but not an academic catalogue of circuses and performers. You will not find your flying trapeze-artist uncle in here or the obscure circus in which he performed, unless by pure coincidence. *Beneath the Big Top* has been written for entertainment and instruction. Those of you who are circus fans will find something new in this book, I hope, some aspect of the circus you never knew about. For those with just a passing interest, I intend to open up the world of the circus as you have never imagined it, uncovering the triumphs and disasters, the trials and tribulations and the downright bizarre.

The writing of this book has been a fascinating journey. In my research, whether trawling through pages and pages of old newspapers and documents, listening to the stories of those who work in the circus or who fondly remember childhood visits to it, I have come to appreciate just how much it is part of our social history. It is a very British institution. I hope very much that as you dip into this book, you too will be drawn into the dream world of the circus.

Steve Ward
Leeds, 2014

Photo by Baron de Rakoczy, A.R.P.S.

COCO
The Clown

With the Compliments of BERTRAM MILLS CIRCUS

Coco the Clown; my childhood hero. Image from an advertising leaflet given out to members of the public in the 1960s. *(Author's collection)*

Introduction

As a small child in the mid-1950s, I was taken to see the Bertram Mills Circus when it made its annual visit to Gloucester. It was the first time that I had ever visited a circus and we went as a whole family. My mother recalls that I was 'spellbound' with the whole event, but what I remember most vividly is the damp, earthy smell inside the tent, the rough wooden seat, the music and the vibrant colours, especially Coco the Clown's crazy costume. To me as a small boy, he was a very tall, painted, ginger-haired monstrosity in a colourfully loud and baggy checked coat. He was terrifying and yet fascinating at the same time – he scared me, yet he made me laugh – and from the moment he pulled me out of the audience to take part in one of his 'tricks', I was hooked! Since that day I have had a life-long fascination with the circus.

So when some years ago my three-year-old granddaughter Chloe suddenly announced, 'Let's play circus', I was pleasantly surprised. For the next half an hour she became the clown with a funny walk, the high wire artiste balancing across an imaginary rope, and the juggler pretending to juggle three balls. Nothing unusual in that, you might think, but she had not yet visited a circus. So how did this three-year-old child have an understanding of what a circus is?

Circus seems to have permeated our culture since the development of its recognisable modern form in the late eighteenth century, through the 'father' of the circus, Philip Astley and his trick riding. Circus imagery has appeared in many forms, some ephemeral, such as advertising.

In the example overleaf, a beautifully painted window display board from 1900 for Greensmith's Derby Dog Biscuits depicts a dog jumping through a paper hoop being held by a painted clown of the period, whilst another hidden clown tempts the dog with a Derby Dog Biscuit. Other forms of circus imagery are more lasting, and many well-known artists, such as Degas and Seurat, took their inspiration from the circus of their time.

Toulouse-Lautrec produced a remarkable series of 39 drawings entitled *Au Cirque* (*At the Circus*), including a beautiful coloured crayon on paper sketch from 1899 of a wire walker, entitled *Danseuse de cord* (*High wire*

Advertising placard for Greensmith's Derby Dog Biscuits, c.1900: Circus themes were common in advertising. *(Author's collection)*

walker). Lautrec has captured the moment of suspense as, gripping her seat with both hands, she stretches her right foot tentatively forward onto the wire before stepping out; one can feel the tension and drama of the scene.

In the mid-twentieth century, popular children's author Enid Blyton produced 15 books featuring the circus. Since the early days of cinema, with the 1928 silent film *The Circus* by Charlie Chaplin and Disney's *Dumbo* (1941), circus has also been a popular subject for filmmakers.

We have long been surrounded by references to the circus – on postage stamps, advertising trade cards, cigarette cards, tea cards and television – and it even appears on walls as street art. Colourful circus posters and flyers are a common sight in many towns and cities. One belonging to the Moscow State Circus depicts trapeze artists flying over the onion domes of St Basil's Cathedral in Moscow, while that of Circus Perrier shows a colourful riot of clown firemen. Street performers entertain us with juggling, unicycling, fire eating and other seemingly mysterious circus skills.

Our lives are surrounded by images of the circus, even if we do not always realise it. Today, for most people 'the circus' is little more than an amusing spectacle, populated by clowns, jugglers, high wire, trapeze, and even performing animals. There would be little, if any, mention made of artistry, drama or beauty.

Sadly, today the circus is still quite commonly perceived as a vulgar form of entertainment. But that is what, in essence, it is. Vulgar, common, of the people, it has its roots deep within the community culture. Many of the basic physical circus skills that we see performed today have roots within folk cultures. The juggler, manipulating a variety and number of objects in time and space has always been a source of wonder – someone who has extraordinary powers. In Japan, according to legend, the overawing power of a nine-ball juggler even put an end to a battle.

A 1960s circus-themed birthday card, which challenges the child to remove both the monkey and the ring from the card without tearing or bending it. (*Author's collection*)

Acrobats, tightrope walkers and stilt walkers were once all given an elevated place in the eyes of society due to their skills. In 1861, at the Alhambra Theatre in Leicester Square, a young Frenchman named Jules Leotard performed daring feats of agility high in the air, swinging from trapeze bar to trapeze bar; he had invented the flying trapeze act. His skills captured the imagination of the public and he became an instant success, to the extent that George Leybourne was inspired to write the lyrics to the popular song of 1867, 'The Daring Young Man on the Flying Trapeze'. Leotard also gave his name to the skin-tight, one-piece garment he used in his performances.

Charles Blondin also enthralled the public when, in 1859, he stretched a rope across Niagara Falls and became the first man to walk the 1,100 feet across the gorge. *The Chicago Tribune* recorded that over 100,000 people witnessed the event. Blondin became so famous that, when the Prince of Wales invited him to re-enact the event at the Crystal Palace in London in 1861, he controversially wheeled his five-year-old daughter across the rope. Blondin remained popular for the rest of his life and even had the 'Blondin March' composed in his honour.

Even today someone who can stand on another's shoulders or juggle with fire is seen as something out of the ordinary, above normal, imbued with

Advertisement for 'Elliman's Universal Embrocation' from the *Illustrated London News*, 1889. (*Author's collection*)

Roll up and enjoy the show! Crowds gather at the main entrance to the circus, c. 1910. *(Library of Congress)*

powers that the average person does not possess. Is this perhaps due to some basic need to have 'magic' in our everyday lives? Ritual, ceremony, dance, physical skills and magic all play a role in our folk cultures creating a feeling of common being, and circus is part of that universal folk culture from which we all developed. Every culture contains these common elements, even if not identified as specifically 'circus'. The circus has been, and always will be, part of our lives.

So let's settle back in our seats and enjoy the show beneath the big top. The lights have been dimmed, the overture has ended with a crash of cymbals and a spotlight picks out the velvet curtains covering the entrance to the ring. Through the curtains steps a tall man resplendent in his scarlet tailcoat, polished riding boots and black top hat. In his left hand he carries a riding whip which he flourishes in the air. He raises his hat and welcomes the crowd, old and young alike, to the big top and the magic of the circus. The band strikes up again, the curtains are drawn back and the entry of the circus artists begins.

Chapter One

From Ancient Roots to the Restoration: The Circus Survives

The sun beats down on the central courtyard in the Palace of Knossos in Crete. It is early afternoon and the crowd, in holiday mood, has been gathering since morning, thronging the Royal Road from the nearby port of Heraklion up towards the palace. Latecomers, pushing through the central gateway, jostle for position with the already eager spectators settled around the edge of the courtyard, as the crowd murmurs in anticipation. The courtyard, covering a space roughly equal to that of half the area of a football pitch, is surrounded by the whitewashed walls of the palace, decorated with brightly coloured frescoes; reds, blues and yellows all reflecting in the bright sun.

Then the rumbling of the crowd swells as, through one of the gateways, the acrobats enter – young men and boys stripped bare to the waist. They acknowledge the crowd as they parade around, waving and smiling, and then turn to face a gateway at the far end of the courtyard. A door swings open and the crowd roars as into the arena explodes a bull; wild-eyed and snorting, it twists and turns in confusion. Gradually the bull settles and the acrobats step forward.

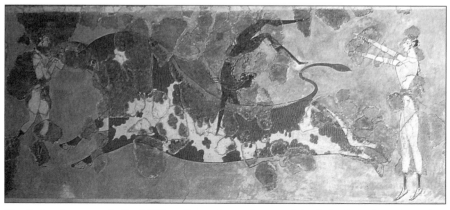

Youths leaping over a bull c.1,500 BC. Scene from a fresco originally in the Palace of Knossos Crete, now in the Archaeological Museum of Heraklion. *(Photograph by the author)*

One, a tall, bronzed young man, moves towards the bull and the crowd holds its breath as the bull fixes its eyes upon the man. It paws the ground, creating a small cloud of dust as slowly it tosses its head and begins its charge. The young man stands his ground fearlessly as the bull approaches until, at the last moment as the bull lowers it horns, he leaps forward in a graceful swallow dive. Passing clean between the horns of the bull and placing his hands on the animal's back, he somersaults to the ground. The crowd roars its approval. In a swirl of dust the bull turns in bewilderment as another youngster steps up. The bull charges towards him and this time the acrobat grasps the horns and uses them as a lever to assist his somersault over the beast. The crowd roars again and the spectacle continues, the acrobats making a fearless variety of somersaults over the charging animal.

This was a scene played out some 2,000 years ago in ancient Crete. Using contemporary fresco paintings, jewellery, pottery and other artefacts, the eminent archaeologist Sir Arthur Evans put forward the idea that 'bull leaping' was a regular occurrence in the Minoan culture. But what has it to do with the history of the circus?

If, for a moment, we strip away the artistry of the performer, then circus is very much an exhibition of physical skill, courage and mastery. The acrobat in the circus ring displays an obvious physical skill and courage, but also a mastery over the natural force of gravity; the animal trainer displays skill, courage and mastery over the animal. Circus at its basic level is a spectacle and as such, according to A. Coxe in the 1951 work, *A Seat at the Circus*, demands that, 'Man, brought face to face with either events or other men, should react to them … there must be something physical about a spectacle; boxing is a spectacle, chess is not'. Presented before an audience this spectacle may take the form of entertainment, ritual or ceremony.

And that is just what the 'bull leaping' of Knossos was – a spectacle. Circus at its basic level and 'bull leaping' still continues today in the town of Mont de Marsan in the Gascony region of France, where brightly clad *sauteurs* (leapers) take part in the *Course Landaise*. This interaction between man and animal as an entertainment is not so far removed from the equestrian acts of the modern circus. As one 91-year-old lady commented on her childhood visit to the circus, 'I liked the bareback riding and the girls who jumped on and off the horses and did pirouettes on their backs. It was all very clever, I thought'.

It is not just the Minoan culture that shows us physical 'circus' activities being presented. A wall painting in the fifteenth tomb at Beni Hassan in

Egypt depicts both women jugglers and acrobats and dates from around 1900 BC. A century earlier, also in Egypt, the young Pharaoh Pepi gave the first recorded performance of a clown. He wrote, 'He is a divine spirit – something to rejoice and delight the heart'. In the ancient Greece of 700 BC, wandering clown figures known as *deikeloktas* were seen in Sparta. Meanwhile, in China the tradition of circus goes back some 4,000 years and is steeped in symbolism. For example, the plates used in the skilful plate spinning acts symbolise the sun, and the performer is the intermediary between the people and the sun.

Some scholars have traced the origins of the circus only as far back as the Roman Empire and the Circus Maximus in Rome. The Circus Maximus was an oval-shaped structure in which chariot races and other large-scale spectacles were held, frequently of a barbaric nature, often with the slaughter of both men and animals. Certainly the slaughter of man and beast as witnessed in the Circus Maximus was physical, yet the physicality

The Circus Neronius in Rome: an oval structure providing a space for chariot races and other spectacles. *(Library of Congress)*

of circus is predetermined. Every move is meticulously prearranged and choreographed, unlike the events of the Circus Maximus.

Other, more recognisably traditional, physical circus skills were presented during the Roman period. In *Dinner with Trimalchio* (part of Petronius' *Satyricon*), Petronius writes about acrobats arriving at a dinner party. He goes on to say that acrobats are a common sight at the circus but hardly the sort of people to have at a dinner party, though the host Trimalchio seems to think that these acrobats are artistic. In his writing, Petronius not only describes in reasonable detail an act that would not be amiss in a present day circus performance but actually uses the phrase 'at the circus'. From this we can assume that such acts of physical skill were common within the Roman period and presented in a specific dedicated performance space. The sixth century Roman historian Procopius gives a portrait of the Empress Theodora, who was trained as an infant in the arts of the stage and the 'floor show'.

As the Roman Empire spread its tentacles across the world it transported much of its culture with it, even to the far-flung outpost of Britain. Large Roman amphitheatres have been excavated at St Albans and at Chester and, as it has been recorded that acrobats and jugglers were used as a 'warm up' to main events in the amphitheatre, it is logical to assume that Romans settling in Britain and other European countries would have enjoyed similar entertainments to those at home in Rome: gladiatorial combat, theatre, dance and acrobats, jugglers and other such amusements. Whereas we might recognise these skills described by Petronius as being a 'circus style' entertainment, the only connection between our modern circus and the Circus Maximus of Rome lies in name only.

With the decline of the Roman Empire in the fifth century AD, Britain entered a period very often referred to as the 'Dark Ages'. Over the next 500 years, until the Norman invasion, Britain saw an influx of differing Germanic and Nordic tribes, each with their own distinct culture. Each had its own tradition of individual entertainers, sometimes retained by a nobleman, sometimes itinerant. These entertainers – frequently referred to as a *scop* and accompanied very often by a harp – were skilled at recitation, story telling, music and singing. From these traditions emerged the character of the jongleur.

The figure of the jongleur appeared somewhere between the ninth and tenth centuries. He was much more of an all-round performer and very often assisted minstrels and troubadours with displays of physical skills – skills that we would recognise today in a circus performance. It is significant that the French word *jongleur* is derived from *jogleur*, the word for a juggler,

Medieval jugglers (one male, the other female) perform together. *(Library of Congress)*

which in itself is derived from the Latin *ioculator* or joker. A jongleur was very often skilled in music, poetry, singing, juggling, acrobatics, dancing, fire eating, conjuring and presenting animals, as well as buffoonery. One unidentified jongleur is referred to by G. Speaight (1980), who writes about, 'his ability to sing a song well, to make tales to please young ladies, and to be able to play the gallant for them if necessary. He could throw knives into the air and catch them without cutting his fingers and could jump rope most extraordinary and amusing. He could balance chairs and make tables dance; could somersault and walk doing a handstand'.

One can imagine the scene in the great manorial halls of the early medieval period. There in the smoky and gloomy interior, lit only by candle or torchlight, with the lord of the manor and his entourage seated at the top table and the lesser beings seated along each side, stands our lonely jongleur. He begins by singing a well-known song before ending this with a back flip. The lord is amused and claps in appreciation. Those seated around him follow suit.

Encouraged by this, our jongleur then takes up some knives from a nearby table and he begins to juggle; first three, then four and maybe even five, to the delight and astonishment of his audience. And so he runs through his routine, each new skill meeting with much approval, until he completes his act by blowing a huge plume of fire into the air. He is pleased with his performance, the audience is pleased and, above all, the lord of the manor is pleased. Our jongleur can eat tonight!

However, jongleurs were not always seen in the best light. The fourteenth century Italian poet Petrarch referred to jongleurs as 'people of no great wit and impudent beyond measure'. But if this was the case for the jongleur, then there was another type of performer who attracted even less respect – the gleeman. Whereas the jongleur often performed for noblemen, gleemen were distinctly individual itinerant performers who plied their trade at fairs, festivals and celebrations. Although often as individually skilled as the jongleurs, as entertainers they were considered the lowest of the low. Already, even at this early stage in history, the travelling performer was considered an 'undesirable' character; someone on the fringe of society who was not to be trusted.

The jongleur is not to be confused with the minstrel and the troubadour, whose main respective functions were to play music and sing, and to recite lyrical and romantic poetry. Minstrels were predominantly musicians and singers of poetry. Of French origin, from the eleventh century they were initially retainers at court and employed to entertain their masters' guests with music and song. Many became proficient on the instruments of that period – the fiddle, the cittern, the bagpipes and the flageolet.

As courts grew more and more sophisticated, so minstrels were replaced by troubadours, who were usually educated men (and sometimes women), and who composed their own lyrical poetry based around the themes of chivalry and courtly love. Often troubadours recited their poetry to a musical accompaniment. As troubadours replaced minstrels, so minstrels became more itinerant and very often the troubadours would attack the jongleurs and minstrels in their poetry.

To maintain a degree of professionalism and quality, King Edward IV ordered in 1469 that all jongleurs should join a guild under his patronage, namely the Guild of Royal Minstrels, thereby placing all minstrels, troubadours and jongleurs under one banner. A guild was a form of professional organisation of the time. A jongleur had to join this guild or else cease performing, although many probably continued to do so illegally. Over 100 years before this, the minstrels of Paris had also been formed into

A poster for the company Maskarás, who base their performances upon medieval-style entertainments. *(Author's collection)*

a guild with the same rule. During the medieval period itinerant performers, once perceived as being on the fringe of society, were now being endorsed and given respectability through royal patronage.

The character of the jongleur has also appeared in literature. In 1892, Anatole France wrote the story, 'Le Jongleur de Notre Dame', which, in turn, was based upon a thirteenth century medieval legend by Gautier de Coincy. Jules Massanet later adapted the story for the stage in 1902 and produced it as an opera in three acts under the same name. In the story a poor juggler becomes a monk and he has no gift to offer to the statue of the Virgin Mary except his skill. Because of this he is accused of heresy but the statue comes to life and blesses him.

Whilst the role of the jongleur continued throughout medieval times, another figure also developed: the jester. Familiar to many of us, he appears on playing cards in his multicoloured clothing, with bells dangling from his fool's hat and clutching a stick with a pig's bladder attached to it. This colourful portrayal of a jester is very much derived from the image of an Elizabethan jester, as described much later by Francis Douce in 1807.

According to Douce, the jester's coat was parti-coloured, with bells at the skirt and elbow. The hose sometimes had legs of contrasting colours. The hood, resembling a monk's cowl, fell down over the head and shoulders and was sometimes decorated with asses' ears or cockscomb. The jester carried an official sceptre or bauble, a short stick ending in a fool's head or perhaps, a doll or puppet. Also sometimes attached was a pig's bladder,

'The King's Fool': A modern interpretation of the court jester, carrying his sceptre topped with a fool's head. *(Library of Congress)*

with which the jester beat those who had offended him. The seventeenth century Flemish artist, Jacob Jordaens, portrayed the figure of the fool in several of his works. In *Merry Company on a Terrace,* the fool can be seen in the background holding aloft his sceptre with a fool's head on it. In the works *Folly* and *Cleopatra and Fool,* the figure is shown in a monk-like cowl, to which are attached bells.

Jesters came from a wide variety of backgrounds; some from simple peasant stock, others from the world of clerics, and even from universities. Some were retained at court whilst others, the greater number by far, were itinerant but there was always the chance of being spotted by a nobleman and moved to higher circles. At a time when social mobility was very constrained and farmers begat farmers, carpenters begat carpenters and so on, the jester could, and sometimes did, move beyond his class. There were also a few notable female jesters of the time, each known as a 'jestress'. A jestress named La Jardinaire attended Mary Queen of Scots in 1543 and a Maria Asquin attended Isabella of Spain for some 50 years during the seventeenth century.

Many jesters had a physical deformity such as dwarfism or were hunchbacked, which was considered a source of amusement at that time. The ability of the grotesque jester to mock their own afflictions created much merriment. The grotesque was a figure on the edge of society and to the medieval mind it represented the chaos outside of an ordered world, and through the jesters' own mockery of this they could be both feared and loved at the same time. This is the paradox of the grotesquely costumed modern day circus clown. Very often they appear with exaggerated features, oversized feet, wild hair and garish clothing. For many children, and indeed adults, clowns can be quite frightening figures, yet they both scare us and delight us. These modern clown characters hark back to the grotesque jesters of the medieval and Tudor periods. The last dwarf jester to be retained by royalty was Copperin, who belonged to Princess Augusta of Wales, mother of King George III, in the mid-eighteenth century.

Jesters sometimes became the close companions of royalty and nobility. Some royal courts even consulted their jesters on matters of state. Duke Leopold of Austria is reputed to have consulted his court jestress on the eve of a battle against the Swiss in 1386. As the story goes the Duke, unfortunately, chose not to heed her advice – and lost the battle. But for the majority of jesters their survival depended very much upon performing at fairs, markets and wherever people gathered in large numbers.

An itinerant jester would have made his way to many fairs like the one portrayed in Pieter Breughel the Younger's early seventeenth century painting *The Village Fair.* Within Breughel's picture the fair is in full swing. A religious procession is winding its way through the street, with music playing and drums beating. It is, after all, a fair to honour Saint Hubert and Saint Anthony but few of the village people are taking any notice of this. Already many of them are drinking, dancing and eating. A fight has broken out near the dancers, and animals wander unattended through the thronging crowd. Our jester already has competition – a rough stage has been set up in the village square and a group of players are already in performance, perhaps enacting a morality play. It is certainly popular and people have climbed onto the roof of a nearby house to get a better view.

The jester chooses his spot carefully; he knows that many people will be heading towards the church and after the service they will be coming out again. He draws a rough circle in the earth with his stick and places his bag of belongings within it. From the bag he takes out a small three-legged stool upon which he sets some of his props. Already his strange and brightly coloured clothing has attracted the attention of some of the children who are drawn towards the circle. He smiles at them, coughs and produces an egg from his mouth. The children gasp in astonishment and then he breaks the egg over the head of a little girl to magic a small bird which flies off into the air.

The girl squeals with delight and the children clap. A few of the adults stop to see what is going on. Our jester takes a small tabor from his bag and begins to drum a rhythm and encourages the children to clap and cheer, so much so that before long a small crowd has gathered around the circle. For the first time he speaks, in a booming voice that rises above the merriment.

"All you good people of the village on this the day of Saint Hubert and Saint Anthony. Gather round and see. Who would like to watch a humble man drink ale whilst balancing this stool upon his chin? In fact, good sir," addressing a passing man, "who would like to drink ale *with* a humble man whilst he balances this stool upon his chin?"

The man laughs and steps into the circle. Much to his surprise, the jester produces a flagon of ale from within his jerkin and hands it to him. The crowd applauds as the jester then proceeds to balance the stool by one leg upon his chin, as the man downs his ale. To the delight of the people, the man having finished his drink then mimics the jester by balancing the flagon on his own head as he returns to his family. The jester in return applauds this parody and pulls a small boy from the crowd. Setting the child upon the stool, he then lifts both into the air and continues to balance both stool and boy upon his chin. The child squeals in fear and the crowd cheers. Setting the boy back to earth, he does a back flip and a bow before returning the child to its mother.

By now he has the full attention of the growing crowd, no more words are needed. Villagers on their way to the church have stopped for a while to see the commotion and even those watching the players have drifted away towards this new attraction. And so our jester continues with his performance, each new trick drawing gasps of amazement and cheers of appreciation. A master of his art, he varies his numbers, sometimes startling the crowd with seemingly impossible and magic tricks, and sometimes softening the moment with a snatch of a ballad or a haunting melody on his flute, but all the while building the crowd towards the climax of his performance – the fire number!

Pulling off his multi-coloured jerkin, he passes a burning brand up and down his arms and across his chest. Some of the women in the crowd look away and some men wince as if they feel his pain. The children stare at him goggle-eyed in disbelief. He then proceeds to juggle with three burning brands, creating ever more complex patterns in the air. Pulling his ale-drinking companion back into the circle, he sets him on the stool and clambers up onto his broad shoulders and continues to juggle again. The climax of his performance comes when he suddenly belches forth a sheet of flame that rises up into the sky, catching the crowd by surprise, and they instinctively shrink back. With a final forward somersault from the man's shoulders, he lands neatly in front of the crowd and makes an extravagant bow.

There are cheers and applause as he moves amongst them, holding open his fool's cap. Willing coins are tossed in, a few shake his hand in thanks. A man from a nearby house brings him some ale and a woman offers him some bread and cheese; the jester is a happy man. His performance has gone down well and he begins to pack away his props. Shouldering his bag, he picks up his stick and sets off down the street, followed by a gaggle of laughing children. Nothing is left of him except the rough circle drawn in the earth but the villagers will talk of him for some time to come. And in this picture we can see perhaps the legacy of all those jesters, jongleurs, minstrels and troubadours of long ago in our modern street entertainers, the buskers, who still operate in the same manner.

The itinerant performers of the medieval period understood that to make people laugh not only filled their pockets but also created a feeling of well-being within the crowd. Medieval doctors believed that health was governed by four 'humours': the choleric, the phlegmatic, the sanguine and the melancholic. Ill health was brought about by an imbalance in these humours. Today it is well-known that laughter and merriment go a long way to help improve health, proving right the saying that 'laughter is the best medicine'. There are organisations such as Clini–Clowns and Clowns Without Borders; groups of performers, mainly clowns, who visit children in hospitals or areas of crisis to help relieve suffering and pain through laughter. Communication is never a problem, for the wise fool transcends language and we can all speak the language of laughter.

During the Tudor period, England was evolving from a medieval way of life to a more sophisticated society, yet jesters were still being retained at court. That royalty liked to be entertained is made clear in the *Letters and Papers of Henry VIII*: 'Poets, harpers, minstrels, players, and tumblers amused his tastes and partook of his bounty'. Thomas Skelton had been a well-known court jester in the late 1500s and the royal court jester Will Somers spanned both the reigns of Henry VIII and of his three children, including Queen Elizabeth I.

Queen Elizabeth herself engaged at least three court jesters – Richard Tarleton, Will Kempe and Robert Armin, all also noted actors of the period. Robert Armin was a recognised expert on jesting and he wrote a volume entitled *Foole Upon Foole* in 1600. Now the court jester had a foot in both camps – he was a licensed fool and a reputable actor.

The jester confidant, or literary fool, is a figure that often appears in literature during the sixteenth and seventeenth centuries, notably in the works of William Shakespeare, the most famous of which is perhaps the Fool in *King Lear*. When all else is lost, King Lear chooses his Fool to advise him. Shakespeare's Fools took on many guises; Trinculo in *The Tempest* is described as a jester; Yorick the king's jester in *Hamlet*, although never seen in person, is referred to by Hamlet as, 'a fellow of infinite jest … Where be your gibes now, your gambols, your songs, your flashes of merriment that were wont to set the table on a roar?'. Launcelot Gobbo in *The Merchant of Venice* is listed as a clown, likewise Costard in *Love's Labours Lost* and Touchstone in *As You Like It*.

Although much has been written about the more celebrated actors, poets and musicians of the period, we sometimes forget that the popular culture of itinerant performers still thrived in England's towns, cities and even rural streets. It never really went away – rather it became overshadowed by its more respectable cousins. In 1550s Shrewsbury, street entertainments were still alive and well. There are records of tumblers and acrobats, of a Hungarian wire walker and a 'very tall man over seven feet' from Antwerp – possibly he may have been on stilts. The names of these performers also appear in local towns around this period, so presumably they were a travelling group of street entertainers.

In London alone between 1570 and 1663 there are 22 references to rope-dancing, 13 to tumblers, seven mentions of vaulting, and five jugglers. Both male and female performers were in evidence at a time when women were not allowed to appear upon the stage. In 1546 a Spanish rope-dancer stretched a rope from the ground to the steeple of St Paul's Cathedral and then slid down it head first, arms outstretched. In 1553, as Mary I was passing through London, a Dutchman balanced on the weathercock of the same cathedral and in 1575 there was recorded the amazing skills of the Italian tumblers in a display given before Elizabeth I at Kenilworth Castle. Itinerant street

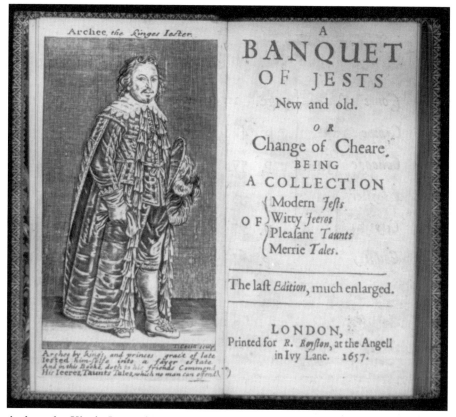

Archee, the King's Jester, from an engraving by Thomas Cecil, 1657: Born Archibald Armstrong, he first entered the service of King James VI of Scotland and later Charles I of England. *(Library of Congress)*

entertainments were now taking on an international flavour. Circus knows no barriers of gender or culture, it has always been an universal art form.

Even the famous Globe Theatre was not a stranger to such 'feats of activity'. It is recorded that during the theatre's off season there were displays of vaulting, fencing and rope-dancing. However, itinerant performers were still viewed with suspicion. In the Calendar of State Papers during the reign of Queen Elizabeth I there are at least two references to foreign spies coming to England 'in the guise of tumblers'.

It took almost another century and a half for the concept of circus to re-emerge, but the important fact is that it never really died. All the skills of the jesters and other itinerant performers endured chiefly because of their popular nature. They are entertainments of the people, and people still needed entertaining during the turbulent reign of Charles I and the following Commonwealth Puritan regime. They survived in events such as Bartholomew Fair, Southwark Fair and other May Fair gatherings.

Bartholomew Fair itself was first created by a character named Rahere, jester to Henry I in the twelfth century, who later became a monk. In the 1859 work *Memoirs of Bartholomew Fair*, Henry Morley gives a contemporary account of the Fair originally written in 1641 by Richard Harper:

> *It is remarkable and worth your observation to behold and hear the strange sights and confused noises in the fair. Here a Knave in a Fool's coat, with a trumpet sounding, or on a drum beating, invites you and would fain persuade you to see his puppets; there a rogue like a wild Woodman, or in an antick shape like an Incubus, desires your company to view his motion. On the other side Hocus Pocus with three yards of tape or ribbon in's hand, showing his art of Legerdemain to the admiration and astonishment of a company of cockoloaches.*

Clearly there were entertainments of all description to be had at Bartholomew Fair. Samuel Pepys, the great diarist, made many visits to Bartholomew Fair and mentions the fair several times in his diary during 1668, 'to visit the mare that tells money and many things to admire – and then the dancing ropes', and 'so to Jacob Hall's dancing of the ropes; a thing worth seeing, and mightily followed'. Rope-dancers were very popular it seems, and not only with the common people. Jacob Hall was a favourite of Lady Castlemaine, the mistress of King Charles II, and she spent much time in his company.

In all of these fairground entertainments we begin to see elements of circus as we may recognise it today. Maybe the advent of the modern circus would have begun here, had it not been for the intervention of the English Civil War and the ensuing period of the Commonwealth, in which the arts and entertainment were almost wiped from the face of the country. During the Interregnum, from 1649 to 1660 performances of dancing and plays by live actors were forbidden, but the state did not challenge performances by puppets or other entertainers such as the jongleur and the rope-dancer. Cromwell himself is reported to have had in his service at least four 'buffoons'. Throughout all of this time the circus was still alive and well and soon, as we shall see in the next chapter, the eighteenth century would provide the springboard for circus as we know it today.

Chapter Two

Acrobats, Ale and Aristocrats:
The Eighteenth Century Age of Decadence

It is 1733 and we are about to visit Southwark Fair on the south bank of the River Thames in London. It is early evening and, as we push our way through the crowds towards the church of St George the Martyr, the first thing that assaults our senses is the noise and bustle of the square; a teeming throng of people taking in the amusements and entertainments all around us.

People are pushing and shoving in their efforts to see what is going on. You had better hold on to your belongings because, look, over there on the

'Danse Aristocrate': A satirical image of a rope dancer from 1790. *(Library of Congress)*

right behind the peep show, a man has just had his pocket picked. In the middle of the square is a very pretty woman playing a drum, accompanied by a small black boy on a trumpet – perhaps her servant or maybe they are in the same company of performers? It looks like they are drumming up customers for a nearby performance and she is certainly attracting attention.

As you push on through the crowd, look up and you'll see a man performing tricks on a slack rope slung between two buildings. He is named Violante and seems to defy gravity itself as he dances in mid-air. Let's hope he doesn't fall upon the heads of those below – this has been known to happen. Between the church tower and a nearby tree another aerial performer, Cadman, known as the 'flying man', has stretched a rope. With his arms outstretched he descends the rope head-first.

Placards advertising the entertainments coming to the fair are all around us. Behind the rope-dancer is an advertisement for Maximillian Muller, the famous 'German Giant', who is reputed to stand over 8ft tall. On the right of the square another placard shows two contortionists. Beneath it, perched on a balcony, is a drumming monkey accompanying the famous Isaac Fawkes, a noted juggler and magician. He is demonstrating some magic trick to the crowd and, no matter how closely you watch him, you will be unable to see how his magic is performed. Many people in the crowd will have seen Fawkes before, at that other great London fair over at St Bartholomew's. There he was working with another magician, a Mr Pinchbeck, who in one trick caused a tree to grow out of a flower pot on a table, which then blossomed and bore ripe fruit within a minute. Also in their show was the famous little nine-year-old 'Posture-Master', who showed several astonishing acrobatic figures. This young boy also performed tricks upon a slack-rope as the crowd waited for the show to begin.

Turning away from Mr Fawkes, you can see a man standing on a small raised platform, somehow breathing fire without setting fire to his wig. Behind him, on a raised balcony, there is some form of performance going on. A bystander explains that it is about the Siege of Troy, but it is a bit confusing because on a nearby balcony is a harlequin character and a hobby horse.

Pushing back through the crowd, you almost stumble across a dwarf drummer leading a man upon a horse. The man is holding a fearsome looking sword in his hand and it is said that he will be giving a demonstration of swordsmanship later. Perhaps he is going to perform with that man dressed in Roman armour over there? The lady drummer is still beating away but now you can see, behind the gamblers and near that blind piper with his puppets, there is a dancing dog. Complete with hat, sword and cane, he is a very miniature of the gallants in the crowd.

Suddenly there is a splintering sound and cries of alarm as the balcony on the left begins to sway and fall. These temporary booths are quite often thrown up very quickly just for the fairs and they are not at all well constructed. Men and women begin to tumble to the ground onto the heads of those below, as a small monkey clings desperately to one of the uprights. It is time now to leave the heady mix of sights, sounds and smells of the fair and head for the safety of home.

This is the scene that William Hogarth gives us in his 1733 engraving *Southwark Fair or The Humours of a Fair*. Southwark Fair was granted its charter in 1462 by Edward IV and, like the other London fairs, began its life as a mercantile market that lasted for just a few days. By the turn of the seventeenth century these markets had become focused less on business and increasingly on pleasure, with a myriad of entertainments, and lasted for up to four weeks. Diarists John Evelyn and Samuel Pepys both visited Southwark Fair and commented on the sights. Evelyn describes seeing monkeys and asses dancing on a tightrope. He observed an Italian girl dance and perform tricks on the tightrope to much admiration, so much so that the whole royal court went to see her. Another interesting exhibition he saw – which could be taken directly from a modern circus – was that of a strong man, who lifted up a piece of an iron cannon weighing about 400lbs using only the hair of his head.

In 1668 Pepys referred to visiting a 'very dirty' Southwark Fair, where he went to see Jacob Hall dancing on the rope. He thought the show was well worth seeing and he later met Hall in a nearby tavern and struck up a conversation with him. Pepys asked Hall if there had ever been times when he had fallen during his shows, to which Hall said, 'Yes, many, but never to the breaking of a limb'. During his visits to Bartholomew Fair between 1663 and 1668, Pepys saw many rope-dancers, clearly a popular entertainment.

There is an old saying, 'Wherever the crowd, there a performer', and the London fairs such as at Southwark, Bartholomew and the Greenwich May Fair became magnets for all kinds of itinerant performers and their followers. Yet, as well as being places of entertainment, these fairs had a darker and seedier side of drunkenness, prostitution and crime, and some people were very wary when visiting them. In the same year that Hogarth produced his engraving, a woman was trampled to death by the crowd at Southwark Fair, and earlier, in 1702 at the May Fair in Greenwich, a constable was fatally wounded during a riot.

Because of the growth of urbanisation within London, many of the boroughs were becoming more residential. There was increasing opposition from residents as the annual fairs caused much congestion and an increase in crime. There was great opposition to the fairs in general, and in 1763 Southwark Fair was banned by the authorities, although Bartholomew Fair continued well into the nineteenth century.

The eighteenth century was a very sensual, visual era and people liked to see and be seen, especially if they deemed themselves above the common classes. They went to the ever-increasing number of theatres; they began to wear elaborate and fanciful costumes which mirrored those of the theatre and they promenaded in the growing variety of pleasure gardens of the period.

Imagine the scene: it is a warm summer's evening and the fragrant scent of flowers drifts through the evening air. Hundreds of twinkling lights glimmer in the trees and the gentle sound of a string quartet mingles with the late birdsong. Ladies of fashion in their fine feathered bonnets converse demurely with a group of gentlemen, resplendent with their cravats and canes, as they stroll along the gravelled pathway towards the rotunda. There, in candle-lit booths, tables are laid ready for the diners. Liveried footmen in powdered wigs stand nearby holding warm kettles with which to serve tea. On a nearby bench a portly gentleman sits and snoozes, oblivious to the crowds around him.

Between two trees a rope-dancer has slung his slack-rope and now performs upon it, balancing and juggling. In dumb show he takes a hoop from a passing young boy and then tosses it over him as if at a funfair. Descending from his rope, he then performs somersaults and back flips before once again ascending and reclining on the rope as if it were his bed. Another tumbler appears from the shadows walking on his hands, much to the amusement of the passers-by. The light begins to fade into darkness and as they take their places at their tables, a firework show begins beyond the rotunda, lighting up the sky around.

At a time when London and other major cities were overcrowded, dirty and smelly, these gardens were created on the edges of the urban sprawl, providing a space where people could go to 'take the air' and, more importantly for those of rank and fashion, to display themselves. These pleasure gardens provided ample opportunities to swagger or stroll through the carefully manicured leafy walks of a romantic, rustic idyll.

Although the idea of a pleasure garden had existed during the reign of Charles I, it was not until the Restoration period that they began to develop.

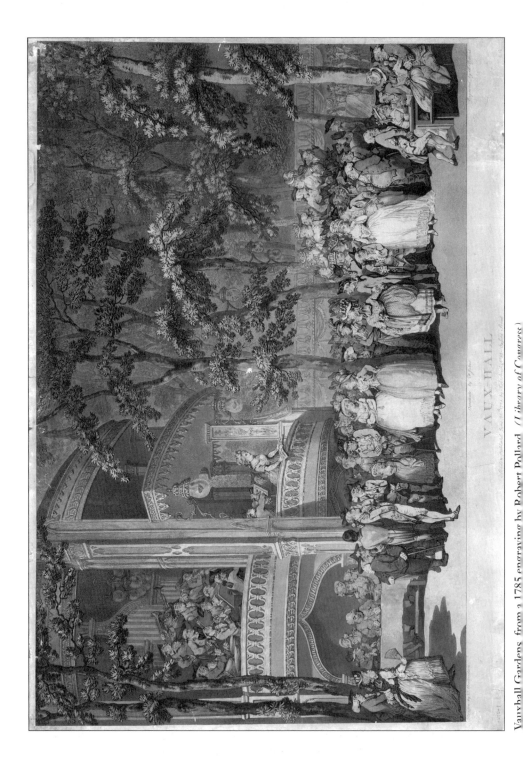

Vauxhall Gardens, from a 1785 engraving by Robert Pollard (Library of Congress)

Charles II had spent a period of exile in France during the Commonwealth period. When he returned to England, he brought with him all the fashionable ideas of the French court, including that of the pleasure garden, very much influenced by what he had seen at the garden at the Palace of Versailles.

By the middle of the eighteenth century there were over 60 pleasure gardens throughout the whole of London. Some were licensed to present music and dancing, whilst those without a licence provided spaces for the playing of bowls or the taking of tea, and as they became more and more fashionable other provincial cities copied London. The gardens were places designed for pleasure, places of intrigue and assignations. A handbill advertising the Bagnigge Wells Gardens, located in the area of what is now King's Cross Road, carries this rhyme, or maybe warning:

Salubrious waters, tea and wine
Here you may have, and also dine
But, as ye through the gardens rove
Beware, fond youths, the Darts of Love.

New Spring Gardens opened to the public in 1661 in Lambeth, south London. John Evelyn, the diarist, called it a 'prettily contrived plantation' and Samuel Pepys picnicked on cakes, powdered beef and ale during a visit

'The Humours of Spring Gardens', 1732: 'Here may the wandering eye with pleasure see both knaves and fools in borrowed shapes agree'. *(Library of Congress)*

to the gardens. On another trip Pepys recalled, 'There came to us an idle boy to show us some tumbling tricks, which he did very well, and the greatest bending of his body that ever I observed in my life'.

In 1732, under the management of Jonathan Tyers, New Spring Gardens was reinvented as the new Vauxhall Gardens and people were charged a one shilling admission fee. The pleasure garden was no longer exclusive and anyone could enter who could pay the entrance fee. However, the owner endeavoured to create an agreeable atmosphere, where the riff-raff of the town were dissuaded from entering and gentlemen were requested not to smoke in the walks. That is not to say that incidents did not occur, and at the opening of the new Vauxhall Gardens a man stole 50 guineas from a masquerader but was apprehended by a night watchman shortly afterwards.

The gardens extended over 12 acres and set into the leafy hedgerows along the walks were recessed bowers, where one could rest or take tea. Royalty were regular visitors and Tyers built the Prince of Wales Pavilion for Prince Frederick. This was the age of the celebrity with many aristocrats, actors, writers and artists using the pleasure gardens for recreation. In 1781, the presence of the Duke and Duchess of Cumberland attracted over 11,000 visitors and in 1784 the centennial celebration of the birth of George Frederick Handel drew a vast crowd. So people now had the possibility of rubbing shoulders with aristocrats or even royalty.

Amongst the walks and greenery, small pavilions and booths were erected so that the visitors could rest awhile from their walking to eat, drink and converse. With gravelled walks bordered by fragrant bushes and overhung with trees, within which hundreds of glowing oil lamps were hung at night, it must have been a fairy-tale sight for the pleasure seekers. However, Tobias Smollett, in his 1771 work *The Expedition of Humphrey Clinker*, gives us a very different picture through the eyes of his character Matthew Bramble:

> *What are the amusements of Ranelagh? One half of the company are following at the other's tails, in an eternal circle; like so many blind asses in an olive-mill ... while the other half are drinking hot water, under the denomination of tea, till nine or ten o'clock at night, to keep them awake for the rest of the evening ... Vauxhall is a composition of baubles, overcharged with paltry ornaments, ill conceived, and poorly executed ... The walks, which nature seems to have intended for solitude, shade and silence, are filled with crowds of noisy people, sucking up the nocturnal rheums of an anguish climate; and through these gay scenes, a few lamps glimmer like so many farthing candles.*

As they developed, the gardens became places of entertainment and excitement; art works were displayed in pavilions and music was played. In June 1764, the eight-year-old Mozart gave a performance on the harpsichord in Chelsea's Ranalegh Gardens. Masquerades were always popular and recitals were given, very often accompanied by firework displays later in the century. But the gardens now also became venues for performers of physical feats. In the late seventeenth century, at the gardens on the site of the present day Sadler's Wells Theatre, rope-dancers were engaged to entertain the public.

Performances also took place inside the building itself. Between 1750 and 1800 there are several recorded performances of what we might term circus-style entertainments. Michael Maddox performed wire-dancing and 'tricks with a long straw'. In 1768 a Mister Spinacutti and his performing monkey made an appearance. There were tumblers such as Paul Redigé, also known as the 'Little Devil', and another named Placido; the Bologna and Sons act of feats of strength and Costello and his performing dogs.

One of Smollett's other fictional characters, the maid Winifred Jenkins, gives a very vivid description of a visit to Sadler's Wells: 'I was afterwards at a party at Sadler's Wells where I saw such tumbling and dancing on ropes

Dancing at Cremorne Gardens, 1847. *(The Pictorial Times, 1847)*

and wires that I was frightened and ready to go into a fit – I tho't it all inchantment [sic]; and believing myself bewitched, began to cry'.

These acts inspired just as much awe and wonder as they do today. I myself have sat in a circus tent and watched the audience gasp in fear and amazement as the high wire artist does a back flip or some other dangerous feat of agility. In Marylebone Gardens in 1738, a tall tower was erected so that a performer could walk across a stretched rope with a wheelbarrow, something that Blondin was to do much later when he famously crossed Niagara Falls.

In 1792, under the management of Tyers' sons, the entrance fee was increased to two shillings. However, this did not deter the public from visiting the gardens. With the opening of Vauxhall Bridge in 1816, it became far easier for the public to gain access to the Vauxhall Gardens, visitors previously having to cross the Thames to enter. The opening of the bridge was celebrated by a tightrope walker, Madame Saqui, who walked up a 300ft long inclined rope to the top of a tower, from which she then descended to a storm of fireworks. She was engaged by Vauxhall Gardens to perform this feat many times over at a fee of 100 guineas a week.

Her performances were well recorded in the newspapers at the time and *The Morning Post* of 15 July 1816 gives a colourful account:

> *There are many attractions here this summer which we have not observed in former seasons; but the most wonderful attraction of all is the incomparable performance of Madame Saqui on the tightrope. In the place where the Cascade was formerly exhibited there is a beautiful stage fitted up; over this there is extended sometimes one, two or three ropes upon which this little Parisian sylph trips along with fearless agility; here she dances and throws herself into different graceful attitudes. Her grandest feat, however, is when she ascends the elevated rope that reaches nearly to the tops of the trees. When she has reached the extremity, the grand fireworks are let off, and then Madame Saqui appears like a Goddess suspended in the air, and nearly surrounded by clouds, descends amid the illumined atmosphere. Like Iris upon her empyreal causeway, the effect produced upon the spectators is like that of magic.*

However, such performances were not always without mishap and on 29 July *The Morning Post* reported that, whilst attempting to perform a new figure on the tightrope, she lost her balance and fell onto the rope. Fortunately she managed to finish her performance but she must have been quite shaken by the accident, as her brother, Monsieur Lallane, performed the rope ascension in her place and *The Times* stated that some of her ribs had been broken in the accident. The excitement surrounding Madame Saqui's performances also created danger for her audience, as on 30 August a fatal accident occurred. A

Madame Saqui

The celebrated Performer on the Rope, at Vauxhall.
Engraved by Alais, from an Original Painting by Hutchisson of Bath.
Published for Ld Belle Assembleux Nº 252, Febᵃ 1ˢᵗ 1820.
by J.Bell & Sold at Nº 16 Bridges Sᵗ Covent Garden.

Madame Saqui performing at Vauxhall Gardens, c.1820. *(Engraving from W. Wroth,* London Pleasure Gardens of the Eighteenth Century, *Macmillan & Co, 1896)*

group of military officers, being driven at speed in a hackney coach to reach the performance in time, collided with another hackney coach. The driver of their coach was thrown to the ground and broke his neck.

Madame Saqui continued performing at Vauxhall Gardens during the summer periods until 1820 and she was always a popular attraction. Within her audiences there were many aristocratic and royal persons, including on the evening of her accident the Duke and Duchess of Cumberland, Prince and Princess Esterhazy, Count Munster, the Earl of Harrowby, Lord Palmerston and many others. In *Sketches from St George's Fields* (1821), a rhyming couplet encapsulates Madame Saqui's magical impact:

> *Amid the blaze of meteors seen on high*
> *Ethereal Saqui seems to tread the sky.*

A survey of popular entertainments during the late eighteenth and nineteenth centuries shows a wide array of activities. On 10 November 1788 *The Times* gave notice of a first performance at the Royal Grove near Westminster Bridge by 'The Grand Troop of Strangers'. Their performance included rope-dancing, horsemanship and several feats of activity on horseback, horse vaulting at full speed, tumbling, slack-wire and a pantomime. Other popular physical feats that could be seen in the pleasure gardens of the time included magicians, balloon ascents, ventriloquists, acrobatics and equilibristics, strong man acts, jugglers, curiosities, animal acts and clowns.

Clowns are synonymous with the circus and are very often referred to as 'Joeys' within the circus world. Although there were several clowns performing at this time, the Joey owes much to one particular clown, Joseph Grimaldi. Grimaldi was born in Clare Market, a slum district of central London, in 1778. He came from a long line of Italian performers and his father, Joseph Giuseppe Grimaldi, was an actor and dancer, known often as 'the *signeur*'. As well as a noted performer, he was also the ballet master at the Theatre Royal in Drury Lane. Joseph's young mother had been an apprentice to his father, who was a strict disciplinarian and often beat his children. He had a morbid fascination with death and would very often feign death to see how his children would react. He even gave his eldest daughter strict instructions that he was to be decapitated after his death, and this was also to be carried out before a group of onlookers.

Despite his quirks of personality, Joseph senior was a successful performer and took his two-year-old son onto the stage at the Drury Lane Theatre in 1780. There is a colourful description of this appearance in his memoirs, published in 1838. His father playing the character of a clown, young Joseph appeared as a monkey, led on stage by a chain attached around his waist. His father would then swing him around on the chain at arm's length with ever-increasing speed. Unfortunately during an early performance the chain snapped and Joseph was hurled into the audience, landing in the lap of one very surprised elderly gentleman, but thankfully uninjured.

Within a year he was appearing as 'the little clown' in a piece entitled *Harlequin's Wedding* and then making regular appearances in another piece named *Harlequin Junior.* By the age of six 'Master Grimaldi' was rapidly becoming a prominent stage actor and reputed to be earning the sum of £1 per week.

Many of the performances in which Grimaldi was involved were centred on the character of Harlequin and these were often referred to generically as Harlequinades. These performances were very often presented as a

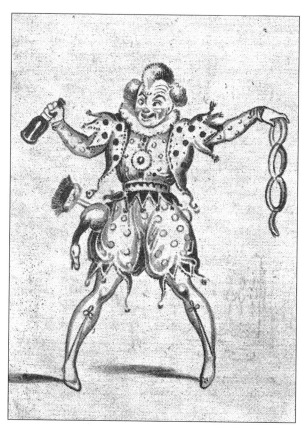

Grimaldi, with his characteristic bottle, goose and string of sausages. *(Author's collection)*

comic closing entertainment at the end of an evening of more serious entertainment. Complete with a magical transformation scene and the increased use of mechanical scenery and effects, these became very popular. Today the Harlequin is a familiar character, with his colourful diamond patterned, close-fitting costume, black tricorn hat and black eye mask, but this character was an English development of the earlier sixteenth century Italian *Commedia dell'Arte* character named Arlecchino.

The *Commedia dell'Arte* was a peculiarly Italian form of entertainment during the sixteenth and seventeenth centuries. Itinerant groups of *Commedia* actors would travel the country performing at markets, fairs and sometimes at the request of the aristocracy. The story-lines were never written down as a script and they were passed on via the oral tradition from master to apprentice. It was not until the mid-eighteenth century that playwrights such as Carlo Goldoni developed the *Commedia* ideas into structured and scripted plays. Fast moving and slick, the *Commedia* performances were always improvised and centred on a series of defined comic routines known as *Lazzis*.

Imagine the scene: Arlechinno the servant, dressed in his multi-coloured suit and wearing a mask covering the upper half of his face, has been called upon to serve dinner to two masters at the same time. He is alone on the stage and, whilst the two masters scream at him from offstage left and right, he turns to the audience and mimes being hungry. He is so hungry he would even eat a fly. A fly buzzes around him and Arlechinno follows it with exaggerated movements until it settles on his nose. Trapping the fly, he then begins to pluck first the legs and then the wings before swallowing it, expressing great satisfaction, then sitting on the stage, replete after his meal.

At this point the two masters increase their shouts and screams. Plates fly in from left and right and Arlechinno, showing all the dexterity of his character catches the plates and passes them on, from left to right and right to left. The plates arrive quicker, followed by knives, forks and then food. All of these Arlechinno deals with, racing from side to side, never dropping an item. If that was not enough he even finds time to throw in the odd somersault or two into this performance and the crowd cheers with delight.

The character of Arlechinno was the same in every *Commedia* troupe. He was a nimble and comic servant, always seeking to get one over on his masters. An Arlechinno actor had to be agile, a master of tumbling and acrobatics as well as a good juggler. Once donning the Arlechinno mask, after seven years of apprenticeship, the actor never played another role. This was the same for the other stock *Commedia* characters; Pantalone, the shuffling old man; Il Doctore, the academic bloated with his own words; Il Capitano, the strutting, cowardly braggart; Brighella, the devious and conniving servant and Polcinello the hunchbacked, evil servant who delighted in hitting people with his 'slap stick', two pieces of wood hinged together to create a slapping noise.

There were also characters without masks and these were the roles played by women. The most well-known was Columbina (later to become Columbine in the English Harlequinade), with whom Arlechinno very often fell in love, much to the disgust of his master Pantalone, who wanted Columbina for himself.

The work of the *Commedia dell'Arte* spread widely throughout Europe, reaching as far as England. Here many of the *Commedia* characters became incorporated into the theatre and entertainments of the time. Even Shakespeare makes reference to the 'lean and slippered pantaloon' character of Pantalone in *All's Well that Ends Well*, in the famous 'All the world's a stage' speech. We can still recognise some of these stock characters today – the grumpy old man, the bumbling professor, the boastful, cowardly landlord, the layabout and the nimble minded wheeler-dealer.

A modern performance of the *Commedia dell' Arte* on a trestle stage in the Piazza San Marco, Venice. *(Author's collection)*

The eighteenth century English Harlequinade changed Harlequin into the central character of the piece. Unlike Arlechinno, this new Harlequin became the romantic lead figure in his quest to win the hand of Columbine against the wishes of her father or sometimes her guardian, Pantaloon. In the early eighteenth century Harlequin was a silent character and gave much of his performance in mime, although later in the development of the Harlequinade dialogue was added. Pantaloon was ably assisted in his comic attempts to keep Harlequin and Columbine apart by a servant named Pierrot and an additional character referred to as Clown. It was as the Clown that Joseph Grimaldi made his name.

Joseph's Clown character was very visual and he developed his own particular style of make-up. A blank white face was topped by a distinctive black wig, very often with upswept hair. His eyebrows were painted as black arches over his eyes. To complete the picture his lips were reddened and he sported a large red triangular pattern over each cheekbone. His costume, consisting of a tunic and knee breeches, was predominantly white, sometimes with multi-coloured spots and sometimes with coloured stripes, complete with a ruff around his neck. Even into the early twentieth century, many clowns still wore a style of make-up and costume that reflected Grimaldi's influence.

His performances were also very physical. In one show alone he would be diving in and out of windows, tumbling across the stage and on the receiving end of all sorts of rough treatment from other characters. In 1813, a review in *The Times* called Grimaldi:

> *The most assiduous of all imaginable buffoons and it is absolutely surprising that any human head or hide can resist the rough trials which he volunteers. Serious tumbles from serious heights, innumerable kicks and incessant beatings come on him as matters of common occurrence and leave him every night fresh and free for the next night's flagellation.*

But Grimaldi was an indefatigable worker and during the height of the pantomime season he would often be appearing at two theatres on one evening, so popular was his Clown character. On one particular occasion he was appearing at Sadler's Wells Theatre and immediately after finishing the performance he then had to make an appearance on stage at the Theatre Royal, Drury Lane. He managed to run there in eight minutes – not bad for a distance of just under two miles after an exhausting physical performance!

In another season he was appearing at Sadler's Wells Theatre but then had to be at the Italian Opera House in the Haymarket, some two-and-a-half miles distant. He managed this in 14 minutes, apparently delayed by knocking over an elderly lady along the way. After a short appearance at the Opera House he then ran back to Sadler's Wells Theatre in 13 minutes, with just enough time to don his Clown costume for the concluding part of the entertainment there.

As famous as Grimaldi became, he was not immune to bad reviews, as seen in the review of the Covent Garden Theatre production of *Harlequin Whittington* in *The Times* on 22 December 1814:

> *The least effective part is a dull song by Grimaldi. Nothing could be more injudicious than to put a long ditty into the mouth of a man who has not a note in his voice; with all his nearly irresistible power of producing laughter, it was almost half an hour before he could, by his ludicrous exertions, do away the stupefying effect of his ballad.*

In spite of the occasional unfavourable review, Grimaldi became the most popular clown of the late eighteenth and early nineteenth centuries. As well as appearing in the London theatres, he travelled widely throughout the country, also giving performances in Ireland. Often his performances were sold out and people had to be turned away from the theatre. On one occasion when he was appearing in Maidstone, the announcement of his performance caused great excitement in the town. By 4.30pm a large crowd had gathered outside the theatre and extra constables had to be summoned by the proprietress; those not able to get tickets were turned away. The same thing happened during the following day's performance. For those two sell-out performances, Grimaldi took a half-share of the total takings and left with the sum of £155 and 17s, a substantial amount for the period.

By the age of 48, Grimaldi was physically worn out. The years of gruelling nightly shows with the incessant physicality of his performance, appearing at times in two theatres in one night, the provincial tours and the personal tragedy of his wife dying in childbirth, had all taken its toll. He had risen to become what we might call a 'national treasure', but by the 1820s he was performing less and less, and in 1828 he took his retirement from the stage. He appeared for a final time at the Theatre Royal, Drury Lane, where he had first begun his career in 1780. During the benefit show such was his infirmity that he was able only to appear in one scene from *The Magic Fire* in which he, of course, played the Clown, to much applause.

At the end of the performance he had to sit upon a chair to make his final address, which *The Times* recorded on 30 June 1828:

Ladies and Gentlemen I appear before you for the last time. I need not assure you of the sad regret with which I say it but sickness and infirmity have come upon me and I can no longer wear the 'motley'. Four years ago I jumped my last jump, filched my last custard and ate my last sausage. I cannot describe the pleasure I felt on once more assuming my cap and bells tonight ... I thank you for the benevolence which has brought you here to assist your old and faithful servant in his premature decline ... and I am sinking fast. I now stand worse on my legs than I used to do on my head ... like vaulting ambition I have overreached myself.

With this he made his final farewells to a standing ovation.

Grimaldi died in relative obscurity at his home in Islington in 1837, a broken and depressed man with an inclination towards alcoholism. He was buried in St James's, Pentonville, and the area around later became the Joseph Grimaldi Park. In the park is a coffin-shaped casket set into the ground with phosphor bronze tiles on its surface. These tiles respond to pressure and create musical notes, and by dancing on the 'grave' of Grimaldi, it is possible to play the melody of his most famous song, 'Hot Codlins'.

Joseph Grimaldi became the most celebrated clown of his time and has left a long legacy. He was often referred to as 'Joey' and this name has become synonymous with circus clowns right through to the present. As Richard Findlater states in his 1955 biography of Grimaldi, 'Here is Joey the Clown, the first of 10,000 Joeys who took their name from him'. Even today clowns from all over the world gather annually on 31 May to lay wreaths on the grave of Grimaldi in homage to the man, and on the second Sunday in February each year since 1940, clowns have come together at the Holy Trinity Church in Hackney for an annual service to celebrate clowns.

Throughout the eighteenth century and into the early nineteenth century physical performance skills not only survived but also developed as highly popular forms of entertainment, supported by all classes of society. They took place in a wide variety of venues – from borough fairs to pleasure gardens and the London stage. The circus, as we would recognise it today, was about to be born and it would take one man to pull it all together. That man was Philip Astley.

Chapter Three

Clowns, Competition and Conflagrations: The Circus is Born!

In 1840 Charles Dickens wrote of a visit to Astley's Royal Circus in his novel *The Old Curiosity Shop*:

> *Dear, dear, what a place it looked, that Astley's; with all the paint, gilding, and looking-glass; the vague smell of horses suggestive of coming wonders; the curtain that hid such gorgeous mysteries; the clean white sawdust down in the circus … the clown who ventured on such familiarities with the military man in boots – the lady who jumped over the nine-and-twenty ribbons and came down safe upon the horse's back – everything was delightful, splendid, and surprising!*

Earlier in 1836 Dickens had also written a short story called 'Astley's' in *Sketches by Boz*, which gives a detailed description of the riding master, resplendent in his military uniform, chasing the clown with his whip. But who exactly was Astley? For the answer we must go back to the latter half of the eighteenth century, when war was looming in Germany, and Britain had committed to fighting alongside the King of Prussia against the French. At this time Britain was entering into an age of revolution. The increasing growth of industry was leading to a decline in the traditional agricultural way of life, and with rapid urban expansion people were beginning to migrate towards the cities.

By the turn of the century, London's population had grown to around one million, bringing with it all the attendant problems of increasing poverty, overcrowding and crime. Raw sewage was deposited in the rivers, causing frequent outbreaks of disease. Around the middle of the eighteenth century, the child mortality rate up to the age of five years was approximately 74 per cent, while general life expectancy was about 35 years of age. By the middle of the century, it was estimated that an income of £40 per year was necessary to keep a family, yet at that time a domestic servant could only expect to earn

£2-£3 a year. A skilled carpenter could earn 2s (two shillings) and 6d (six pence) a day, but a porter could only expect 1d per bushel of coal carried. Many families received money from the parish relief fund and might expect a few shillings per week at the most.

Drunkenness was rife in the big cities, and in London during the mid-eighteenth century 11.2 million gallons of gin were consumed a year – approximately seven gallons per adult. Public hangings and floggings were treated as entertainment for the masses. There were still religious tensions across the country and London was to see outbreaks of rioting between Catholics and Protestants. It was a turbulent time.

Amidst all of this, in 1759 a young apprentice cabinetmaker, tired of endless arguments with his father, took himself off to the November Fair in Coventry and joined Colonel Elliott's 15th Dragoons. That young man was Philip Astley. Born in 1742 in Newcastle under Lyme, Staffordshire, he was put to work from an early age with his father Edward, also a cabinetmaker. Philip's interests, however, lay with horses, and whenever he was able to, he would disappear from his workbench to help out with the horses as they pulled into the nearby coaching inn, much to the disapproval of his stern father. By the age of 17, Philip was already a skilled horseman and it is little wonder that he enlisted with a cavalry regiment at the first opportunity.

Broad-chested, 6ft tall, and with a voice to match his size, Philip was put in charge of breaking in the new mounts. He soon caught the eye of the renowned Italian riding master and notable fencer, Domenico

PHILIP ASTLEY.

Born Jan.ʸ 8ᵗʰ 1742

'Twas here the Painter's Task to trace
But the mere Semblance of his Face,
The Portrait of whose Mind more true,
Lo! his own Work presents to view.

Philip Astley: Silhouette from the frontispiece of his book *The System of Equestrian Education*, 1802. *(Reproduced with permission of the National Fairground Archive)*

Angelo Tremamondo. Tremamondo had been engaged to train the regimental riding instructors in the newly developed method of schooling horse and rider to fight as one unit. Astley soon became an accomplished horseman and was already performing a variety of tricks upon horseback; leaping off his horse travelling at full speed and then remounting without breaking pace, or cantering round in a circle standing on his head, heels in the air. It is not surprising that the local people thought that Corporal Astley, as he had become, was the 'devil in disguise'.

Astley saw active service against the French in Germany. At the Battle of Emsdorf in 1760, he is recorded as having captured the enemy's regimental colours, and in the same year, at the Battle of Warburg, he rescued the Duke of Brunswick from the French lines. By this time Astley had risen to the rank of Sergeant Major but his dream was to open his own riding school. On the regiment's return to England he became taken with the idea of performing 'feats of riding' as a means of earning a living and, having been granted a discharge in 1765, made his way to London.

Although horses were his passion, at this stage, due to a lack of funds, he occasionally reverted to his father's old trade to provide a decent income. In September 1766, Philip Astley took on John Hughes as an apprentice in his cabinetmaking business. Around this time Astley also met and married his wife, Patty Jones, a horsewoman herself.

The demonstration of equestrianism was by no means new. As far back as the seventeenth century horses were taught the art of *menage*, in which they would learn to circle, leap and kneel in carefully choreographed sequences. Much of this training was related to the skills required by horses in battle. William Cavendish, the first Duke of Newcastle, was a keen horseman and he built a riding house at Bolsover Castle, where he could demonstrate his theory of the training of horses. The riding school is still in existence and demonstrations can be seen there. Cavendish became known as the 'father of modern dressage' and many of his techniques would have been known by Astley.

Such demonstrations and trick riding were already being given in the pleasure gardens around London. According to a later account by Thomas Frost, a Mr Price was giving displays of horsemanship alongside tumblers and rope-dancers at Dobney's Place in Islington, a popular tea garden and bowling green. At the same time a Mr Sampson was also giving an equestrian demonstration at the Old Hats Public House.

Astley gave demonstrations of horsemanship in similar venues and is thought to have exhibited in the New Spring Gardens. In 1768 he eventually acquired a piece of land on the south bank of the Thames between Blackfriars and Westminster bridges, the site now covered by Waterloo Station. The area was always referred to as 'Halfpenny Hatch' because there was a narrow short cut between the two bridges, along which was set a tollbooth where hurrying pedestrians could pay their halfpenny at the 'hatch'. Alongside this, Astley pegged out a rough circular arena and made the first tentative steps towards creating his riding school. The circular ring, or 'ride' as Astley always called it, was a natural space to present horses to the public, it being easier to watch horses moving in a circle rather than backwards and forwards. Contrary to popular belief, Astley did not invent the 'circus ring' as such, nor did he ever refer to his demonstrations as the 'circus'.

"A REPRESENTATION OF THE SURPRISING PERFORMANCES OF MR. PRICE" AT DOBNEY'S. *Circ.* 1767.

Mr Price performing feats of equestrianism at Dobney's, a well-known tea garden and bowling green in the Pentonville area of London. *(Engraving from W. Wroth,* London Pleasure Gardens of the Eighteenth Century, *Macmillan & Co, 1896)*

A larger than life figure, resplendent in his full military uniform and astride his white charger, Gibraltar, given to him by his commanding officer on his discharge, Astley would parade through the streets around Halfpenny Hatch announcing the forthcoming entertainment:

Activity on horseback of Mr Astley, Serjeant-Major in His Majesty's Royal Regiment of Light Dragoons. Nearly twenty different attitudes will be performed on one, two, and three horses, every evening during the summer, at his riding school. Doors to be open at four, and he will mount at five. Seats, one shilling; standing places, sixpence.

(Quoted in Walford, 1878).

Astley's performances were given in the open air and very much depended upon good weather. However, adjoining the ring were some open fronted wooden sheds, little more than stables, which for the inflated price of two shillings functioned as seating for the more genteel classes should the weather be inclement. Such was the popularity of Astley's performances that on a warm summer's day he could take over 40 guineas, a significant amount of money for that time. There was something about Astley's shows that caught the imagination of the public.

Demonstrations of riding skills had existed long before Astley began his performances in London, so why had he become such an overnight success? The truth is that he was a showman and perhaps this made all the difference. He knew how to interact with his audience and how to build up their expectations, galloping around his ride at full speed before standing on the saddles of two horses and proceeding to jump hurdles. His shows continued in this way, with numerous tricks being performed by Astley himself before he would introduce his 'Little Military Learned Horse' named Billy, bought for five pounds at Smithfield Market. The horse would lie as if dead in the middle of the arena and Astley would begin his prologue:

My horse lies dead, apparent at your sight,
But I am the man who can set things to right,
Speak when you please, I am ready to obey,
My faithful horse knows what I want to say,
But first pray give me leave to move his foot.
That he is dead is quite beyond dispute.

At this point Astley would lift the leg of the horse, which would not react at all. He would then continue in his loud and commanding sergeant major's voice:

> *This shows how brutes by heaven were designed*
> *To be in full subjection to mankind.*
> *Rise, young Bill, and be a little handy,*
> *To serve that warlike hero Granby.*

And at this point the horse would rise to its feet with no obvious command from its master. To conclude, Astley would then turn to his audience and announce:

> *When you have seen, all my bills expressed*
> *My wife, to conclude, performs the rest.*

(Quoted in Wisher, 1937)

He would then lead off Little Billy to thunderous applause as his wife Patty entered the arena, ready to conclude the show with a display of her

Views of Astley's Amphitheatre at Halfpenny Hatch, c. 1770. (*From an engraving published in* Old and New London *by E. Walford 1878)*

own trick-riding – standing on her head, also firing a pistol while balancing on two horses. Sometimes Astley would join his wife and they would both ride the same two horses around the arena simultaneously. Mrs Astley's performances came to a halt in 1767 when she produced their only child, John Conway Philip Astley, who would later continue the work of his father.

With his success at Halfpenny Hatch, it soon became apparent to Philip Astley that he needed to build something bigger and better. As well as providing shelter for his audiences, he needed a structure that was more than just a pegged out arena in a field, something visible which made a statement. In 1769 he managed to secure a plot of land between Westminster Bridge Road and Stanton Street, now occupied by much of St Thomas' Hospital. Coincidentally, Joseph Grimaldi also had lodgings in this street, although at a later date.

Astley managed to secure a mortgage on the site but was still short of funds to complete his project. Fate then intervened and, so the story goes, he found a diamond ring whilst crossing Westminster Bridge. It was unclaimed and he sold it for £60, providing enough funds to build a wooden fenced enclosure. Although the new Astley's Riding House was still an open–air arena, the high wooden fences provided some shelter and it gave the impression of a substantial structure created solely for the purpose of equestrian displays.

On the opening day, Patty Astley paraded around the area's narrow streets, banging a drum and accompanied by two pipers, whilst the imposing figure of Astley stood before the entrance inviting all to step inside. The road around Astley's Riding School soon became blocked with a throng of people and extra constables had to be sent for. It was not long before he made sufficient profit to build a covered entrance way and roofed stands around the arena, providing more shelter for the ever-increasing numbers who flocked to his shows.

During this period Astley also began to realise that displays of horsemanship alone would not retain the interest of the public. A consummate showman, he understood that people wanted to be entertained and so he expanded his performances to include a clown named Fortunelly, who performed on the slack-rope, and a strong man, Colpi. The Italian Colpi performed feats of strength by balancing his children on the soles of his feet, a style of circus performance known today as a 'Risley Act', named after the nineteenth century American circus athlete Richard Risley. Astley also engaged a troupe of tumblers who performed acrobatic feats, including building a human pyramid, standing upon each others' shoulders. The circus had been born – and yet it was left to another to officially adopt the term 'circus'.

Astley was a man gifted with luck, always seeming to be in the right place at the right time, and in 1771 another piece of good fortune fell his way. King George III was processing over Westminster Bridge when his horse was suddenly startled by the mass of people crowding to see him pass. The horse reared and plunged and would have thrown the King had not Astley stepped forward and calmed it. To show his gratitude, the King invited Astley and his company to give a command performance before the royal household in Richmond Park performance. The performance was so well received that Astley was subsequently invited to Paris by the French Ambassador, who happened to be present at the Royal Court that day.

Artistic rivalry is nothing new and it has been said that imitation is the highest form of flattery. Astley's company included a young horseman named Charles Hughes. An equally accomplished horseman and trick rider, he must have seen how lucrative such performances had become. Whilst Astley travelled to France in 1772 and performed before the royal household at Fontainebleu, Hughes left Astley's company and leased a plot of land south of Blackfriars Bridge. Here he set up a wooden palisade similar to Astley's and opened the Hughes' Riding School.

Astley immediately returned to London to confront this upstart competitor, declaiming Hughes as nothing more than a 'pretender'. Unfortunately for him, people flocked to Hughes' Riding School to see how well this 'pretender' could do, and so their rivalry began. Hughes performed an increasing variety of equestrian tricks; Astley presented military spectaculars, showing how the 15th Light Dragoons had charged the French infantry in Germany. The more vocal the animosity between them, the better it was for business, although is it more than probable that they capitalised upon this very open rivalry as a means of publicity.

Then fate took a hand. At that time theatres had to be licensed in order to allow performances to take place. Neither Astley nor Hughes had applied for a licence and accordingly the Surrey Magistrates closed both riding schools in 1773. Dispirited by this, Hughes took his company on a long tour of Europe, and after performing before heads of state in Portugal, Germany, Italy and even Morocco, he ended up presenting his equestrian acts in St Petersburg before Catherine the Great. His feats of riding captured her imagination and she ordered that two circus rings be built for especially for him, in St Petersburg and Moscow. Because of this, Hughes is commonly credited with bringing the circus to Russia.

Astley, meanwhile, went on a tour of the British Isles, establishing an amphitheatre in Dublin and drawing crowds wherever he went. In 1774 he travelled to Paris and performed with his company at the rue des Vielles Tuileries before returning to England later in the year. The tour continued throughout 1774 and in addition to riding skills, he also gave a much more bizarre and dangerous exhibition, as advertised in the *Caledonian Mercury* at the New Tumbler's Hall in Bailie Fyfe's Close, just off the Royal Mile in Edinburgh:

> *On Monday next (besides the usual diversions of this place) Mr Astley will perform the grand Experience with a LOADED PISTOL. He will suffer any man in the company to Fire at him, when he will receive the Ball at the Point of a Knife, on a principle never attempted by anyone before (Sieur Comus of Paris excepted).*
> *Admittance one shilling*
> *Doors to be open at six o'clock and to begin precisely at seven.*
> (10 and 14 December 1774, Caledonian Mercury)

For the audience, it must have been a terrifying sight to see the popular hero Astley face a loaded pistol. What trickery was involved in this act we will never know, as there was no report that he was injured during this act. The only injury he ever encountered was when he 'cut his hand by lifting up a sashed window' and therefore had to cancel a performance, in 1777.

Throughout this time Astley was applying for a licence to perform in his own amphitheatre, which was granted in 1775. In the same year as the American War of Independence began, the Amphitheatre reopened to much acclaim; as his rival Hughes was still abroad, he now had no real competition. Realising that the building now needed to be bigger and better, he started to make plans to have the structure roofed as this would allow him to present performances the whole year round.

Timber was very expensive but Astley realised that there would be a lot of spare wood left over after a large public event that year in the city, which would otherwise have been burned. There was also an election taking place at the time and much wood was being used to build the hustings. By making his need known to the people responsible for taking down these structures – with the promise to reward them well for bringing him timber – he gathered enough wood and planking together to complete the task. The roofing of the Amphitheatre was completed by 1780. Astley advertised 'Winter Evening

The interior of Astley's c.1810: One of a number of colour plates reproduced by the Dutch Dairy Bureau for their album 'The colourful world of the circus', produced in the 1950s. *(Author's collection)*

Amusements', involving horsemanship, vaulting, balancing, feats with ropes and ladders, as well as a clown number.

His amphitheatre was now fully enclosed, with two tiers of private boxes and a gallery. The performance area consisted of a pit (or ring) fronting a stage upon which pantomimes could be staged. The domed roof was painted with trees and foliage '*à la mode Française*' and Astley renamed his building the 'Royal Grove'. His son John began to make a name for himself in the new arena. Posing as only five years old, although he was nearer 10, John performed feats of horsemanship. An advertising bill of the time shows him standing on his head on the saddle, leaping on the saddle and standing with one foot on the saddle, the other on the neck of the horse, and all at the gallop. A speech balloon issuing from the mouth of Astley junior declares, 'I'm only five years old'.

In 1781, after spending eight years abroad, mostly in Russia, Charles Hughes returned to England and went into partnership with Charles Dibdin, a noted songwriter and musician. They leased a plot of land in an area known as St George's Circus and set about constructing a stone building that was grandly named the 'Royal Circus and Equestrian Philharmonic Academy', later known as the 'Royal Circus'. This is the first record of the word circus being given to a building or structure specifically used for such entertainments. Although Astley is credited with being the 'father of the circus', it is his rival Hughes who should be recognised for popularising the actual term 'circus'.

The Royal Circus was bigger and better than Astley's Royal Grove and Astley was consumed with jealousy. An increasingly acrimonious war of words began: Astley was accused of poisoning Hughes' horses, Hughes was accused of performing without a licence. The recriminations continued until both were arrested in 1783 for performing music and dancing without a licence. Hughes won his case in court but Astley had to agree not to perform music and dance, although he later continued to do so in spite of the ruling. Instead, Astley turned to using fireworks in his shows, employing a well-known pyrotechnical expert, Signor Hengler, who would also become famous in the world of the circus.

The performances given in both establishments were a mixture of equestrian and physical skills, music, song and dance, and very often some form of burlesque or harlequinade to complete the evening's entertainment. Today these would seem more like Variety or Music Hall acts. *The Times* of 20 June 1786 gives advertisements for three different venues featuring similar styles of performances. At Jones' Equestrian Amphitheatre in Whitechapel one could see the Egyptian Pyramids represented by 12 strong men; the celebrated English Hercules; Horsemanship and various other Feats of Manly Activity; and the Child of Promise (only three years old) on the tightrope.

At the Royal Grove it was possible to see Young Astley's new exercises on several horses, 'and which no other horseman in the world can perform'; two different musical pieces, a new dance, tumbling and other exercises, an astonishing monkey rope dancer, horsemanship 'in the highest perfection', the best mandolin player in the world, nine strong men performing 'real Venetian exercises', and a concluding pantomime.

The Royal Circus was offering the public Signor Charini and his troupe performing on the wire, tightrope and trampoline, 'far superior to any that have appeared in this Kingdom', including a 10-year-old boy whose performances are 'so extraordinary that Mr Hughes will give 100 guineas to anyone who can equal him on the tightrope'; Monsieur Balmat who will throw a back somersault 22 feet in the air and flip-flaps with his legs tied together; a Burletta, New Dances, and Horsemanship by Hughes. The circus had arrived!

After losing his monopoly in London, Astley continued to develop his work in France. No longer performing on horseback but still very much the 'equestrian director', he was now taking on the recognisable role of the 'ring master'. In 1783, as a result of his son performing before Queen Marie Antoinette in Versailles, Astley was granted a Royal Privilege, giving him permission to open a permanent amphitheatre on the rue de Faubourg du Temple (now in the area of the Place de la Republique), which he called the '*Amphitheatre Anglais des Sieurs Astley, père et fils*'. He now owned two amphitheatres in two European capital cities and he was soon also granted a Royal Patent to open a further permanent amphitheatre in Dublin.

The outbreak of the French Revolution in 1789 curtailed Astley's work in France and he had to lease his property in Paris and return to England. One of the lessees was an Antonio Franconi, who later became known as the 'father' of French circus. During this period Astley continued to tour the British Isles successfully, as well as performing in London. While Astley was expanding his empire, Hughes and the Royal Circus were experiencing increasing problems. Endless internal disputes eventually saw Charles Dibdin leave the company and growing financial difficulties, along with licensing issues, saw the Royal Circus go into decline. The West family, who had leased the property to Dibdin and Hughes, repossessed their land.

In 1792 a young man of the company named John Bill Ricketts departed to the newly-formed United States of America to establish his own riding school there. Ricketts, a Scot by birth, was a skilled horseman and known for his trick riding at the Royal Circus. He had already gone into partnership in 1791 with a John Parker at the Circus Royal in Edinburgh. Now with his own company, he founded a riding school in Philadelphia, then the capital of the United States. He went on to construct a roofless arena, based upon Astley's principles, which he named 'The Circus', and apparently even George Washington attended at least one performance there.

Ricketts' shows were a mixture of equestrian demonstrations, trick riding, clowns and tightrope walkers. He spent seven years touring the United States, introducing his own brand of circus, travelling from the south right up to the province of Quebec. Wherever he went he built amphitheatres but Philadelphia was always his base. He developed 'The Circus' into an impressive roofed building named 'Ricketts' Art Pantheon and Amphitheatre' but, like many other amphitheatres of the time, it burned to the ground in 1799. After the fire, Ricketts decided to travel to the West Indies, but not long after he arrived there he decided to return to England. Selling all his horses and chartering a small ship, he set sail but the ship was never seen again and was presumed to have been lost at sea. In spite of his relative youth, Ricketts is rightly considered as the founder of the circus in America.

While this was happening, on the other side of the Atlantic, although he continued to impress the Russian court, Hughes did not have Astley's business acumen and was unable to capitalise on this. Returning from Russia, he had little success – his audience in London began to drift away and the building gradually fell into a state of disrepair. It is said that the final loss of his licence led to his death, at the age of 50, in 1797. Astley may have laid down the form but it had been Hughes who coined the name of the circus.

Astley continued to go from strength to strength, despite a succession of near-disasters. When war broke out in 1793 against Napoleonic France, he immediately re-enlisted in the Dragoons and was sent again to France as a 'horsemaster'. The Royal Grove was left in the capable hands of his son John, but in 1794 it too was destroyed by fire – the fate of many wooden structures in London at this time. Astley returned immediately and organised the rebuilding of 'Astleys New Amphitheatre of the Arts', which opened in 1795. It was modelled on the Royal Circus, with an equestrian ring and a full stage. During the rebuilding phase Astley still gave performances, although he was beginning to diversify and experiment with new technology, as advertised in *The Times*, 19 September 1794:

> *Exhibition of the Telegraphe*
> *Astley's New Circus at the Lyceum, Strand*
> *This and every evening (until further notice) will be presented a pleasing variety of capital entertainments which for the very first time these five years*, [includes] *Les Ombres Chinoise* [a form of shadow play].

But for all this he still returned to the love of his life – his horses, for at the foot of the same advertisement appear the words, 'After which a grand display of the most surprising feats of horsemanship'.

The New Amphitheatre of the Arts had a short existence; in 1796 it was seriously damaged by fire. Undaunted, the Astleys rebuilt the wooden structure yet again and continued to perform. After the Treaty of Amiens, Astley senior returned again to France in 1802 to negotiate with the French authorities for the return of his lease on his amphitheatre in Paris. Much to his surprise, this was granted but in May 1803, with the failure of the Peace Treaty, Napoleon declared that all British nationals should be detained in

France. Astley was now a prisoner of war and to make matters worse his London Amphitheatre was burned down yet again.

A vivid contemporary account paints an horrific picture:

FIRE AT ASTLEY'S AMPHITHEATRE

On Friday morning, between two and three o'clock, this beautiful and superb edifice situated on the Surrey side of Westminster bridge, was discovered to be on fire. The flames, which must have been long collected in the interior burst from the roof of the building like a volcano, illuminating for a while the whole horizon, and threatening with destruction a considerable part of the very crowded and populous neighbourhood. How or in what part of the Theatre this calamity began has not yet been ascertained.

It is the second visitation of this kind which has befallen the always loyal and patriotic but now unfortunate Astleys – the old gentleman is at present captive in France; an affectionate wife, a prey to death in his absence, but two days buried; and now the whole of his property, and with it the means of his family's subsistence, a sacrifice to an all devouring conflagration, which, raging with uncontroulable [sic] fury for upwards of three hours has desolated not less than eleven houses in the rear of the Amphitheatre. These were inhabited by persons in ordinary circumstances who, shivering and naked in the streets, were glad to escape with their lives.

To add to the calamity, Mrs Woodman, mother-in-law to young Mr Astley, perished in the flames. She was far advanced in life, but was seen running from window to window, imploring that help which two neighbours, Mr Burton and Mr Moor, were hastening with a ladder to afford her, when the floor fell in and put a period, for ever, to her sufferings. Her headless trunk has since been dug out of the ruins. Two children belonging to a poor man who inhabited one of the houses that has been destroyed, had nearly perished, but were most providentially saved.

(*The Aberdeen Journal*, 7 September 1803)

Astley somehow managed to make an escape, and by trickery and deception made his way to Holland and from there back to England. On his return, he rebuilt the amphitheatre with a larger stage than ever, reputedly the largest in London at that time, and the interiors were lavishly painted and fully lit by a huge chandelier, a present from the Duke of York. It must have been a spectacular sight, a truly glittering palace full of the promise of the wonders to come. It is easy to imagine the excitement of a visit to Astley's and you are now invited to step inside and take a look.

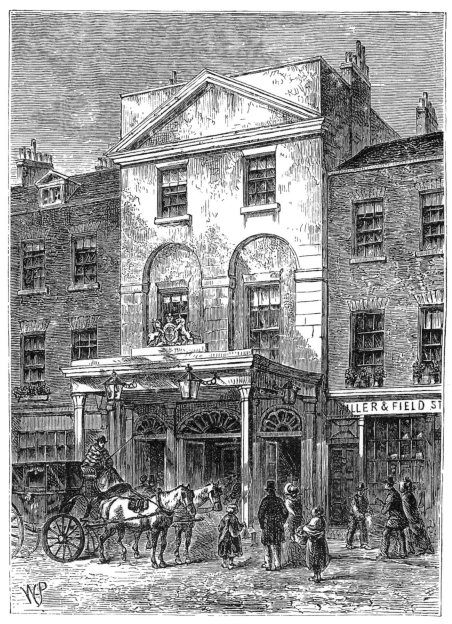

The entrance to Astley's Amphitheatre in 1820, from an engraving published in *Old and New London* by E. Walford (1878). *(Author's collection)*

It is 8.30pm. You have paid your half-price late entry fee of one shilling and you join the throng of people. You will have to stand at the back and join the other latecomers, for the place is crowded. Those who came earlier have paid the full price of two shillings for a seat in the pit and are packed tightly around the ring. An enormous glittering chandelier lit by hundreds of candles, is suspended above the circular ring and casts a warm glow on the proceedings. The first thing you notice is the smell – of burning tallow candles, of the sawdust in the ring, the odour of horses and the stink of the crowd packed tightly together.

The galleries soar above the ring, almost disappearing into the gloom of the ceiling beyond the chandelier. There are two galleries of boxes full of seated people, ladies and gentlemen in their finery and some men in military uniforms. They have paid the princely sum of four shillings a head to sit there. Above them the people in the upper gallery must have a marvellous view of that chandelier for the entry price of one shilling! It is hot up there and the heat from the candles and the crowd below gathers beneath the roof. The crowd in the upper gallery are three deep, the first row sitting, the next standing behind them and the third row standing on a bench with their hands on the shoulders of those in front to stop them pitching forward.

Much of the woodwork is gilded and the candlelight bounces and dazzles around the arena; it looks as if the whole building is made out of gold. Plush red panels are painted on the fascias of the ring boards and the galleries, and this matches the dark red of the velvet curtains covering an enormous stage opening that reaches almost to the top of the building. The orchestra is seated between the front of the stage and the ring and are playing a merry tune. In the ring at this moment is a young woman astride three white horses. As they gallop in a circle she balances on one leg on the middle horse and her diaphanous costume billows out behind her. The clown in the middle of the ring laughs and claps. He looks comical in his brightly striped costume, white pointed hat and garish make-up. The crowd claps and cheers and those in the upper gallery strain forward to see more. And so the show continues.

The Amphitheatre opened to the public on Easter Monday 1804, but for all its apparent opulence, a closer examination of the structure may have alarmed the audience. Recycled ship's timbers had been used for the framework of the building and the roof was little more than a canvas-draped scaffolding covered with pitch and tar. Astley wanted more. His amphitheatre was still restricted by a magistrate's licence issued in Lambeth and he was technically unable to present performances during the winter months. He needed a Royal Licence from the Lord Chamberlain to give performances throughout the year.

When Astley had been discharged from service in 1794 he had received a letter from the Duke of York recommending him to Queen Charlotte as a good and bold soldier. He had kept the letter all this time and now he was to use it for his benefit. He appealed to the Queen, who then instructed the Lord Chamberlain to grant him the licence he required.

Astley was now free to build a theatre in Westminster and he chose a site on the Strand for the 'Olympic Pavilion', which opened to the public in 1806. This was a substantial stone building with a large ring and full stage, which at times had to be used for part of the equestrian displays as so many horses were now involved. All his advertising for the new Olympic Pavilion carried the line 'established by authority of the Lord Chamberlain' to prevent any competitors making false accusations of licence infringement. Although his shows still featured tightrope artists and clowns, he began to lean more towards large-scale equestrian displays and horsemanship rather than trick riding.

An advertisement in *The Times* of 1807 shows how his performances had changed:

Haydn's minuet danced by two horses … concluding with a third horse dancing a Pas Seul to the popular air of the Yorkshire Gala; the whole exhibiting a pure example of the noble elements of the Equestrian Art and Science, so strongly necessary in the field of honour and to victory!

The performance also included large equestrian spectacles called *The Polish Tyrant* and *The News from Copenhagen*, various equestrian exercises, and concluded with a popular harlequinade of the period, *The Will of Fate*.

The Olympic Pavilion had a limited success for a few years but it was moving away from circus-style performances to equestrian theatre. The larger the displays, the more complicated the stage machinery became and the audience often found themselves waiting for lengthy periods for scene changes. They began to drift away towards other, more immediate, entertainments and in 1813 Astley took the decision to close. He had lost a significant amount of money and he sold the building, and the licence, to an actor named Elliston who reopened the Pavilion as the 'Little Drury Lane Theatre'.

Astley now returned to his home in Paris, where a year later, in 1814, he died aged 72. He was buried in the Pére Lachaise Cemetery in Paris, where sadly his grave is no longer visible. His son John continued for a short while as co-manager of the Amphitheatre in Lambeth with William Davis. Seven years later, John died and the reign of the Astleys had come to an end.

What had begun in an open field at Halfpenny Hatch was beginning to grow into an international entertainment form. The legacy of Astley and

Hughes would form the basis of circus as we know it today. The ring had been established, great houses were being built and known as the 'circus'; the basic format of the show had been founded with animals, physical skills and clowns, and the role of the ringmaster had been invented. Not only had the circus become established in amphitheatres across the United Kingdom but it had now also spread across Europe, through France into Russia and across the ocean to the United States of America. Companies had been formed to present this style of performance and artists of all nationalities were now training.

No longer would they perform on street corners and at fairs; now they had venues in which to present their skills. The circus had been born and the forthcoming period would give rise to some of the most famous names in its history.

Chapter Four

The Queen and the 'Lion King':
The Rise of the Nineteenth Century Menageries

During the first years of the nineteenth century Britain was in a state of flux, with the Napoleonic Wars, growing industrialisation, political unrest and rapid urban development. However, for the majority of the rural population this was all far removed from their everyday lives, and for them the major concerns were keeping bread on the table and a roof over their heads. In market towns and villages around the country a visiting fair provided a time of light relief from the daily toil.

Modern fairs are geared towards satiating pleasure seekers, with gaudy fluorescent lighting, stomach churning rides, hot dogs and loud music. The country fairs of the nineteenth century were very different. They provided opportunities to socialise with friends and family. People came together, very often from isolated rural communities, to share news and gossip over a mug of ale. They played games, and races were common, as was bowling for a pig. Goods and animals were bought and sold, produce was displayed and contracts made. They were very much working fairs and it was against this background that the travelling circuses provided an element of pleasure and excitement.

Social revolutions very often lead to artistic revolutions. It could be argued that circus was born of war, for the wars of the late eighteenth century produced many skilled horsemen who, on discharge from service, turned their hand to demonstrations of trick riding. Philip Astley was not unique in this, but he gave an artistic structure and form to these skills and, in doing so, spawned many imitators. While Astley and Hughes were vying to create their circus empires in major cities across Europe, many smaller circus groups were still travelling the British countryside.

Although there had always been itinerant performers at fairs and markets, these groups brought together a variety of different performance skills. They sought to emulate the popularity of the new circus form being displayed in London and other major cities. They were on a much smaller scale and often had only a few acts – maybe two or three horses, a clown, a tumbler and perhaps a rope-dancer. Their patched and worn canvas enclosures were nowhere near as large or as opulent as the amphitheatres of Astley and Hughes, merely simple rectangular structures with a ring pegged out inside.

Sometimes they had no enclosure at all and instead pegged out their performance space in an open field, just as Astley had done early in his career. It was not until 1836, when a circus owner named Thomas Cooke returned from a tour in America with a portable canvas structure, that the recognisable circus tent became regularly used.

The day before a country fair, a small group of horse-drawn wagons would arrive and the circus would be pitched. If it was wet, then wooden hurdles were laid on the ground to help the fairgoers across the mud. A platform was set up in front of the tent and on the day of the fair, the circus owner, resplendent in mock military uniform, would stand upon it banging a drum to gain attention. With loud cries of 'Roll up!' or 'Step up!' he would gather the crowd to him and then offer them sights they had never seen before. He might promise 'riding skills as seen on the battlefields of Germany,' or 'feats as witnessed only before in the mighty amphitheatres of London'. Often he might display his dappled or piebald horses upon the platform with him, while his clown bantered with the crowd.

As soon as the crowd had parted with their money and entered the tent, the horses would be led around the back to the ring. Standing or sitting on straw bales, the audience was then entertained with a comparatively brief show led by the circus owner as the 'ring master', keeping up a continuous banter with the clown as he performed his antics. Acrobats and tumblers might perform flips and somersaults and a pretty girl often graced the tightrope. The main focus was on the horses and the tricks that riders performed upon them.

At the end of the show as the crowd departed, the horses were led back round to the platform and the circus owner would begin his patter again for the next show. And so this pattern continued throughout the day, often well into the evening, with shows being given as long as seats could be filled.

Sometimes the circus owner took no payment from the crowd, preferring to sell lottery tickets instead. As soon as he had drummed up enough interest and the tent was full, while the first act was going on, the other performers would move amongst the audience selling tickets. At the end of the show, the tickets were drawn and prizes such as plated teapots, silk handkerchiefs and other trinkets were handed out to the winners. Of course, the cost of the tickets sold far exceeded the value of prizes given out.

Often the audience was drawn into the fun of the show. Climbing a greasy pole to reach a leg of lamb or pork was always a popular challenge and members of the audience would pay a small fee to try their hand at this, much to the amusement of the rest of the crowd. At the end of the fair, the circus would take down its tent, load its wagons, harness up the horses and move on to the next pitch, leaving only a well-trodden patch of grass and memories behind it.

British travelling circuses tended to work in regional areas. Thomas Frost, in his book *Circus Life and Circus Celebrities* (1881), records that the northern counties were toured by circuses belonging to Bannister, Holloway, Milton and Wild. The southern areas were covered by Clarke, Cooke, Samwell and Saunders. Circuses were very secretive about their plans and often would not reveal too much information about where they would be visiting, unless another competitor should 'steal their pitch'. Even today, circuses will not reveal their itineraries too far in advance for the same reason.

Several performers who started out in the provincial travelling circuses went on to become famous names in the larger circuses. William Wallett, a well-known clown (who we shall meet again later in connection with Pablo Fanque), began performing on the northern circuit with Holloway's circus at fairs in Hull, Gainsborough, Keighley and Leeds, before moving on to the more established circuses of the time.

Alongside the circus, another popular fairground entertainment of this period was the travelling menagerie exhibiting wild and exotic animals. At this time circuses and menageries were quite separate arrangements and it was not until later in the nineteenth century that wild animals became a regular part of circus entertainments. Horses were still the principal animals being used in performances at the time. During the eighteenth and nineteenth centuries, ordinary people rarely travelled beyond their own counties, let alone to foreign lands.

Whatever our modern views concerning wild animals in captivity, the exhibition of wild animals provided a great source of wonder and education at that time. As reported in *The Morning Chronicle* in 1813: 'The study of natural history is now considered as forming a necessary part of the education of young persons and in no place can so much instruction and information on the subject be obtained save by visiting the splendid menagerie of Mr Polito'.

The exhibition of wild animals has an ancient tradition. Egyptian pharaohs, Roman and Chinese emperors and even Alexander the Great all kept menageries for their amusement. In England, wild cats, hyenas, bears and even an elephant were kept as part of a menagerie in the Tower

A Frost Fair held on the River Thames in 1682. *(Engraving from* Old and New London *by E. Walford, 1878)*

The menagerie at the Tower of London c.1820. *(Engraving from* Old and New London *by E. Walford, 1878)*

of London until 1835. The Close Court Rolls of Edward III in 1337 instruct Dinas Forcetti and Peter Byrne of the Society of the Bardi (Italian merchant bankers) to deliver to the keeper of the king's lions and leopards three shillings and one pence daily; one shilling for his daily wage and the remainder for the maintenance of the animals. In the eighteenth century the menagerie was opened to the public and the admission price was one and a half pence, or a cat or dog to feed the lions.

Outside the royal menagerie and other privately-owned aristocratic collections, one of the earliest recorded exhibitions of animals is attributed to a James Chipperfield. During the extremely cold conditions of the winter of 1638, the River Thames froze solid to a depth of one foot. People were able to walk across it in safety and a great 'frost fair' was held on the frozen river. For two months, streets of booths and stalls were laid out on the ice and around them were entertainments of all descriptions; puppet plays, horse races and bull bating. It was here that James Chipperfield exhibited his menagerie and established the Chipperfields as possibly the oldest British family continuously involved in fairs and circuses.

During the eighteenth century, Pidcock's Wild Beast Show became the most famous public menagerie in London. It was regularly exhibited at St Bartholomew's Fair. and the winter quarters were at a building called the Exeter Exchange, off the Strand. In 1773, he made it a permanent exhibition space, and renamed it the Royal Menagerie. Contemporary paintings show a well-lit, paved area surrounded by cages full of animals. When Pidcock died in 1810, his collection was put up for auction and according to *The Morning Chronicle*, it included: 'An elephant, lion and lioness, the male nylghaw [an Indian antelope], the great camel, male panther, North American elk, Pensacola deer, Bramin bull only twenty one inches high, several rare monkeys and birds'.

Stephanus Polito subsequently bought the Pidcock menagerie. Polito was born in Italy in 1763, but by 1790 he must have moved to London as there is a record of his marriage to a Sarah White in that year. He went on to develop the menagerie over several

Entry token to Pidcock's Exhibition, early nineteenth century. *(Author's collection)*

years and, while still maintaining the Exeter Exchange, he toured his Royal Menagerie extensively throughout Britain and Ireland. Polito was never one for modesty and made extravagant claims in newspaper advertisements. During a visit to the Leeds Fair in 1811, Polito offered his: 'Grand exhibition of living curiosities … the largest menagerie that ever travelled the kingdom' (*The Leeds Mercury*, 1811).

By this time he had expanded his collection to include a sloth, a black swan, baboons and a condor. Most of his descriptions of the creatures in the collection included the phrase 'the only one'. By 1812 he had added more animals to the travelling show and was still making extravagant claims:

> *To avoid imposition S. Polito respectfully assures the public that neither lion, male elephant, ostrich, pelican, crown crane, adjutant* [crane], *black swan, male and female royal tigers or perfect* [sic] *hyenas are to be met with in any travelling exhibition at this present time in this kingdom.'*
>
> (*Trewman's Exeter Flying Post*, 1812).

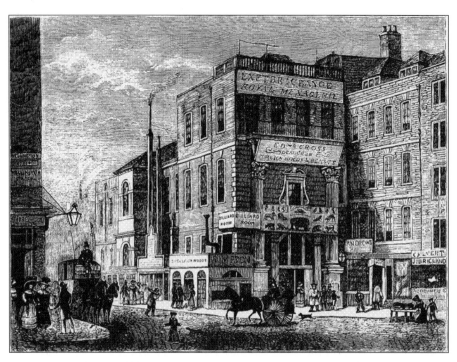

The Exeter Exchange c.1826. *(Engraving from* Old and New London *by E. Walford, 1878)*

Even after his death in 1814, when his manager Edward Cross bought up the Exeter Exchange, the menagerie still toured under the banner of 'Polito's Menagerie'.

Polito's was not the only menagerie touring at this time. In 1810, *The Derby Mercury* refers to a rattlesnake and a crocodile on display at Mr Kendrick's Menagerie in Piccadilly, London. Atkins, Wombwell, Jamrach and Cross certainly had menageries in operation at this time. George Wombwell, a shoemaker from London, began his collection by buying two boa constrictor snakes from a South American ship in London and displaying them in taverns. His rival, Thomas Atkins, later became the director of the Liverpool Zoological Gardens. William Cross and Charles Jamrach were both dealers and importers of wild animals, who kept small menageries that they exhibited.

Menagerie proprietors were keen to assure the public that their animals were well kept. Polito's advertisements usually concluded with a statement in small print, such as, 'the clean and secure state of all the animals is generally noticed with the highest credit to the managers'. In this Polito was almost anticipating the debate on the legal position of wild animals that took place in Parliament in 1819. With specific reference to the animals in Polito's menagerie, a motion was put forward by a Member of Parliament, Mr Lawson, to protect 'all animals reclaimed from their savage nature and subjected to the use of man'. His object was to punish the offence of their theft with seven years' transportation or a whipping.

The timing of this proposal was fortunate for the two men who had been arrested the year before, for attempting to release a lion and a tiger from a menagerie. Whether their motives were pity, avarice or sheer vandalism is not recorded. The Royal Menagerie at the Exeter Exchange was inspected regularly and the inspectors' findings were reported in the press. In 1819 the inspectors were 'pleased to signify their entire approbation with the security, cleanliness and order with which the different apartments were kept'.

That is not to say that there were no critics of the keeping of animals for exhibition. The writer and journalist Thomas Frost makes the following point in his 1875 book, *The Old Showmen and the Old London Fairs*:

It is impossible to do justice to animals which are cooped within the narrow limits of a travelling show, or in any place which does not admit of thorough ventilation. Apart from the impracticability of allowing sufficient space and a due supply of air, a considerable amount of discomfort to the animals is inseparable from continuous jolting about the country in caravans, and from the braying of brass bands and the glare of gas at evening exhibitions.

Unfortunate incidents did, however, take place. On 24 October 1816 an 'Extraordinary Occurrence' was reported in the *Caledonian Mercury*:

> *The Exeter mail coach, on its way to London, was attacked last night at Winterlow Hut, seven miles on this side of Salisbury, in a most extraordinary manner. At the moment when the coachman pulled up to deliver his bags, one of the leaders was suddenly seized by a ferocious animal. This produced great confusion and alarm, two passengers who were inside the mail got out, ran into the house, and locked themselves up in a room above stairs; the horses kicked and plunged violently, and it was with difficulty the coachman could prevent the carriage from being overturned.*
>
> *It was soon perceived by the coachman and guard, by the light of the lamps, that the animal which had seized the horse was a huge lioness. A large mastiff dog came up and attacked her fiercely, on which she quitted the horse and turned upon him. The dog fled but was pursued and killed by the lioness, within about forty yards of the place. It appears that the beast had escaped from a caravan that was standing on the road side, belonging to the proprietors of a menagerie on the way to Salisbury fair.*

The lioness was subsequently recaptured and returned to her cage. The dog and horse died but fortunately there was no loss of human life. Although it was not reported in the press, it is possible that the lioness escaped from Ballard's Grand Collection of Wild Beasts, which was advertising in the area at the time.

Escaping wild cats always caused alarm and sometimes resulted in fatalities. In 1834, a lion and a tigress escaped from Wombwell's menagerie after their caravan collided with a wagon loaded with timber, near Wirksworth in Derbyshire. Although hasty repairs were made to the caravan, the animals managed to escape and attacked several sheep and a cow. The keepers and nearby farm labourers hunted down the animals but not before the lion turned on one of the men and killed him. In the meantime the tigress had gone in a different direction and went on to attack a woman and baby, then a young boy, killing all three before being recaptured.

In 1820, three wild buffalo went on the rampage through the streets of London. They were being driven to the Exeter Exchange on the Strand, when they became startled by the boisterous crowd gathered to see them. From the report in *The Morning Chronicle*, it appears that they took in most of central London, passing around Charing Cross, Pall Mall, St James's Square, Piccadilly, Bond Street, Oxford Road and Park Lane. They were eventually recaptured without any undue damage or injury, after a protracted chase, although two horses were gored in the escapade.

Even at sea it was not always safe to travel with wild animals. On 15 April 1877, *Reynold's Newspaper* reported that a rhinoceros, being transported as part of Montgomery Queen's Circus and Menagerie, had broken free in rough seas. It terrorised the crew, gored and killed a fine horse and trampled two dogs to death.

Such mishaps occurred all over the world. An elephant was being transported in a mobile cage to the fair at Leipzig. Unobserved by its keeper, the elephant managed to remove some of the wooden spars of the cage and walk free. Whilst the keeper and cage continued on their way to Leipzig, the elephant set off in the opposite direction for Pirna. There it came across some women on their way to market who, never having seen such an animal before, ran off in consternation, abandoning their carts and provisions. The elephant took advantage of the free breakfast before being recaptured by its keeper.

Menagerie proprietors began to expand their collections with ever more exotic creatures, Wombwell's even obtaining a polar bear in 1820. Public

Feeding the lions was a popular attraction at the menagerie, as shown here in an 1891 print. *(Library of Congress)*

safety became a concern and it was necessary to reassure the public. With the arrival of an 11 foot-long boa constrictor snake to Polito's menagerie, he gave this assurance in *The Aberdeen Journal* of 1816: 'It is large in proportion and perfectly secure. The most timorous may approach it with safety'.

For all this, accidents did happen, and all too frequently. Most common of all reported were accidents caused by members of the public either standing too close to a cage or attempting to stroke or feed the animals. In Paris in 1816, a celebrated engineer was killed by an elephant at the menagerie in the Garden of Plants. While he offered the elephant something to eat, the animal, accidentally provoked, struck the man so forcibly that his arm was driven into the palisade surrounding the enclosure. In spite of efforts to save the injured man, he died.

In other recorded incidents a man had three fingers bitten off by a hyena because he decided to 'pet' the animal, against the advice of the keeper. A boy was mauled by a lion because he had walked too close to the bars of the cage. In a famous case of 1877, a lady was so badly bitten by a dromedary camel that her arm had to be amputated. The menagerie owner, John Day, was taken to court and the judge ruled that his menagerie should be seized and sold.

Menageries were chiefly places to observe strange and exotic animals, yet they also became places of entertainment. Animals were now performers, as their keepers showed what tricks they could do. Lord Byron visited the Exeter Exchange in 1813 and described how an elephant took his money and then returned it to him. It removed his hat, opened a door, held a whip in its trunk and behaved so well he commented that he wished it could be his butler.

In 1812, Polito advertised another performing elephant in the Royal Menagerie in Exeter which: 'By the command of his keeper will perform so many wonderful tricks that will not only astonish and entertain the audience but justly prove him the half-reasoning beast' (*Trewman's Exeter Flying Post*, 1812). Elephants, however, were not always so obliging towards their keepers. In 1877, the *Liverpool Mercury* reported on an incident where an elephant turned on his keeper and trampled him to death. In 1814, the *Morning Chronicle* reported on an advertisement at the Jubilee Fair in Hyde Park that read: 'To be seen two lions in one den – The keeper will put his head in their mouths'.

Such a stunt is never without danger for in 1820:

A showman named Henry Kraul, who was last month at Cologne, exhibiting a small menagerie of foreign animals, was in the habit of putting his head in the mouth of a young lion, to show the tameness the animal had been brought to by his care. It seems however that the trick was at last displeasing to the brute, for he tore in pieces the unfortunate showman.

(Jackson's Oxford Journal, 1820)

Life on the road with a travelling menagerie was always fraught with difficulties. Apart from cleaning and feeding there was the logistical problem of moving them from place to place. Prior to the expansion of the railway network later in the century, transport had to be made by horse-drawn wagons and caravans. Even on the finer days, progress would have been painstakingly slow, along rutted and potholed roadways. When the weather turned cold and wet, progress would have been even slower and the animals, some more used to tropical climates, must have suffered. In 1820 a lioness is reported to have died of the intense cold in Edinburgh.

Even when much of the later transportation was being done by rail there were still problems:

A tiger travelling by rail from London to Liverpool on Monday, with a sublime disregard of the bylaws of the railway company, descended from the train while in motion and started on a tour on its own account through the midland counties. It was, however, pursued, when its flight was discovered and its career was cut short by a bullet ... little remains to be said of an incident which might have lead to serious results beyond expressing a hope that in future when beasts of prey are conveyed by trains, care will be taken to prevent their escape from the compartments in which they are placed.

(The Pall Mall Gazette, 1877)

If the transportation of animals around the country was difficult enough, then the rivalry between menagerie owners could create even more problems. By the middle of the century there were several menageries in existence, with the better known ones belonging to Polito, Cross, Wombwell, Atkins, Brookes, Manders and Day.

Competition was fierce and in 1805 Atkins promoted his menagerie as the only wild animal show at that year's St Bartholomew's Fair. At the time Wombwell had his menagerie on display in Newcastle upon Tyne but, with a supreme effort, he managed to strike his exhibition and move down towards London, arriving early on the morning of the fair. However, the journey had proved too difficult for his solitary elephant, which died shortly after the menagerie arrived.

His rival Atkins saw this as a golden advertising opportunity and set up placards stating that he had the only living elephant at the fair. Not to be outdone, Wombwell set up rival placards stating that he had the only dead elephant at the fair. Living elephants are a wonder, but a dead one was even more of a curiosity and Wombwell drew the larger crowd!

Seasonal storms, thefts, and occasional violent acts were all a part of the difficulties of life on the road. Thefts from private apartments or caravans were not uncommon, as happened to Polito in Edinburgh in 1811, when robbers forced the three locks on his caravan and got away with £100. Wild winter storms could blow over caravans and rip off roofing. In 1817 the roof of his temporary menagerie erected on the Earthen Mound in Edinburgh, was blown off and carried away in fragments towards the loch.

Polito seems not to have had much luck in Edinburgh, for in 1818 the menagerie was again damaged by high winds when the wooden structure was blown to pieces. And it was not only bad weather with which he had to contend. The following item appeared in *The Times* in 1820:

> About a fortnight ago, the Isle of Man was in some danger of being overrun by beasts of prey. Some caravans belonging to Polito got into a deep drift of snow, on the road between Douglas and Ramsay ... and forth issued tigers, bears, hyenas and other terrific animals.

Sometimes other more extreme incidents took place. On 30 June 1827, *The Leicester Chronicle* carried the following report:

> It will be recollected by many persons that a very serious affray took place at Boughton Green Fair last year ... Wombwell's Menagerie was twice attacked, and one of the assistants who was particularly active in repelling the assailants disappeared at the close of the conflict, and was supposed to have absconded with the receipts of the day. Nothing was heard of him until Saturday last, when preparations were making for the present fair. On clearing out the cellars ... a fur cap was found and shortly afterwards the body of the poor fellow, who could only be known by his dress, was discovered. His head appeared to have been dreadfully fractured and there can be no doubt that he fell a martyr to his own exertions, by some one of the assailants. The ruffians were headed by a pugilist of the name of George

Catherall, who had assumed the name of Captain Slash, and was executed at Northampton July 21 for an aggravated assault.

Attacks upon menageries were not uncommon, although they didn't always result in fatalities. Also in 1827, *The Morning Post* reported on an arson attack on Wombwell's menagerie whilst it was resting in Dewsbury on its way to the Leeds Fair. Fortunately the keepers were able to extinguish the fire before any major damage was done.

Sometimes the menagerie owners themselves made the headlines. On 23 March 1816, the menagerie proprietor John Brookes had a violent argument with an acquaintance, Edward Thompson, apparently over a woman, Sarah Tookey, with whom Brookes had been living. Thompson confronted Brookes with a loaded pistol and Brookes had struck him twice on the head with a metal poker in retaliation. A close quarter struggle ensued in which the loaded pistol was fired, the ball entering Thompson's head. Brookes was apprehended and placed in custody while Thompson died in hospital, fatally wounded by the pistol ball, after managing to give a statement. Brookes was charged with 'wilful murder' and appeared at the Surrey Assizes in the April.

The crux of the case was as to who had actually been holding the pistol when it was discharged. Witness statements were inconclusive, eyewitnesses giving conflicting testimonies. After an impassioned plea from Brookes, the judge directed the jury that they should either find Brookes not guilty, the death being accidentally self-inflicted, or that he could be found guilty of manslaughter if they believed he had been holding the pistol. After only 15 minutes the jury returned the verdict of manslaughter and Brookes was sentenced to six months' imprisonment. The judge went on to hand out several death sentences on the same day, mainly for offences such as burglary and theft; at this time property was apparently perceived as more valuable than life.

Stories of menageries always made popular reading and it is hardly surprising that the death of an elephant belonging to Edward Cross in March 1826 drew an enormous amount of press coverage around the country. During the afternoon of 2 March 1826, a great crowd was reported to have gathered outside the Exeter Exchange in response to gunfire being heard. A rumour had spread that many of the animals had escaped and that Edward Cross had given orders that they should be shot.

In fact it was an attempt to destroy an elephant named Chunee that had caused all the gunfire. Cross had bought the elephant for the Exchange in 1809 and it had even appeared on stage at the Covent Garden Theatre. Chunee had been a very popular exhibit at the Exchange and was valued at more than £1,000 – around £42,000 today. In the preceding months the elephant had become very restive and Cross was concerned that it may eventually cause damage to the building and, more importantly, pose a serious threat to both keepers and the public. He attempted to give the animal medicine himself but Chunee became wise to this and, according to *The Morning Chronicle*: 'If an apple was given to him he would open it, to ascertain whether anything was concealed inside, and on making the discovery would, in great anger, dash it on the floor'.

Eventually Cross managed to administer some medicine but this caused the elephant to become even more aggressive and it managed to bring down two of the heavy supporting beams of its enclosure and also damage the heavy wooden door.

Mr Cross found it necessary, lest human life should be sacrificed, to give orders for his being put to death. It was ultimately resolved to obtain some of the Foot Guards from Somerset House and to put him to death by firing ball. On the arrival of the soldiers, they loaded their pieces and took deliberate aim at the head, but the depth of the flesh was so great, that for a long time, the balls appeared not to have the least effect. The first indication of pain that the animal gave was after one hundred balls had been lodged in his body ... His eyes instantly appeared like balls of fire; he shook his head with dreadful fury and rushed against the front of his den, and broke part of it, and it was expected every moment that the massy pillars, strengthened with plates of iron, would have given way. The keepers armed themselves with pikes and the soldiers continued their firing and near two hours having been spent before a vital part was touched. It was advised that a piece of cannon be procured, to put an end to the lingering torments of the noble animal. When one hundred and fifty two balls had been fired, his fury subsided, his legs began to totter, he groaned and fell, and when the 'mountain of flesh' came upon the floor on his right side, the concussion shook the whole building.

Never being one to miss an opportunity, Cross charged the throng of people the usual admission fee after the beast had been dispatched and allowed the crowd to view the body of enormous, dead elephant. If this report was not graphic enough, the following day *The Morning Chronicle* and *The Times* went on to publish fully descriptive details of the subsequent dissection of the poor animal.

To what extent the newspaper reports were accurate is questionable, because the report of the incident in *The Times* prompted letters from both Edward Cross and Joshua Brookes of the Theatre of Anatomy:

Sir – There having appeared in one of the morning papers a very erroneous statement that I appropriated the flesh of the elephant to the feeding of the different animals in my menagerie. I shall deeply feel the obligation if you will state in your valuable paper, that is far from that being the truth, I actually had a quantity of meat which came from Newgate market destroyed in consequence of its having been some hours in the room where the carcass of the immense beast was, from a fear that it might have been impregnated with the effluvia which arose from such a mass of flesh.

E. Cross

Sir – On reading your paper of this day I perceive that you assert that I had dressed and ate part of the putrid elephant, on Sunday last, which was shot on the preceding Wednesday at the Exeter Exchange. Your motive for doing so I am at a loss to conjecture; and as the statement is altogether devoid of truth, I trust that you will now do me the justice to contradict your former publication on this subject.

Joshua Brookes,
Theatre of Anatomy

The nineteenth century popular fascination with the natural world allowed both travelling and permanent menageries to flourish. People wanted to see exotic and strange animals. Seeing these creatures was informative and educational but merely viewing them was not enough; now the public also wanted to be entertained. Menageries and circuses existed side by side, often at the same fairs but, apart from horses and dogs, other animals were seldom seen in the circus.

The first recorded occasion when lions and tigers were exhibited in a circus was in 1832, when the big cats from Atkin's Menagerie were shown at Astley's Circus. By this time Astley's was under the management of Andrew Ducrow, a renowned equestrian. Ducrow also displayed a 'zebra hunt' in which he pursued four of the animals on horseback. But these displays were still very much an exhibition; animals were yet to be involved as performers. At some menageries keepers did perform tricks with their animals but it was not until the arrival of Isaac Van Amburgh that true wild animal shows became an integral part of the circus.

The lion tamer, as popularly depicted (possibly based on Van Amburgh), 1873. *(Library of Congress)*

Van Amburgh was born in America in 1811 and began working with animals as a cage cleaner at the Zoological Institute of New York. By 1833 he had developed a performance with big cats which included placing his head into a lion's open jaws. Although certainly not the first keeper to have done this, he soon became known as 'The Lion King' and established his own company, which travelled to England to perform at Astley's Theatre in August 1838. His arrival caused quite a stir and some concern, as reported in *The Literary Examiner* on 26 August 1838:

A Mr Van Amburgh has just arrived from America with a collection of very splendid lions, tigers and panthers, over whom he has acquired the most extraordinary ascendency, and these are about to be exhibited at Astley's ... One of Mr Van Amburgh's experiments on the forbearance of the larger lion, however, we decidedly protest against, and trust that, for the sake of all parties, it may be discontinued. We allude to his thrusting his head within the lion's jaws, which appears to us at once a piece of gratuitous impertinence towards the animal, a very disagreeable exhibition for the spectators, and above all, a highly hazardous proceeding for the exhibitor.

The feminine version of Van Amburgh, looking equally as brave: 'The Lion Queen', 1874. *(Library of Congress)*

Despite the critics, his performances played to packed houses and people marvelled at his ability to work with these fierce beasts.

As predicted by *The Literary Examiner*, Van Amburgh's performances were not without danger. Within a month the headlines were showing a 'Furious attack on Mr Van Amburgh, of Astley's Amphitheatre, by one of his tigers'. During a rehearsal a tiger had turned on Van Amburgh, who had been whipping him, and pinned him to the floor. In the struggle that followed, Van Amburgh managed to force the animal into submission. Onlookers thought that this was just a rehearsal for a routine to be performed later.

Three days after this report a short entry in *The Examiner* states: 'An account, in which there is no truth, has been copied into all the papers, of a deadly struggle having recently occurred between Mr Van Amburgh and one of his tigers'. Maybe this was just a good publicity stunt generated by Van Amburgh himself, because a week or so later he addressed a letter to *The Morning Post* stating that the attack was nothing more than part of the performance and he offered to repeat the incident to remove any doubts. Van Amburgh's performances went on to play to full houses when he transferred his show to the Drury Lane Theatre.

His popularity was tremendous and even the young Queen Victoria attended a performance in 1839. Afterwards she went on stage to view the lions devour their food with 'violent rapacity'. She was so interested that she returned to the theatre the following week to see Van Amburgh and his lions once more. *The Operative* newspaper of 10 February gave a colourful account of her visit:

> *Her Majesty's visit in state drew an overflowing audience to Drury Lane Theatre on Tuesday night. The house was packed in every part, not a single place was unoccupied, and hundreds went away who could not find room. The doors were besieged as early as two o'clock and, not withstanding the inclemency of the weather, multitudes remained for the chance of gaining admission in the first rush to the pit and boxes. The usual scene of noise and tumult occurred when the doors were opened, and shrieks of women in distress were heard at every side. No less than 2,800 persons were admitted before the curtain, independently of the one hundred friends of the management, who were accommodated with places upon the stage. The boxes displayed a fashionable company, the pit a closely wedged mass of respectable persons, and the galleries a pyramid of heads, one rising upon the other to the distant roof ...*
>
> *On the conclusion of the opera the lions were brought on the stage and Mr Van Amburgh went through his extraordinary performances. The Queen appeared to take great interest in the exhibition, and Mr Van Amburgh excited the animals more than he usually does, for the purpose of displaying before her Majesty his wonderful command over them.*

So fascinated was the Queen by Van Amburgh, that she later commissioned the artist Edwin Landseer to paint a portrait of him with his big cats. The portrait went on to be exhibited at the Royal Academy.

Popular as Van Amburgh was, he was not without rivals. While he was performing feats of bravery at the Drury Lane Theatre, a Mr Taudivin was presenting his wild animal show, with lions, tigers, leopards and jaguars, at the St James Theatre. His performance included the animals jumping through hoops and leaping over his back. He then wrestled with them before feeding them in front of the audience. Ducrow, across at Astley's, was also engaging a man named Carter and his lions to perform.

Working with wild animals was a hazardous occupation and accidents did sometimes happen. Whilst working on stage at the St James Theatre, a young man named Haynes was attacked and badly bitten by one of Taudivin's

THE RUSSIAN VAN AMBURGH TAMING THE
BRITISH LION ;

SHOWING THE POWER OF AN EMPEROR'S GOLD.

A satirical cartoon based on Van Amburgh and his lion, published in *Punch* in 1847. *(Author's collection)*

leopards. At the Drury Lane Theatre, while viewing the lions after a performance, a female friend of Van Amburgh dropped her handkerchief near the cage. As she bent down to pick it up, a lion lashed out at her and tore away part of her scalp.

Animal acts were very much a part of the traditional circus until the 1980s: Vistascreen 3D Viewer Cards showing *(top)* Alex Kerr and his tigers and *(bottom)* Jean and her baby elephants. *(Author's collection)*

Van Amburgh himself was quite badly injured during a performance in 1839. During a performance in Paris, one of his lions turned on him and severely gashed his leg. He continued with the performance, placing his head in the lion's mouth, despite the blood flowing from his wound. However, when it came to his curtain call he was unable to take the stage and had to be attended by a surgeon. This injury was exacerbated by his premature return to the stage against medical advice and the wound turned septic. In the end he had to stop performing until the end of the year and Carter took the opportunity to transfer his show from London to Paris, to perform at Franconi's Cirque Olympique during Van Amburgh's confinement.

Wild animal shows were becoming the 'in thing' during the mid-nineteenth century. The fascination with viewing the animals was turning into a fascination with the fear and almost expectation that the trainer might be attacked. This sense of apprehensive anticipation underpins any circus act today. We hold our breath as the high wire walker 'slips' and then recovers, as the trapeze artist flies high in the air, and we let out a collective sigh of relief when the move is completed. The audience knows that the performer is in control, but there is always that possibility that something might go wrong. Therefore, the audience fears for the performer, but from a position of safety as they are not physically involved in the act.

The 'Lion King' eventually returned to America, where he continued to tour his wild animal show, one of the largest in America. Unlike many of his contemporary big cat trainers, Van Amburgh died in his bed in 1865 as a result of a heart attack. He was only 54 years old, but his name lived on after his death as the Ringling Brothers leased the name at the end of the nineteenth century. Van Amburgh may have received ferocious criticism for his attitude and behaviour towards his animals, but through his performances he paved the way for the coming together of menageries and circuses and the beginning of the great age of the Victorian circus.

Chapter Five

Spectacles, Disasters and Murder:
The Victorian Circus

The nineteenth century saw rapid social and economic change within the United Kingdom. With the advent of the Victorian era, Britain was becoming an industrial nation and one of the wealthiest in the world. Its empire extended around the globe and pink, denoting British territory, was the predominant colour on the world maps hung in Victorian schoolrooms.

The Victorians attempted to impose their way of life and values wherever they colonised and much of our social infrastructure was laid down at this time – education, the law, religion, government. Many people grew wealthy through this brisk industrial expansion, but the period also saw great hardship. Rapid urbanisation of the cities created ghettos of poverty, and the divide between rich and poor grew. It is estimated that within the major cities of Britain up to one third of the population lived below the poverty line. Merely to exist, many had to rely upon poor relief or the workhouse. For the masses, a visit to the circus was a welcome escape from the drudgery and toil of everyday life.

By the middle of the nineteenth century, circus was a thriving industry not only in England but in the colonies as well. When the First Fleet sailed with convicts to Australia in 1788, circus was in its infancy but some of those convicts would have seen, or at least been aware of, this new form of entertainment. In 1833 the first recorded instance of a circus-style entertainment was given, when two rope-dancers performed at the newly-built Theatre Royal in Sydney.

That some convicts themselves were performers is quite possible. Alexander Greene, a circus tumbler, was transported to the notorious Hyde Park Barracks in Sydney in 1824 for pickpocketing. He later went on to become the public executioner for the barracks. Yet, it was not until the 1840s that the first full circus-style performance was presented in Australia, by a Signor Luigi Dalle Case at the Australian Olympic Theatre, on Hunter Street in Sydney.

What Astley and Hughes had begun at the end of the previous century was now being developed by a number of performer-managers across England. Equestrianism was still the backbone of the circus and many managers were skilled horsemen in their own right. Andrew Ducrow, possibly the most talented of them all, later gained great fame with his large scale 'equestrian dramas'. Elaborate scenery, exotic costumes and a cavalcade of horses all added to the appeal of this dashing young man displaying his trick riding skills around the ring.

Ducrow was born into a circus family in 1793. His father, Peter Ducrow, was Belgian by birth who came to London to work for Astley as a strong man act under the name of the 'Flemish Hercules'. He made such a big impression that when Astley built his first house near the Amphitheatre he named it 'Hercules House' in Ducrow's honour, although some claim it was named after Astley's own equestrian performance of the *Labours of Hercules*. Hercules House has now long gone but Hercules Road, on which it was built, still exists today.

In Astley's Amphitheatre, Ducrow's son Andrew had begun to perform with his father at just four or five years old. Peter Ducrow was immensely strong and was reputed to have carried several children, Andrew included, on a table held high above his head as part of his act. The Ducrows performed in flesh coloured, skin-tight body stockings, known as 'fleshings' and they have been referred to as the 'Chippendales' of their time, as they were certainly popular performers with the ladies.

Andrew also had a passion for horses and he soon learned to ride as well as any man. As part of their act, he and his father would create '*poses plastiques*', or physical statues, and gallop around the ring standing on the backs of their horses. These *poses plastiques* would later become a trademark of Andrew Ducrow's performance style. By his late teenage years, around 1812, Andrew Ducrow was presenting his own act called 'the flying wardrobe'. During the act he would gallop around the ring in a drunken fashion, dressed in rags. With each circuit of the ring, and with many comic 'falls', he would divest himself of layer after layer of clothing, whilst standing upon his horse, until he eventually revealed himself as the star rider of the show.

With the deaths of both Astley senior and junior, the management of Astley's Amphitheatre was taken on by William Davis, for whom the Ducrows worked. Davis was himself a fine horseman, as were his two sons, but they found that their own equestrian performances were overshadowed by Andrew Ducrow. Exactly what happened is unclear but Ducrow's contract was terminated. He then moved to the continent for a short period,

Riding acts were still the main attraction of the circus: *(top)* A circus performer leaps through a ring of fire, while another *(bottom)* rides several horses at once. *(Library of Congress)*

appearing to great acclaim at the Cirque Olympique in Ghent, and at Franconi's Cirque in Paris. The European circus audiences had never seen anything like Ducrow's *poses plastiques* and such was the impression he made that soon other circus performers were copying his style of riding.

Ducrow travelled widely throughout France but not without mishap. Whilst his company were in Lyon, presenting a large-scale equestrian drama, which involved a simulated battle, a female member of the audience was inadvertently shot in the neck. A member of the company playing a soldier had rammed a blank charge into the muzzle of his musket with the ramrod, in readiness for the 'battle'. Unfortunately he forgot to remove the ramrod before discharging the musket. The authorities closed the circus for three weeks and only after Ducrow agreed that no more battles would be represented was he allowed to reopen.

Whilst Ducrow was making a name for himself throughout Europe, back in London, William Davis was contesting his claim over Astley's. After the death of John Astley in 1821, he rather arrogantly wanted to change the name of the amphitheatre to 'Davis's Royal Amphitheatre'. Astley's widow Hannah and the licensees of the Amphitheatre, the Gill sisters, contested this and at the Kingston Sessions in 1822 the licence was granted under the name of 'Astley and Davis'. Davis persisted in renaming the amphitheatre 'Davis's Royal Theatre' but to satisfy the licensing agreements, he included the words 'late Astley and Davis' after the advertising title.

The shows at Astley's, as it was still commonly referred to, were very much dependent upon Davis' horsemanship skills. Just like the performances at the Surrey Theatre (formerly the Royal Circus) and at Covent Garden, Davis presented large equestrian dramas, supported by a few other circus acts. The programme advertised at Davis's Royal Theatre in May 1822 showed an equestrian drama called *Tom and Jerry*, supported by a Monsieur Decour, 'the French Hercules' and a young American on the *corde volante*, a length of rope attached at two points from the ceiling of the theatre to form a simple rope swing. This was to be followed by equestrian exercises from the Yorkshire Phenomenon, without saddle and bridle, then the evening would be concluded with an equestrian spectacle entitled *Richard Turpin, the Highwayman*.

Unlike Astley or Hughes, Davis found that his performances did not draw the crowds as well as they had once done. He lacked the drive and energy that the others had shown and he was beginning to feel the financial strain. What the circus needed was a larger-than-life figure who would capture the public's imagination and, fortuitously, at this point Andrew

Ducrow returned to London. In a way Davis had been the maker of his own downfall, for he had lost Ducrow when he had not renewed his contract at the Amphitheatre.

Ducrow was now an international star in his own right and with his small company he first appeared at Covent Garden with a performance of the equestrian drama *The Conquest of Mexico*. But he had his eye on Astley's and now offered himself to Davis but under his own terms. Davis could do little but accept; to turn down such a star would have been financial suicide but, in accepting the offer, he was effectively handing over the management to Ducrow.

On Easter Monday of 1824 Ducrow opened with the spectacular *Battle of Waterloo* and took the place by storm. In February 1825 it was reported in the *Hampshire Telegraph* that, 'Astley's has been taken by Ducrow, the equestrian, at an increased rent'. Although not yet a licensee (his name first appears on the licence in 1828), Ducrow now had, in effect, the day-to-day control of Astley's. The final blow to Davis came when the circus owner James West returned from a financially successful tour of America and offered to invest and place his stud at Astley's. Ducrow and West became partners and Davis realised that he had to go.

Ducrow now embarked upon large, lavish equestrian dramas and spectacles, far surpassing anything that Davis had previously offered. The crowds now began to return to witness performances such as *The Battle of Waterloo*, *Raphael's Dream*, *The Blood Red Knight*, *St George and the Dragon* and, most famously of all, *Mazeppa and the Wild Horse*. Ducrow's performance of *Mazeppa* was loosely based on the legend of the Ukranian folk hero Ivan Mazepa who, in the story, falls in love with a beautiful young married Countess. As punishment for this affair, the Count orders Mazepa to be strapped naked to a wild horse before setting it free to roam the steppes. Ducrow used this tale to demonstrate his trick-riding skills, galloping around the ring on two horses. All his spectacles were full of noise, colour and pageant, with large companies of several hundred performers and many dozens of horses. Amongst all of these would be Ducrow himself, the star rider of the shows. His popularity was immense, as illustrated in an article in the *Liverpool Mercury* on 11 May 1831:

> *I witnessed, a few evenings since, some of the wonderful specimens of the versatility of character and truly novel performances of that inimitable actor, Mr Ducrow. I cannot find language to express my admiration of the beauty and variety of his scenes both upon the stage and in the ring. A man*

who can (I think I may say) identify himself with the ghastly Mummy of Egypt, and the enegetic [sic] *and the apparently inspired Egyptian Prophet; with the warrior in the height of his daring spirit, and with the fabled thief of heavenly fire writhing beneath the vulture's beak and talons; with Hercules and Eleatreas* [sic]; *with the gladiator fighting and the gladiator dying; with Mercury with his light and graceful attributes; and with the gigantic Atlas writhing and struggling beneath the ponderous globe; with Apollo with all his majestic elegance; and Pan with all his fun; and finally with Samson bending, crashing, and overthrowing the temple which contained his enemies;– a man who can do this, as Mr Ducrow does it, must be allowed a man of universal talent; a man of unequalled genius in the line upon which he has bestowed his care.*

However, for all his popularity, Ducrow was not without his critics. In February 1832 he was forced to write a letter to the editor of the *Liverpool Mercury* in defence of his production of *Raphael's Dream*, which had been heavily criticised in the press. Ducrow had an ego on the same scale as his performances. On his return to London he had styled himself as 'Monsieur' Ducrow and claimed French ancestry, which had an air of truth about it as his father was Belgian. He also possessed an arrogance that could irritate people. In a tour of northern cities during 1831 an incident in Sheffield ruffled a few feathers. The Mayor of Sheffield and other elected officials went in procession to Ducrow's circus. Expecting to be officially welcomed by the man himself, they were very much put out when he did not appear and Ducrow is reputed to have stated that he, 'only received crowned heads not a set of dirty knife grinders'. The mayoral party then left in high dudgeon and returned to the town hall.

Sometimes Ducrow's bravado created problems but there were times when his flamboyant personality stood him in good stead. In November 1831, Ducrow and his company had a lucky escape from Bristol, where they had been engaged to perform for one month. Arriving on a Saturday, they suddenly found themselves caught up in serious rioting. Several hundred people had rampaged through the city, looting and burning property in a protest against the authorities. It was expected that the theatre in which Ducrow was housed would be attacked and he, showing a keen and brash presence of mind, armed his company with the swords, pikes and muskets held in the company's property wagon and awaited the rioters. Perhaps fortunately, the rioters left the theatre alone and directed their attentions elsewhere. Ducrow was then able to evacuate the company from the city on the following evening. It had been a lucky escape as over 100 people had been either killed or wounded during the riot, with at least 200 rioters arrested.

Despite Ducrow's success, Astley's seems to have been doomed to destruction. Having risen from the ashes of two previous disastrous fires, on the morning of 8 June 1841, Ducrow and his family were awoken by smoke. *Freeman's Journal* gives one of the first reports of the fire:

> *Astley's Amphitheatre, the scene of the glories of old Philip Astley, and of the more recent triumphs of Ducrow, is now a heap of ruins. Shortly after four o'clock this morning (Tuesday) a tremendous fire broke out at the back of the Theatre, and in less than three hours the whole of the premises, with the exception of the front towards the Westminster Bridge Road, was totally destroyed. The fire is supposed to have had its origin in the stable facing Stangate Street, and to have arisen from some defect in the gas pipes but on this subject it is impossible at present to obtain any accurate information.*
>
> *Three of Mr Ducrow's valuable horses have perished in the flames, and an unfortunate donkey, which was in the stables at the time, has also fallen a sacrifice. We are sorry to add, that this calamitous fire has not been unattended with loss of human life. One of Mr Ducrow's female servants was suffocated in the flames and the body, dreadfully burned, was this morning dug out of the ruins.*

Perhaps it is a reflection upon the status that Astley's Amphitheatre enjoyed at the time that the reporter lists the disaster in the order of the loss of the building, the loss of livestock and then, almost as an addition, the death of the servant. Ducrow himself was able to give a little more information on the events in an interview for *The Standard* on 12 June 1841. In the interview he told the reporter:

> *after the performances on the Monday night he never quitted the theatre and went to bed, with his family, at about half past 12 o'clock. When he retired the establishment was apparently perfectly safe. The first intimation which he received of the fire was, he thinks, by being awoke by Mrs Ducrow, who was aroused from her sleep by the room being full of smoke. They instantly jumped out of bed and rushed to one of the back windows, when they discovered the theatre all on fire. The rest of the family were asleep and he had some difficulty in arousing them, and not before the flames had broken into the rooms through the windows; finding that not a moment was to be lost in effecting their escape he, Mrs Ducrow, family and servants immediately ran downstairs to the entrance leading to the Westminster road ... Until he*

saw an account in the newspapers the following day he was not aware that the unfortunate female, Elizabeth Briton, who had been in his service a great number of years, had perished in the flames ... Mr Ducrow appeared to have been deeply affected at the melancholy death of the deceased to whom he was much attached from the number of years she had been with him.

The cause of the fire remained a mystery for some time, but at the inquest into the death of the servant, Elizabeth Briton, it was found that the fire was caused accidentally but that the theatre's fireman had been negligent and should have seen the fire earlier on his rounds before it had managed to take hold of the largely wooden building. The fire probably started under the stage, and it was suggested that paper from fireworks used during the performance had fallen through cracks in the stage boards and lain smouldering on the wooden joists before later igniting.

Whatever the cause, the experience deeply disturbed Ducrow and he fell into a deep depression, as reported in *The Bradford Observer*, 12 August 1841: 'Ducrow, who had been for so many years a popular favourite and a nonpareil in his own peculiar way, is so seriously affected by his recent loss, as to be under restraint. The aberration of mind is too marked to be mistaken'.

His condition worsened and he died in January 1842. Ducrow had been a flamboyant figure in life and continued to be so in death. A huge crowd gathered around the streets where he had lived to witness his funeral procession and there was confusion caused by a state procession then on the way to Buckingham Palace. Some of the crowd thought that the state carriage was the one belonging to Ducrow, as it resembled a vehicle used in performances at Astley's.

In spite of the loss of his amphitheatre, Ducrow died a significantly wealthy man. His estate was valued at £50,000, (equivalent today to well over £2 million). But his legacy was far more than financial. Ducrow had elevated the art of the circus to a new golden age, he had become a household name. As well as horses, Ducrow had introduced lions, zebras and elephants into the ring; Astley's Amphitheatre was now synonymous with the circus and the circus was as popular as it had ever been.

The circus was not confined to London during this period. Several travelling circuses of the period were also becoming very successful, and amongst them were those of the Powells, the Sprakes, the Cookes, the Henglers and William Batty. As Ducrow was making a name for himself largely in London, so Batty made his name on the touring circuit. For all the popularity of the circus, there was still a place for the flamboyant individual who could capture the imagination of the public, and the next big name arose through Batty's Circus. In December 1821, a young man of African descent made his début with this circus in Norwich, under the performing name of 'Young Darby'.

Little is known about the childhood of William Darby. There is some debate over the year of his birth, which various sources place from 1796 to 1810. What is known is that his father was African-born and had been in service in Norwich before William was born. Unlike Andrew Ducrow, William had no background in circus and the story of how and why he came to join Batty's Circus is unrecorded. In his first few years with Batty he developed the skills of horsemanship and rope-vaulting. As he became more established he changed his name to Pablo Fanque, perhaps to give himself a more exotic stage name to match his exotic looks, and it is under this name that he became famous.

By 1835 Fanque was achieving the top billing with Batty's during a season in Dublin, and by 1837 his five-year-old son was appearing with him on the tightrope. In fact it was not so long before his son was gaining more advertising coverage than his father!

The Northern Star and Leeds General Advertiser carried the following advert on 2 June 1838:

BATTY'S NEW ROYAL OLYMPIC CIRCUS ARENA – LEEDS (Bank Street) – IMMENSE SUCCESS! The wonderful leaps of Pablo Fanque … Master Pablo Fanque the youngest performer in the world, whose precious talents have obtained for him the appellation of the Gem of Africa, the wonder of the world, will go through some pleasing feats on the tightrope.

Newspaper reports did not often mention Pablo Fanque's African heritage but occasionally reference was made to his colour, as in the *Caledonian Mercury*, 18 November 1838: 'Among the different feats of the evening the leaps of Pablo Fanque, a gentleman of colour, were conspicuous'.

The public took Fanque to their hearts and in 1839 he performed for a season at Astley's with Ducrow, where he proved very popular. By 1841 he had returned to work for Batty and was in Dublin when the disastrous fire at Astley's Amphitheatre took place. On hearing the dreadful news, William Batty immediately set out for London with the intention of assisting in the rebuilding of the Amphitheatre and left his circus under the management of Pablo Fanque and the clown William Wallett.

While Batty was in London, Fanque decided to leave and set up his own company, leaving Wallett in charge. Taking his son with him, he bought a small stud of horses, gathered together a small company and began to tour mostly in the north of England. In doing so, Pablo Fanque became the first black circus proprietor in Britain, maybe even in the world.

By 1842 he was clearly well established and presenting a full programme, as an advertisement in the *Preston Chronicle*, 28 May 1842, shows:

PABLO FANQUE'S CIRCUS
In the orchard
NIGHTLY OVERFLOWS!!

Mr Pablo Fanque respectfully informs the inhabitants of Preston and vicinity, that the circus has been fitted up with every attention to comfort, having been thoroughly lined – particularly the Boxes, every crevice has been stopped, to prevent draughts, and fitted up with taste; in short every care has been taken to render the place as comfortable as possible, the Proprietor having spared neither pain nor expense to ensure him patronage and support.

It is Mr P. F.'s intention to give the proceeds of one night to some Charitable Institution in Preston; due notice of which will be given.

Programme of Performances

1st   Mr Pablo Fanque's leaping over a number of difficult objects
2nd First of May; or Frolics of Cupid in the Soot Bag. Master Pablo Fanque
3rd Two Nondescripts – Messrs Griffiths and Heath
4th Principal Acts of Horsemanship – Mr Moffatt
5th Statues of the Ancients – Messrs Smith and Taylor
6th Horseman of all work – Mr Pablo Fanque
7th Corde Floxe – Mr H Walker
8th Serious Pantomime – Three Fingered Jack – Mr Moffatt and the whole company
9th Tight Rope – Master Pablo Fanque
10th Merry Millers; or Old Grubb's Wedding Day

Boxes 2s; Side do [side boxes] 1s; Pit 6d; Gallery 3d
Sole Proprietor Mr Pablo Fanque; Riding Master and Acting Manager Mr Moffatt; Clowns Messrs Kemp and Griffiths.

Pablo Fanque's Royal Circus visits Leeds c.1850. *(Reproduced by permission of Leeds Library and Information Service)*

For the accommodation of Families and Country Visitors, a GRAND PERFORMANCE will take place on Saturday June 4th commencing at two o'clock.

For the poorer members of the audience, a visit to the circus could be quite expensive, especially if they had a large family. In *Victorian London* (2006), Liza Picard gives the weekly living expenses of a single labourer in London as follows:

2 rooms	*5s*
Coal for fire	*1s 1d*
Bread	*4s 6d*
Vegetables	*1s 1d*
Meat	*2s 6d*
Milk	*3d*
Coffee / tea / sugar	*2s 6d*

An unskilled labourer might expect to earn between 2s and 3s per day and even if he were being paid the upper daily range, the balance left over between his income and expenses was only 13d. The figures above are for a single man, and a family would have even less money left over at the end of each week, certainly not a lot to spend on luxuries. And yet the circus was always well supported.

It seems that Fanque spared no expense when it came to the comfort of his audiences. The amphitheatres that he had built were well-appointed and weatherproof, and in 1843 he forbade smoking in any part of the circus. This may have been primarily a safety measure, more in response to the frequent fires in circuses, rather than the health of the audience.

During the 1840s, Fanque's old friend William Wallett joined his company and together they created a very successful circus in the north of England. Their circus was popular with local civic dignitaries because they invariably gave charity performances or donated takings to charities in the towns and cities that they visited. Fanque himself was a member of the Order of Ancient Shepherds, a charitable organisation associated with the Freemasons, which gave assistance to families in times of distress. Fanque's circus was called upon at many different events, such as the half-day holiday declared by the Lord Mayor of Leeds, to celebrate the repeal of the Corn Laws in August 1846.

(Top, l–r) William Darby, known as Pablo Fanque; Mrs Elizabeth Darby, the second wife of Pablo Fanque. *(Bottom, l–r)* Edward 'Ted', Pablo Fanque's son; This large headstone in St George's Field, Leeds, marks the grave of Susannah Darby, first wife of Pablo Fanque. At the foot of her headstone lies Pablo Fanque's own grave. *(Photographs of the Fanque family were originally published in* The Worlds Fair, *reproduced by permission of the National Fairground Archive Sheffield. Image of gravestone copyright the author)*

However, popular as it may have been, Pablo Fanque's circus was not without its fair share of disasters. The year 1847 seems to have been particularly bad. In the January, a member of the audience suddenly collapsed and died during a performance in Leeds. In March a petition was submitted to the Magistrates in Wigan to remove his circus from the town on the grounds that the petitioners could not afford their own rates and taxes, without the authorities paying to have the circus in town. Fortunately for Fanque, the local authorities attested to his good conduct, and the police also noted that there had been a decrease in the number of incidents of drunkenness in the town since the arrival of the circus.

But it was later in March 1847 that the most disastrous event of all took place in Leeds, here reported in *The Leeds Mercury*, 25 March 1847:

SHOCKING ACCIDENT AT MR PABLO FANQUE'S CIRCUS DEATH OF MRS FANQUE AND NARROW ESCAPE OF MANY OTHER PERSONS

A serious and fatal accident occurred at the Circus – a temporary wooden erection – occupied by Mr W. Darby, better known by the name of Pablo Fanque, and his corps of equestrians in Kings Charles' Croft Leeds, at about a quarter to ten o'clock on Saturday night last. The performances were for the benefit of Mr Wallett, the celebrated comic jester or clown, and the circus was crowded in every part, many persons having had to be refused admission owing to the want of room.

All went on well, till the hour above named, at which time Pablo Fanque Junior was performing some feats on the tightrope, when suddenly that portion called the pit, which was a kind of wooden chamber, built in a sloping position upon a framework of wood, fell to the ground with a tremendous crash. There were upwards of six hundred persons, of all ages and both sexes, in the pit at the time and the most of these fell with the broken and loosened timber and planks of which it was composed; some of them fell into the gallery which adjoined the front of the pit, but was on a lower level; and many fell into the lobby of the building, and others out at one side; the weight of the falling timber and the people together bursting out a portion of that side of the circus the nearest to Land's Lane.

Mrs Darby and Mrs Wallett were both in the lobby at the time of the melancholy occurrence. They were both thrown down and, we regret to say, that two heavy planks fell upon the back part of the head and neck of Mrs Darby and killed her on the spot. Mrs Wallett received some severe bruises and contusions but she is fast recovering. Many other persons were injured but none, we believe, seriously. The gas with which the circus was lighted was put out by some of the pipes being broken in the fall and the scene presented immediately after the erection had given way was one of indescribable alarm and confusion.

One can only imagine the horror and panic of that night. The area around King Charles Croft, now the site of a shopping centre, was a warren of narrow, cobbled, gas-lit ways. The audience, plunged into darkness, struggling to find the exits and, stumbling out into the poorly-lit streets, must have been terrified. Pablo Fanque discovered the body of his wife, as he gave witness at the inquest, reported in the same article:

I was present when the accident occurred. The house was very full, but I thought we had more money than was in that night; there certainly was more money then taken for the gallery, and consequently more persons in the gallery than there had ever been before ... I believed all was safe or I would not have done what I did and placed my good lady there.

The moment before the accident I had put my boy on the tightrope and had turned my eye off the audience upon my boy, when the whole party in the pit came down. I heard the crash, turned round, and they appeared to have come down bodily. I ran into the stable, got into the street and to the end where my wife was. I broke the window, cutting my hand in doing so, and I pulled out Mrs Wallet, who I thought was my wife; for I was not aware that there was any person in the lobby but my wife. Mrs Wallet was a good deal cut.

I found Mrs Pablo laid on her face, with two planks laid upon the back of her head. They were eleven inch planks and had formed a seat. I believe they had dislocated the vertebrae at the base of her neck ... I lifted the planks up and got my wife out. I got her out in seven to eight minutes, or ten at the furthest, after the fall. I got her to this inn [the King Charles Hotel]. I believe she was dead when I first got her out. Her head hung down on her shoulder, and I never observed her breathe at all. I sent for Mr Hey the surgeon, but she was dead.

There was of course a lot of speculation as to what had happened to cause the accident and fingers were pointed in several directions. Pablo Fanque explained that he had taken the circus on hearing that it was safe and had had it examined by his own architect. The joiner who had built the circus

Entertainments at Hengler's Circus, images from the *Illustrated London News*, 1883. *(Author's collection)*

then stated that he had built it for a previous circus owner, Charles Hengler, under the direction of his architect. He was rather vague as to how the gallery had been propped, but he suggested that some of Hengler's men may have removed some of the props when they took their equipment from the circus.

He had let the building 'as it stood', agreeing that Fanque was to make any alterations 'at his own expense'.

So, who was responsible for this calamity? The coroner could not find any culpable negligence and declared that the accident had arisen, in all probability, from some error of judgement and that the death of Mrs Sarah Darby, the wife of Pablo Fanque, was 'accidental'. With due ceremony Sarah Darby was laid to rest in the Woodhouse Cemetery in Leeds (now St George's Field and situated within the university campus). A crowd of at least 10,000 turned out to watch the funeral cortège pass. The hearse was drawn by four cream coloured horses and followed by her favourite horse, led by a groom. Then came the mourning coaches, followed by the entire stud of Pablo Fanque bearing mourning emblems.

In spite of his loss, Pablo Fanque's circus was soon back on the road and he also remarried the following year. In April 1847 the circus was at Cook's Amphitheatre in Manchester; in May, based in the orchard at Preston; in June, at Tourniaire's Royal Amphitheatre in Hull; and in July he was back in Leeds with his Royal Marquee. But 1847 had further problems to come. His circus was robbed whilst performing at Preston and in November, in Manchester some members of the audience feared the gallery was collapsing and raised a false alarm, resulting in panic and a few injuries.

Collapsing galleries seems to have been a regular occurrence because in the August of 1849 Fanque's circus experienced yet another incident. Whilst performing in the Pavilion at Buxton, *The Derby Mercury* reported that:

About the middle of Wednesday evening's performance, nearly one fourth of the gallery fell in with a tremendous crash, and hundreds of spectators were thrown in all directions … Happily no lives were lost, nor any limbs broken, although from the nature and extent of the accident we can scarcely conceive how so favourable a result could be brought about.

A visit to the circus was potentially dangerous for the audience and even the performers sometimes suffered mishaps. Whilst at the Queen's Theatre in Hull in 1869, a terrible accident occurred to a gymnast:

ACCIDENT TO A GYMNAST

Mr Pablo Fanque's troupe have occupied the Queen's Theatre, Hull, for the past fortnight. Les Frères Trevannion, 'the greatest sensational star gymnasts of the age' appeared for the first time in their 'thrilling and exciting act – the

*double fall for life' – a significant title and ominous of what was to follow.
The 'leap for life' consists of swinging through the air by the aid of two ropes
with rings attached, from a perch near the roof of the theatre, immediately
over the front boxes, to a trapeze suspended from the roof at the other end of
the theatre, in a line with the perch. Hanging on the trapeze by the legs was
the other gymnast, ready to catch his adventurous companion immediately
he had swung through the air and let go the rings ... He reached his hands
certainly, but from some unexplained cause he slipped from his grasp and
commenced his 'second fall for life', from the roof of the theatre to the floor,
amidst the agonising and painful shrieks of men, women and children.*

(*Liverpool Mercury*, 20 March 1869)

The year 1869 continued to be a difficult one for the performers in Fanque's
circus, because another, almost disastrous, accident happened in an outdoor
stunt in Bolton, when a tightrope walker tripped over a knot in the rope:

*She approached the knot cautiously, and partially crossed it but just as her
hind-most foot was leaving it she stumbled. At once she threw aside her pole,
and by a desperate effort she grasped the rope. She is a strong, muscular
woman and she exerted herself greatly to regain her position on the rope; but
despite her endeavours, she remained suspended by the hands. The wildest
excitement prevailed amongst the thousands of spectators. There was [sic]
loud cries of, "Lower the rope", and the rope was lowered but only a few feet.
A number of men then massed themselves together directly below the woman,
and begged her to fall. She did as advised, and was caught by the men, and
although the distance she fell was almost fifty feet she sustained no injury
beyond the fright and shock.*

(*Reynold's Newspaper*, 9 May 1869)

The Illustrated London News carried an engraving of what the scene might
have looked like at the moment of her fall but whether the tightrope dancer
performed in the future is not recorded.

In 1871, two years after the Bolton incident, Pablo Fanque died of
bronchitis in Stockport. He had achieved much in his circus career,
including performing before Queen Victoria and Prince Albert at Astley's
Amphitheatre. His body was carried by train from Stockport to Leeds and
the cortège began its final journey from King Charles Croft, the site of the
dreadful accident in which his first wife died, to Woodhouse Cemetery.
Thousands of silent people lined the streets of Leeds as the hearse passed.

Fanque was buried alongside Sarah and their headstones can still be viewed today.

Pablo Fanque achieved immortality through the lyrics of the Beatles song 'Being for the Benefit of Mr Kite', in which he is mentioned. Whilst working in Kent, John Lennon bought an original 1843 poster for Pablo Fanque's Circus Royal in Rochdale. The performance was for the benefit of Mr Kite, who was Fanque's resident tightrope walker at that time and the wording on the poster inspired Lennon to write the song for the 1967 album *Sgt Pepper's Lonely Hearts Club Band*.

As one dominant figure in the circus world faded, another would arise to take his place. At the time of Fanque's death, George Sanger was negotiating to take over Astley's Amphitheatre. The Sanger family had been involved in the fair and circus business for some time. George and his elder brother John were the sons of an ex-press-ganged sailor, who had fought at the Battle of Trafalgar and had become a showman on being pensioned off from service.

Originally appearing at fairs with a sideshow booth, they later developed the 'Sanger's Travelling Circus' and menagerie and performed throughout the country. George was a natural showman and as a young boy he acted as the frontman for his father's booth, drumming up the customers with his slick patter. Even then, George had aspirations to emulate his hero Ducrow and to be the owner of Astley's. By 1868, the year in which William Batty died, George had been fronting the family circus for almost 20 years and his dream was about to come true.

Astley's was then in decline and the quality of its performances had dropped since the heady days of Ducrow. The management changed hands several times after Batty's death, but with little success. In a performance of the *Battle of Waterloo* at this time the management was reduced to

Lord George Sanger, as pictured in the frontispiece to his autobiography, *Seventy Years a Showman. (Author's collection)*

using only one horse in the entire show; the same horse appearing under both Wellington and Napoleon. The Sangers had already acquired the Agricultural Hall in Islington as a performance space and in 1871 Batty's widow sold the building to George and John Sanger for £11,000, equivalent today to over £500,000.

Their first task was to completely refurbish the building to bring it back to its former glory. In October 1871 a lengthy article appeared in *The Pall Mall Gazette* about the re-opening of Astley's by the Sangers:

> *The Messrs Sangers, late of the Agricultural Hall, Islington, and long known as the managers of a travelling company of riders and gymnasts, have become the lessees of Astley's Theatre with a view to reviving the 'equestrian drama' and the 'scenes in the circle' for which that establishment was so renowned … The Messrs Sanger have redecorated the theatre in the most liberal manner, and restored the circus … The managers boast that the theatre is lighted by no less than 200,000 jets of gas, and the statement is almost credible, for the heat and glare of the illuminations are painfully excessive.*

The article then continues to describe in colourful detail the opening performance and concludes with, 'The house was crowded to excess by a most enthusiastic audience, and there would seem to be good ground for believing that the spirited efforts of the new lessees of Astley's will obtain complete and enduring success'.

George Sanger was the driving force in the partnership and they presented large-scale equestrian spectaculars in the style of Ducrow. By December 1871 the Sangers were performing three separate shows in the capital. At Astley's New Royal Amphitheatre, the company was presenting a varied programme, opening with the popular pantomime of *Lady Godiva*, with the well-known equestrienne Miss Amy Sheridan in the starring role on her Arab steed. The show also included *The Derby Day*, an amusing escapade of follies, female jockeys and thoroughbred horses, before concluding with a grand tableau of *Britannia and a Living Lion*. This was presented by Mrs George Sanger, formerly Miss Nellie Chapman. Nellie had been known earlier as the 'Lion Queen' when she had worked with Wombwell's Circus.

Across at Astley's Grand Amphitheatre, the Sangers were presenting the Great Equestrian Troupe; their advertising claiming the best riders, the most skilful gymnasts, acrobats and contortionists and the finest performing horses in the world. And at the Royal Agricultural Hall they were offering *The*

War in China, a large-scale equestrian spectacular involving over 1,500 men, women and children. *The Pall Mall Gazette* of 28 December 1871 recorded that 28,683 people viewed this production in the first two performances.

A natural showman, George Sanger did not shy away from publicity. Shortly after the opening of the new Royal Amphitheatre, Queen Victoria had arranged a day of thanksgiving for the recovery from illness of the Prince of Wales. The festivities were to include a state procession through the streets of London. With a view to self-promotion, George Sanger decided to mount his own parade from the Agricultural Hall to Astley's that would 'attach' itself to the royal procession. Having friendly relations with the local police, and maybe even with a little bribery, he arranged that, although his parade might be stopped, it would be at a point where he would be unable to turn around and therefore had to be allowed to continue. This happened as planned and his glittering cavalcade was received enthusiastically by the crowds.

He gives an account of it in his own words, in his book *Seventy Years a Showman* (1910):

> *We had our Britannia, Mrs George Sanger, with her living lion on the top to typify the nation and its strength. The Queen, too, was impersonated, in her crown and robes, surrounded by representatives of her dominions all in correct costume. At the top of Park Lane there were about a dozen carriages that had fallen out of the Royal procession and as our mimic pageant came along, the occupants of these carriages, amongst whom Lord Beaconsfield was conspicuous, rose and acknowledged the endeavour of your humble servant to enhance the circumstances of the great occasion.*

Only George Sanger could have pulled off such an audacious stunt and it captured the public's imagination. He had rekindled the former greatness of Astley's and there was a renewed vigour in the world of the circus.

In 1872 a Bill was presented in Parliament to outlaw the employment of children under the age of 16 in acrobatic performances. George Sanger did not hesitate to write to the press about the matter:

> *A Plea for Acrobats*
>   *Sir – I see in last week's Parliamentary news that Lord Buckhurst was successful in the reading of the Acrobats Bill the second time, the object of which is to prevent the employment of children under sixteen years of age in acrobatic performances, such performances being dangerous to life or injurious to health … his Lordship will be, I have no doubt, surprised to*

hear that the acrobatic profession cannot be acquired after the age of sixteen. It would be much easier for his Lordship to perform the feats of the street Arabs at his time of life than for any person to learn to turn a somersault after attaining sixteen years of age.

(The Era, 14 July 1872)

Sanger continued to employ children in his large-scale spectaculars, although not always as acrobats. He continued to mix circus with displays of animals, expansive equestrian dramas and pantomimes. Astley's became well suited to these forms of performances, but during the summer season he also took a tenting show on tour. These proved very popular and the arrival of a circus in a provincial town caused great excitement.

Sanger's Circus travelled with upwards of 60 horse-drawn vans and wagons, sometimes stretching as far as two miles along a road, many containing strange and exotic animals – camels, lions, ostriches. Bill stickers would have already put up posters in the area advertising the forthcoming event, so it was with great anticipation that the circus hit town. A weekly column by 'Uncle Jack' especially aimed at children appeared in one local newspaper of the time:

FOR YOUNG FOLKS

My Dear Bairns – I think there are but few of you who will not have been to see Lord George Sanger's splendid circus and exhibition during the past week, and those of you who have not will have seen the grand procession that has paraded the streets each day. The gigantic panorama of the war in Soudan [sic] has given us some idea of the terrible things that happen on the battlefield, and Lord George Sanger has spared no pains to make it realistic. I dare say you have never seen such a number of animals of all kinds together. In the battle scene alone there are five hundred people and three hundred and fifty horses, to say nothing of the elephants, the camel– battery, with the huge cannons on their backs, firing away at the enemy. Another great attraction is the talking horse Robert the Devil, who foretells the horses that are to win the great races all through 1895. I do not quite like to see Madame Paulineda Vere's awful risk, in dancing a serpentine dance in the den of African lions. It is dreadful to think that these animals might kill the brave lady. Far nicer to my mind are the performances of the marvellous circus riders, the tricks of the animals and the antics of the clowns. Lord George Sanger certainly provides us with a wonderful entertainment.

(The Newcastle Weekly Courier, 18 May 1895)

The circus was not only for entertainment, it also educated and informed, although as the mention of the elephants in the Soudan shows, not always accurately. For all the jingoism and patriotism shown in these displays, they were the Pathé News items of their day, giving the public a living, moving representation of current events.

George Sanger had by now acquired the title of 'Lord', but he had not actually been elevated to the peerage. The acquisition of his title came out of the disastrous year of 1887, Queen Victoria's Jubilee. For George Sanger it had begun very well. In January he was in Margate and to celebrate the beginning of such an auspicious year he distributed an 1887 shilling to 500 elderly people and 500 children in the town. But after such a generous start, his year began to go rapidly downhill.

The Honourable 'Buffalo Bill' Cody, c.1911. *(Library of Congress)*

As part of the Jubilee celebrations, an American circus had been invited to perform at Earl's Court; the British public were about to be entertained by 'Buffalo Bill' Cody and his 'Congress' of Wild West riders. They were new and exciting and the public flocked to their performances. Even the Queen and other members of the royal family paid visits to the Honourable Colonel W. F. Cody and his show. Sanger was not particularly averse to American circuses – indeed he had had previous dealings with P.T. Barnum in 1874, when he had sold to him all the equipment and costumes for the show *The Conquest of Monarchs*, which Sanger had staged at the Agricultural Hall. But Buffalo Bill Cody's new entertainment was attracting a large proportion of the crowds.

Whilst on a provincial tour in Southsea in the July of 1887, the *Hampshire Telegraph* carried a general advertisement for Sanger's Circus:

IMPORTANT NOTICE
THE GREAT SCENE FROM BUFFALO BILL

The Stopping of the Mail Coach – with the Indian Horses – and great Fight and Defeat
Manager and Director for the company Mr GEORGE SANGER.

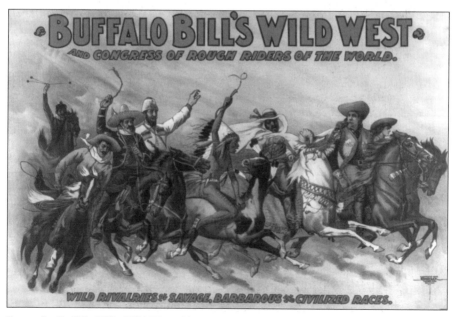

Poster for Buffalo Bill's Wild West show, 1896. *(Library of Congress)*

Colonel Cody was outraged that Sanger should steal his programme titles and successfully applied for an injunction against Sanger to prevent him from using the terms 'the Wild West' or 'Buffalo Bill' in his advertising. The following month Cody made a further appeal for Sanger to be committed to prison for breaching these orders. Sanger's defence was that he had: 'Not committed a breach of the undertaking but merely issued notices that his entertainment was not connected with that of 'Buffalo Bill' (*The Liverpool Mercury*, 1 September 1887).

The case rumbled on and Sanger simply pasted over his larger posters with a sticker that read 'no connection with Buffalo Bill now playing in London'. Cody once again challenged Sanger for breaching the undertaking. He claimed that, although Sanger had indeed altered the wording, he had still used an illustration that was a copy of Cody's own advertising. The court ruled that the compliance order related to words only and not pictures and Sanger was discharged. The bitter experience left bad blood between them for the rest of their lives. Sanger felt that his good name had been dragged through the mud. In a fit of temper he was heard to declare that if Cody could be an 'Honourable' then he could be a 'Lord' – and so the name stuck and he became known as 'Lord' George Sanger.

After that time Sanger continued to use the term 'Buffalo Bill' in his advertising but he was very clever about it, as shown here in *The Leeds Mercury* 3 October 1887:

> *GEORGE SANGER'S WORLD FAMOUS CIRCUS*
> *ROYAL OLYMPIA MENAGERIE and*
> *GEORGE SANGER'S*
> *BUFFALO BILL WAINER and his BULLY BOYS.*

After the events of 1887, Lord George Sanger's brushes with the courts continued. In December 1887 he was again in court over a copyright issue concerning a song performed in one of his shows. This was later thrown out of court, when it was found that the solicitor acting for the actress who had brought the complaint had been practising unqualified; the bogus solicitor received a three-month sentence. The following year he appeared in court in connection with some of his employees, who had been arrested in a serious riot with police in Motherwell.

His final appearance in 1888 concerned the barely believable arrest of one of his horses:

SANQUHAR – THE ARREST OF A CIRCUS HORSE FOR CUSTOM DUES

The solicitor to the Sanquhar Town Council has given it as his opinion that under the Roads and Bridges (Scotland) Act the burgh has no longer power to exact custom, the Council has returned the horse arrested by them last Sunday from Lord George Sanger and agreed to pay all expenses connected therewith. We understand, however, that the action by Mr Sanger for illegal detention will still be proceeded with.

(*The Glasgow Herald*, 11 July 1888)

For all these trials and tribulations, Lord George Sanger continued to produce bigger and better spectacles. His name became synonymous with showmanship and he was even popular with royalty. Queen Victoria, Prince Albert, other members of the Royal family and visiting foreign royals all attended Sanger's Circus at Astley's. In 1899 his circus was summoned to Windsor, where he gave a private performance before the Queen and was rewarded with an engraved silver cigar box. He was, as he always proudly

Royalty supports the circus. The Prince and Princess of Wales at the Crystal Palace (*Illustrated London News*, 1876). (*Author's collection*)

announced, the last entertainer to receive a gift from the Queen before her death.

Sanger was an ardent royalist and patriot and his shows reflected this; the brave red-coated soldier facing the horde of Zulu savages; the intrepid British army fighting in the Soudan; the Battle of Waterloo – even the pantomime of *Cinderella* contained a patriotic element, when she dreams of a parade of British military might. But for all these spectacles, the lustre of Astley's was beginning to dim and civic politics were beginning to interfere with Sanger's work.

In 1888 the Metropolitan Board of Works demanded expensive repairs to the building. Sanger complied and also installed a huge water tank in the Amphitheatre so that he could present water spectaculars. With the founding of the London County Council in 1891, pressure was applied to Sanger once again with a request for major building work. Undaunted, he continued that year by presenting *St Petersburg on the Ice*, in which he innovatively placed the whole company on roller skates. The final performance at Astley's came the following year with a water and equestrian spectacle entitled *The Jockey Club*.

The days of Astley's were now numbered and, in 1893, Sanger bowed to pressure and sold the property and land to the Ecclesiastical Commissioners. After over 100 years and several reincarnations, the building would never again echo to the laughter and applause of the crowd. Lord George Sanger continued with his tenting circus for a few years but finally retired in 1905. He settled in the circus winter quarters in Finchley and, for a man of such immense stature and character, the circumstances of his death were tragic.

On the 29 November 1911, *The Evening Telegraph and Post* carried the news:

LORD GEORGE SANGER THE WELL-KNOWN SHOWMAN MEETS WITH A TRAGIC END
Attacked by an Employee

Lord George Sanger ... was attacked by a young man who was employed on the farm. His skull was fractured and he died later.

The full circumstances of the attack were never fully understood but it is believed that the young Herbert Cooper, employed by Sanger, had been suspected of stealing from the house. Sanger had heatedly confronted him but the matter had never been referred to the police. Some time later, Cooper had entered the house in a deranged state and attacked two other men in the house, before striking Sanger with an axe, causing the fatal head injuries. Cooper then escaped but his body was found four days later on a nearby railway line. At the inquest into both deaths, the Coroner found that Sanger died of 'wilful murder' by the hand of Cooper, who committed suicide.

On the day of Sanger's funeral, shops and businesses closed for a time as a mark of respect for a man who had given his life to showmanship – a rather muted end to a splendid life. On 8 December 1911 *The Courier* ran a short, if somewhat prophetic, article about Lord George Sanger:

THE PASSING OF THE CIRCUS

That prince of showmen, the late 'Lord' George Sanger, is said to have held the opinion that the days of the circus were numbered. We are afraid (says a correspondent) he was right. Music Halls and variety theatres, the popular passion for witnessing athletic contests, especially football, and above all the amazing growth in cinematographic shows, have already in large measure eclipsed in populous places the ancient and time-honoured glories of the circus.

'Lord' George Sanger had lived through and contributed to a 'golden age' of circus. Now the circus in Britain was to enter a dark and gloomy period, yet across the Atlantic this very British institution was about to blossom.

Chapter Six

Railways and Rings: The Circus in Nineteenth Century America

When John Bill Ricketts had taken the idea of 'circus' as a form of entertainment across the Atlantic in 1792, the United States was still a fledgling nation of only 16 years standing. The West was yet to be tamed, a civil war was yet to be fought and General Custer was yet to make his infamous last stand at Little Big Horn. Ricketts was not to know that by the end of the nineteenth century the American circus would have grown into a vast business empire. When he sold up after the disastrous fire of 1799 and returned to England, losing his life at sea on the way home, Ricketts left behind a handful of small travelling shows, which toured mostly just the eastern states.

If England was the birthplace of the circus, then America gave us the iconic and enduring image of the 'big top'. The idea of a large portable canvas structure in which to perform revolutionised the circus, and it was credited to a menagerie and circus proprietor named Joshua Purdy Brown. He erected the first circus tent in Wilmington, Delaware, in 1825, with previous travelling circuses having performed either in the open air or within roofless canvas enclosures. A year later, Nathan Howes, another circus proprietor, erected the first circular tent. With this innovation circuses could now perform almost anywhere.

Until the 1830s, when the railway was first introduced into America, circuses had to travel by horse and wagon. Although the introduction of the canvas circus tent allowed greater mobility, they still could not travel much further than from town to town. This sometimes created problems, as people who had seen the show in one town might well follow the circus to the next town, as recounted by Frank Van Hoven, talking about his early days in the circus ring:

> *we were caught several times. Our equipment in horses was small, and we only moved eight or nine miles a day, so it happened that people who had*

seen the show followed it to the next town and gave the gag away about the alligator that was only fed once a month. "Why, I saw it fed yesterday," they would say, and then the people ran us out of the town.

(*The World's Fair*, 19 October 1915)

During the nineteenth century, America was a country still waiting to be explored, a land of opportunity where anything could happen. In 1825 the Eerie Canal opened and by 1842 the Oregon Trail was mapped out, and the gradual settlement of the west of America began. Within a few years gold was discovered in California and so, as the population began to move ever westwards, the circus duly followed. By 1860 the railway stretched for 35,000 miles across America and, by 1869, the transcontinental line was completed. The circus was now on the move in a big way.

The development of the circus in America would follow a very different path to what was happening in England. By the 1840s, the use of the circus tent was commonplace, whereas in England most performances were still given in the permanent amphitheatres, theatres or specially erected semi-permanent structures. In America, menageries often travelled as part of a circus – add to this the very American creation of the 'sideshow' and we have the typical American circus of the day.

Performers had to be multi-skilled and fulfil several roles, as Claude M. Roode, the American wire walker, recounted to *The World's Fair* in 1914:

There were only a handful of us in the company, all told, but we could all do two or three acts, and we filled out quite a long and varied programme. Before the show opened we always paraded the town with the whole outfit, the company in the band wagon – we all had to be musicians as well as performers – and the employees and workmen riding the horses and driving the wagons. In the band wagon stood a loud voiced man who at frequent intervals advertised the show adding, "And don't forget the free attractions on the show ground". The free attractions were several. In the first place we had a high diving dog which was trained to run up a ladder outside the show and jump from the top into a net below. Then a girl did a fire eating act, and all together we got the crowd gazing good before ever we asked them to go inside.

(*The World's Fair*, 14 February 1914)

The sideshow was to become an American institution and grew out of a natural curiosity for the strange, wonderful and weird. Any individual who

Portrait of Charles Stratton, known as 'Tom Thumb', 1863. *(Library of Congress)*

was different in some way – who was exceptionally tall or exceptionally small, who had a deformity or disability, who was in possession of a physical peculiarity, such as being tattooed all over or being exceptionally hairy – was worthy of being displayed to the public.

Charles Stratton, known as 'General Tom Thumb', was perhaps the most famous curiosity of his day and stood only 102 centimetres (3ft 4 in) tall by the time of his death in 1883, at 45 years. The master of the sideshow, P. T. Barnum, took Charles Stratton under his tutelage, and it was he who created the character of General Tom Thumb. He toured this 'performing midget' across Europe, including presentations before Queen Victoria on two occasions.

In 1841 Barnum opened his American Museum in New York and put on public display such attractions as snake charmers, jugglers, an orangutan, performing fleas and a model of Paris. Barnum was first and foremost a showman and it was not long before he was also regularly presenting mermaids, giants and midgets as part of his exhibitions. He reputedly said that the public was happy to be deceived, as long as they were being entertained. Barnum also had a flair for advertising and promotion, manipulating people in their thousands, so that they flocked to view his exhibits.

The museum was popular for over 20 years, before it burned down in 1865 during the Civil War. Barnum then retired and entered politics, but his political career was to be shortlived. In 1871, he was persuaded to join circus proprietors Dan Castello and William Coup to create 'P. T. Barnum's Museum, Menagerie and Circus'. Within a year they had expanded to a six-tent outfit covering five acres – approximately the size of five football pitches. The outfit included a menagerie, a museum and a hippodrome.

Not only were they beginning to operate on a large scale, they also brought about innovations that were to change the face of the American circus industry. Tents were growing larger and larger, so Barnum and his colleagues added a second ring to the performance space. The American style of tent easily allowed for this expansion. The 'King Poles', the central supporting poles for the structure, were arranged in single file, which meant that additional rings could be laid out between each pole. This was unlike the British style where the four King Poles were placed in a square, with one central ring between them. Now two acts could perform simultaneously, offering the audience even more spectacle. But even more significantly at this time, they also put their circus on the railways.

The first recorded instance of an American circus using the railways for travel was in 1838, but it was not until the 1850s that the railways began to be used in earnest by performers. The year 1853 saw the first show to tour its entire season by rail and in subsequent years many more circus owners chose to use the railways. By the 1890s, seven circuses were using the railways solely as a means of transporting their outfits around the country. America is an immense country and by using the railways a circus could travel a long distance in a comparatively short time. They could finish performing in one town and the next day set up in another, simply by moving the whole outfit by rail overnight. They were also able to offer ticket discounts or charter trains to draw the public to their performances from the surrounding areas.

Underwood & Underwood Stereoscope viewer card depicting a small travelling circus in Mexico c.1890. *(Author's collection)*

'The Grand Lay-out', c.1874: A circus sets up and parades near the railway. *(Library of Congress)*

But rail travel and larger tents brought more problems. As well as the increased costs of transporting larger and larger outfits, there was always potential for disaster. In 1877, *The Era* reported that seven men on the 'advance' car of Barnum's Great American Circus were killed in a railway accident in Iowa, and in 1884 *The Penny Illustrated Paper* described how a train carrying a circus in Colorado caught fire, resulting in nine deaths, with several others severely injured.

Audiences were equally at risk, for in 1898 the same newspaper carried this item:

> *Disaster at an American Circus – A terrible occurrence is reported from Sioux City, in Iowa. A circus performance was being given in a huge marquee, erected on the banks of the river, when a cyclone which suddenly sprang up caused the tent to collapse. Hundreds of people were buried beneath the structure, many of them being thrown into the river, and a terrible scene of confusion ensued. Up to the time of telegraphing, ten dead bodies had been recovered from the river.*
>
> (*The Penny Illustrated Paper*, 2 July 1898)

When a circus arrived in town it would take on casual labour from the local community. Manpower was needed to set up the big top and a queue of men would line up to sign on for a variety of tough, physical jobs. A circus proprietor could never be sure about the men he was signing up and often there would be friction between hired hands and the regular circus employees.

George Holloway, renowned for originating his perpendicular ladder act in the 1880s, recalled an incident in Phoenix City, Arizona, when a circus employee by the name of Gardiner got into an argument with a local hired man and ended up hitting him. The local man went immediately to the sheriff's office and complained about being assaulted by 'one of those circus folk'. The sheriff asked to be taken to Gardiner and for some reason he then drew his revolver and shot Gardiner dead where he stood. The circus could do nothing, as the sheriff would have claimed he had acted in self-defence and his word would have been accepted by the authorities.

Circus folk were not held in much esteem in those days and, according to Holloway, human life was cheap in the States then. He also pointed out the poor treatment meted out to the Afro-American section of the circus community, with their role limited during this period largely to that of the sideshow band, a 'tribal' warrior or simply manual labour. This contrasts markedly with the British circus, which had embraced Pablo Fanque wholeheartedly as he rose from respected performer to the owner of his own circus.

Popular though circus may have been, the attitude of some sections of the public towards the perceived dishonesty of the circus is reflected in a sarcastic letter from an American circus manager to the press:

I am pleased to learn that you intend writing a book on the subject of 'The Circus and other Noxious Institutions' and I cheerfully give you all the information in my power concerning our last season.

We are somewhat fortunate in several things, one of them being our elephant. Not knowing the feeling of the public on elephants this summer we started out with a milk-white sacred elephant from Interior India, captured at the usual great expense and appalling sacrifice of human life. We had only reached Johnson's Creek, O. [Oregon] when the whitewash began to flake and rub off, which necessitated the application of two coats of white paint at considerable expense. This weather-cracked and blistered some, and when we reached Poseyville, Ind. [Indiana] the public was wild for a black elephant, and it took three coats of dark paint, applied at some expense, but fortunately no loss of life to please 'em.

When we reached Illinois I found that by keeping my finger on the public pulse, that it wanted a trick elephant, and ours was accordingly trained to stand on a barrel and kick at the clown. The paint was allowed to come off gradually, and when we reached the Mississippi river our elephant showed several square yards of black, considerable white, besides a number of spots of simple elephant.

Our Orang-utang [sic] left us at Keokok, Iowa, going to work on a new brick livery stable at that place carrying a hod. This forced me to put on his skin and grab the bars of the cage and howl for three hours a day myself. Our Mermaid was struck by lightning at Paris, Mo. [Missouri] and the sheet-iron ripped down the back.

Our lion went on a strike early in the season and refused to roar. This made it necessary for the treasurer after he got through selling tickets to get down behind the cage and roar for him, while a canvas man prised the furious beast's mouth open with a picket. This was satisfactory to the public but the treasurer's throat was badly calloused.

An inquisitive gentleman at Atchinson, Kas. [Kansas] punched the hump off our sacred cow with an umbrella and the audience used it for a football, completely ruining it. The buffalo in our Wild West show about the same time got so it would not run for the cowboys, and the ringmaster was obliged to go ahead of it with an ear of corn. I soon after traded with a man from Hay Creek Township for a buffalo with a little more spirit.

During the season we gave 260 performances; lied about the next performance 259 times; number of spectators shot by cowboys, 19; number of cowboys injured by falling from horses, 10; number of men who attempted to ride the trick mule in Missouri, 27; in other States, 1. We escaped without paying our licence 12 times; the zebra was re-striped four times; the clown attempted a new joke one time, which was met with groans and eggs. Number of questions asked by spectators 64,000,000; number of answers given, four; number of answers understood, 0. The proprietors made disrespectful remarks concerning the Inter-State Commerce law 875,000 times. One hundred and thirty thousand tickets were sold, 12,800 complimentaries issued, and 118 Kansas men passed in on account of bringing hay for the elephant. Number of small boys who paid, 34; number who crawled under the tent, 138,274. Number of Iowa men who had spotted horses they wished to sell, 1,700.

We have gone into winter quarters here and now have our agents ransacking the known earth for curiosities. Nothing is purchased which is not warranted to howl all summer, as the treasurer and myself do not feel that we could in justice to ourselves or to the public again undertake to conduct the howl department for the season.

(The Hampshire Telegraph, 3 December 1887)

Publicity poster for the Sells Brothers' Enormous United Show, c.1880s. *(Library of Congress)*

Poster for P. T. Barnum's 'Greatest Show on Earth and Great London Circus', 1879. *(Library of Congress)*

During the 1870s and 1880s, circuses in America seemed to grow at a rapid pace, and Barnum, Coup and Castello now dubbed their circus as 'The Greatest Show on Earth'. The popularity of circus was at an all-time high in America and many well-known names were active at this time; Cooper and Bailey, Adam Forepaugh, Van Ambergh, the Sells Brothers, Stone and Murray, and Buffalo Bill Cody.

The merging of Barnum and Bailey in 1880 created a huge circus empire. Barnum now extended his performance space to include three circus rings surrounded by a hippodrome; George Sanger had tried this in 1871 in the Agricultural Hall in London but never developed the idea further. Now the audience could witness three simultaneous performances, whilst also being treated to a parade. The emphasis became more on spectacle and mass entertainment and there was a growing physical distance between the performers and their audience; gone was the more intimate nature of the British circus.

By the time Barnum died in 1891, the United States was into its second century; the Statue of Liberty had been unveiled five years previously; the Civil War was a distant memory; almost 50 years had passed since Blondin had crossed Niagara Falls on a tightrope; the electric light and the camera had been invented, and Wyatt Earp had had his shoot out at the OK corral. The American circus was about to take another leap forward.

James Bailey took over the sole management of the company on Barnum's death, still trading under the name of Barnum and Bailey. In 1897 the Barnum and Bailey circus embarked on an ambitious six-year tour of Europe. The show took England by storm, as recorded in *The Era:*

Nothing has ever achieved such a phenomenal success as the Barnum and Bailey 'Greatest Show on Earth' which for the past six months has been exhibiting in all of the principal cities of the United Kingdom, winning for itself everywhere the highest encomiums of public approval. It is no exaggeration to say that the big American circus has exhibited to between twenty-five and thirty thousand people daily during its provincial tour, and so marked has been its success and so overshadowing its superiority over anything of a similar kind ever seen in this country before ... The whole country has been aroused to a fever heat at the marvels of the big Yankee institution ...

It is freely admitted that nothing so gigantic has ever been seen on this side of the Atlantic, even as a permanent institution, and when it is considered that this immense show, with its 840 people, 420 horses, hundreds of wild animals and over 100 wagons necessary to transport its material, has travelled all over Great Britain, exhibiting in some cities for one, two and three weeks, while its stay in others has been confined to a single day, erecting its tents in the morning, giving a street parade and two complete performances, and then being loaded on its specially constructed cars, 74 in number (each 54 ft in length), making railway runs of from 15 to 184 miles and arriving in the next city in time to follow out the same programme, we are bound to admit that our Yankee cousins have taught us a few lessons in the art of catering to public amusement and the rapidity of getting from one city to another and presenting their show ... None will dispute that Mr Bailey has revolutionised the circus business on this side of the Atlantic.

(*The Era*, 15 October 1898)

The absence of Barnum and Bailey from the American scene allowed their competitors to grow in strength and number. In particular, the Ringling Brothers circus became extremely successful. So large was their company that, by 1902, they filled 65 railway cars when they moved their outfit. At that time there were 98 circuses and menageries within America, of which 38 used the railways to tour their shows. When Barnum and Bailey had left America for their European tour they had been the most eminent circus company in the country.

They returned to face stiff competition, especially from the Ringlings. Bailey had already earlier taken over part control of both the Forepaugh and Sells circuses and in 1905, a year before his death, he transferred some of this interest to the Ringlings. His widow later sold the interests in Barnum and Bailey's circus to the Ringlings and they continued to tour the two shows separately until 1919, when they combined as one unit. The Ringlings became a byword for the circus in America and the largest outfit of its time:

The biggest circus in America, of course, is that of the Ringling Bros., who also own the Barnum and Bailey outfit ... It is a real travelling town – a community to itself. I have several times known us play in towns where we had twice or even three times as many people with our show as there were in the population of the place ... and yet we should play to 12,000 to 15,000 people because folks knew beforehand that the show was coming, and came from miles around to see it. They rode in on bronchos, fellows and girls, and made it a public holiday. It takes ten acres to set up the Ringling Show – the smallest it can be compressed into. There are 600 horses, 50 clowns, 30 or 40 bareback riders and 50 acrobats. I have known as many as 48 acrobats working at once.

(*The World's Fair*, 14 February 1914)

American circuses had a huge impact upon the circus industry in Europe, and Barnum and Bailey's was not the only American circus to make the long journey across the Atlantic. As early as 1842, an American circus was reported to be performing in Liverpool, with demonstrations of 'clever gymnastic and equestrian exercises' (*Manchester Times*, 30 April 1842), and between 1843 and 1844 the circus of the equestrian Richard Sands and Lewis Lent was also touring Great Britain.

During the next four decades almost 20 different American circuses toured the United Kingdom. Prominent amongst the earlier visitors were 'Howe and Cushing's Great American Circus' and 'Macarte's Monster Circus'. Howe and Cushing first arrived in 1857 and made an immediate impression. The *Liverpool Mercury* reported that, 'the singularity of their dress and appearance has rendered them objects of attraction amongst our townspeople'. Wherever they went, this circus created a spectacle that drew the crowds.

The parade alone was worth seeing, according to *The Leeds Mercury* (13 June 1857):

> *Howe and Cushing's American Circus – Quite a sensation was created in some of the principal thoroughfares of Leeds, yesterday morning, by the arrival in grand procession of this United States Company of Equestrians. Foremost amongst the novelties was an immense musical instrument, denominated an Apollonicon,* [large chamber organ] *drawn by forty cream-coloured horses, four abreast … The entertainment is altogether very much above the ordinary run of travelling equestrians, and is wholly free from anything objectionable.*

Spectacular as these American circus parades were, they could also be dangerous. In Hawick in 1858, during their entry parade into the town, two children were seriously injured when they were caught up in the wheels of the carriage carrying the monstrous Apollonicon. Later in the same parade the carriage came into contact with a wall and overturned. Several people were injured and the legs of a man and a child had to be amputated as a result of the accident.

Despite such disasters, Howe and Cushing's performances attracted many thousands of spectators and were frequently sold out. The venues were packed and often people had to be turned away, as here in Birmingham:

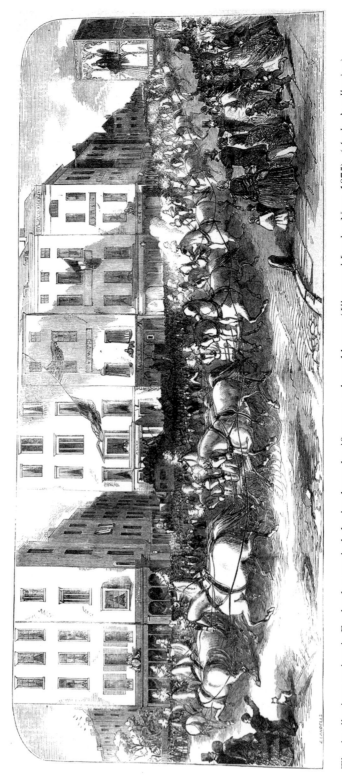

The Apollonicon arrives in England: a musical chariot drawn by 40 cream-coloured horses (*Illustrated London News*, 1875). (*Author's collection*)

There could not have been less than four thousand persons, and these packed together in as small a compass as ever we saw four thousand people before. Hundreds were sent away disappointed from the doors … Every corner, and rail, and gangway was choked with spectators, and here and there might be observed batches of youngsters positioned in inconceivably outré places, clinging to low rafters, perched on window ledges or comfortably adjusting themselves on the shoulders of their taller mates.

(*Birmingham Daily Post*, 28 December 1857)

However, like many other circuses of the time, Howe and Cushing's were never entirely free of mishap. In 1858, *The Bristol Mercury* gave an account of a 'Disgraceful outrage at a Circus': 'In the evening there was such an overwhelming audience admitted that the performances were interrupted and a very serious disturbance ensued. The pressure became so great that numbers were forced into the ring'. Because of this many of the acts could not be performed and the whole performance was curtailed early by the playing of the National Anthem.

This caused a violent reaction from the audience who felt they had been cheated out of their money:

Stones were thrown at the lamps which lighted the arena, all of which were quickly smashed, some ruffians on the outside forced their way underneath the canvas and joined the turbulent mob within … and attempted to pull down the tent, whilst some of those present pulled knives from their pockets and proceeded to cut away at the canvas, doing great damage to the tent.

The mob went on to demand their entry money back and, when this was not forthcoming, they turned their attention to the pay office housed in a caravan. They attacked it with stones, causing a lot of damage. Such was the disturbance that: 'A large body of constables was instantly despatched to the scene, but for a considerable time their efforts to restore order were unavailing … On the following day the circus left the city without waiting to give a second night's performance' (*The Bristol Mercury*, 22 October 1858).

Fires, storms and tent collapses still seem to have been quite commonplace in American circuses. Hernandez and Stone's American circus was devastated by a terrific fire in their tent during a performance in Halifax, though fortunately there was no loss of life. The large tent belonging to Pawe's American circus overturned in a gale during an afternoon performance at

Wirksworth in Derbyshire. Again there were only minor injuries and no loss of life among the audience, which was mainly made up of children.

Other notable American circuses, such as Hernandez and Stone, and those of Bell, Smith and Gibbs, appeared in England during this period. The three circuses of Hutchinson, Tayleure and Transfield also made an appearance on British soil. All carried the banner of the 'American Circus', along with some other hyperbolic term such as 'Great', 'Monster', 'Mammoth' or 'Supreme'. James Washington Myer, another American circus proprietor, spent many years in England. He retired from the business in 1882 and sold off his entire circus. Many well-known English circus owners benefited from this, and Sanger, Hengler, Ginnett and Cross were there ready to snap up a bargain or two.

The circus was always newsworthy, and not always for dramatic reports of accidents. Circus could provide amusing and sad items as well as violently tragic ones. Sometimes the circus was bizarrely placed alongside other seemingly unrelated, less important pieces of news, such as in *The North Country News* of 7 May 1885, in which an item advertising Captain Transfield's American Circus in Middlesbrough came eighth in a news column headed by the item, 'Sixteen fine mushrooms have been gathered in an open field near Stainton-in-Cleveland'.

Keely and Hogin's American circus appear to have offended a section of the community in the village of Beauly, in the north of Scotland, when they arrived on a Sunday. Devout worshippers in the village attempted to boycott the circus in what they saw as, 'a daring act of Sabbath desecration on the part of the 'diverting vagabonds' (*The Belfast News-Letter*, 15 August 1885). However, the boycott seems to have had little effect, as the evening performance was still attended by roughly half the population of the village.

A sad but amusing tale appeared in *The Bristol Mercury* of 13 July 1880, in which the proprietor of an American circus advertised a performance by his elephant, which would play some pieces on the piano. Crowds flocked to see this wonder and much money was taken at the door. When the time came for the elephant to perform:

Raising his foot, he placed it on the keys, suddenly he uttered a fearful cry, which sounded like weeping, and occasioned no small alarm. The proprietor came forward and stuck his head in the animal's jaws to learn the reason. Taking his head out again he ordered the tusked virtuoso to be led away; then, turning to the audience said the elephant could not perform on that piano, as in the keys of the instrument he recognised the teeth of his mother.

An even more poignant story was told in *The Era*, concerning a visit of Howe and Cushing's American Circus to Rotherham in 1864. It would seem that during the parade, the horses pulling a nearby private carriage took fright and bolted. The driver leapt from his box leaving the passenger, an elderly lady, to her peril. A clown from the parade, named the 'Tenderfoot Tramp', dashed forward and grabbed the bridles of the runaway horses and brought them to a halt, but in doing so he fell beneath them. The unconscious clown was carried to the home of the lady, a Mrs Windrath, where he was cared for. It was only then that the lady recognised the clown as her long-lost son Robert, who had been banished from his home by his stern Quaker father several years before. The circus went on its way but Robert, the 'Tenderfoot Tramp', stayed with his mother.

There is a tendency to think of American circuses in England only in terms of Barnum and Bailey or Buffalo Bill Cody and his Wild West show. These two outfits certainly had a big impact on the circus business in the latter part of the nineteenth century, but we must also acknowledge that the American circus had a long presence in England, almost half a century

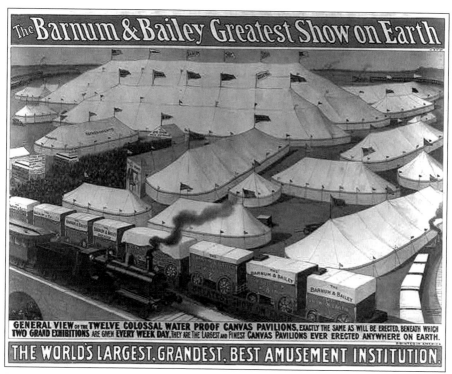

Poster for the Barnum & Bailey 'Greatest Show on Earth'. *(Library of Congress)*

before these big names appeared. This influence was not merely a one-way flow. As much as American circuses were popular in England, so British circuses and circus artists also had an input into the American circus.

Circus performers are, by the very nature of their work itinerant as, they undertake contracts in different circuses throughout their lives. Many British-born circus artists performed in the big American circuses, such as Paul Minno (a stage name), a Scottish-born contortionist who went to America with his family around 1900 and worked with the Ringling Brothers' circus. He started his performing career with Duffy's circus and then went on to appear with many others, including Sanger's, Bostock's and Fossett's.

In a letter to *The World's Fair* newspaper (25 July 1914), Minno talks about the British artists being 'the finest performers with the show', and he goes on to mention them by name. He talks about the Clark family, whose members present an aerial act and the 'finest somersault riding act in the world'. Also mentioned are Fred Stelling, a great clown of his time, and 'J Evans and Sister', who perform, 'the finest foot juggling act I have ever seen'. Originally from Norwich, the Evans duo came to the Ringlings via Circus Pinder in France.

At the end of the nineteenth century, the American circus had developed from a small group of independent travelling shows to a large conglomerate circus industry. Its impact upon American culture was immense and its very terminology became part of the language. We still use terms today that originated in the circus; to 'get the show on the road'; to 'jump on the band wagon'; to 'toss a hat into the ring'; and to regard something as a 'white elephant'. The circus embraced the growth of urban centres and the rapidly expanding railway communications network. In her book *The Circus Age* (2002), J. M. Davis contends that the circus had 'helped consolidate a shared national leisure culture at the turn of the [nineteenth] century'. The American circus had become a major source of live entertainment for the masses and was about to enter a golden age.

In contrast to this, times were changing in England. The Victorian era was soon to pass and a new age was dawning. The circus would face new challenges in a mechanised age; challenges from other forms of entertainment and the upheaval of an impending war that would transform the very nature of society.

Chapter Seven

Magic, Movies and Music Halls: Stiff Competition for the Late Nineteenth Century British Circus

The gaslights reflect off the gilded hieroglyphs and papyrus-leaved columns of the Egyptian Hall, as the expectant crowd chatters restlessly. Upon the narrow stage stands a wooden cabinet set on trestles, which is picked out by the limelight. The closet is the size of a small wardrobe, perhaps 6ft tall by 6ft wide, with three doors to the front. In the centre door is an aperture covered on the inside by a dark curtain.

A tall American named William Fay enters and opens the doors of the cabinet. Behind each of the two outer doors is set a narrow wooden seat; the centre section is empty. He turns to the audience and invites volunteers onto the stage to examine the cabinet. Several men step up and examine both the inside and outside of the contraption, nodding their approval that all seems in order. Standing the volunteers to one side, Fay then introduces the two performers of the evening, the brothers William and Ira Davenport. The crowd applauds as two striking figures walk on stage. Although slight in build, their handlebar moustaches, goatee beards and long black curly hair swept back from their foreheads give them a dramatic appearance. They say nothing but position themselves downstage, on either side of the cabinet, as the crowd settles to an expectant hush.

Only the sibilant hiss of the gas jets breaks the silence. The two men remove their frock coats and Fay invites the volunteers to examine the brothers for hidden devices. Their pockets, cuffs and collars are searched and then their hands are tied behind their backs with lengths of cord. Taking their seats in the cabinet, facing each other, the cords are pulled through holes in the planks and tied around their ankles before being passed across the floor of the cabinet and tied to those of the other brother. With other cords the men continue to secure the knees and arms of the two brothers, until they are securely constrained in their seats.

The volunteers stand aside as Fay closes the three cabinet doors and the lights dim, leaving only the cabinet in the limelight. Almost immediately, to the audience's amazement, a pale, ghostly hand flutters through the curtained hole in the centre door. The audience gasps as the outer doors swing open and the unbound Davenports step forward, their restraints coiled on the floor of the cabinet. There is applause, although hesitant, as the audience is not sure exactly what it has witnessed. Are these two men simply escapologists or are there other 'spirit' forces at work?

The Davenports step back inside the cabinet and Fay swings the doors closed again. Within moments he opens the two outer doors to show the brothers again securely fastened with knotted cords. The volunteers on stage are once more asked to check the restraints. The outer doors are closed and Fay hangs a series of musical instruments from hooks on the back wall of the centre section before closing the door. Immediately there begins a devilish hullabaloo. Instruments are banged, blown, twanged or thrown through the aperture onto the stage. At one point a pale arm is thrust through the curtain and it madly rings a hand-bell. Fay leaps forward and wrenches open the outer doors to reveal the brothers sitting calmly, fully bound to their seats.

Fay replaces the instruments and then, with great showmanship, places dry flour into the bound hands of the brothers and pours water into their mouths. With a flourish he closes the doors and again, within seconds, the cacophony begins once more. Fay claps his hands and the noises stop. He steps forward and opens the doors to reveal both brothers still fully tied, with flour in their hands and water in their mouths. The volunteers are then invited to untie the two men and spend several minutes unpicking the complicated knots before freeing them. William and Ira Davenport step free from the cabinet to tumultuous applause ...

The Davenports gave the first performance of their 'spirit cabinet' at a private function, organised by the actor and playwright Dion Boucicault at his London residence in 1864. At this event the second part of their presentation took the form of a séance, and after a short period of darkness the brothers were discovered bound hand and foot by mysterious 'spirits'. The séance continued in the dark with the sounds of instruments being blown or plucked, and hats and coats pulled away from the invited guests. When the lights were again raised, the brothers were found tied securely in their seats as before, but this time one of them was wearing a guest's coat. The spectators could only conclude that some mystical and spiritual force had been at work.

The Davenport brothers in their spirit cabinet. *(Library of Congress)*

During the nineteenth century, Victorian Britain was swept with a fascination for all things 'magical'; the art of illusion; mysticism and the relatively new movement of spiritualism. Many famous names in the world of magic and illusion began their careers at this time and the Egyptian Hall in Piccadilly, London, became known as the home of British magic. In an age when scientific enquiry was at its highest, other venues such as Philosophical Halls and Scientific Institutes around the country hosted lectures and demonstrations of the mystic arts. Opinions were divided, especially in the matter of spiritualism. Some dismissed it as mere illusion and trickery; others firmly believed in the presence of spiritual forces, and eminent Victorians such as Sir Arthur Conan Doyle and Elizabeth Barrett Browning became ardent followers of this movement.

Poster advertising Harry Kellar and his levitation act c.1894. *(Library of Congress)*

The rise in popularity of magic and illusion was only one form of competition that the British circus industry was now facing. During this period more people than ever were now living in large towns and cities and the focus of life had changed. Previously, life had moved at the pace of the changing seasons. Rural entertainments had been tied to seasonal and religious events such as spring fairs or harvest festivals, and circuses, fairs and menageries had often linked their performances with these celebrations. The visit of a circus became a highlight in the calendar and whole communities would attend; families, the old and young, single or married. The circus had little against which to compete.

Once people had begun migrating to the cities, the pace of life changed. Now that people lived their lives to the rhythm of machines the seasons lost their meaning. It began to matter less to communities whether it was winter or summer and even, sometimes, if it was day or night. Many rural migrants to the growing industrial centres found themselves working in mills or forges. The 1871 Census for Blackburn in Lancashire shows that 32 per cent of the total population was employed in the cotton mills in and around the town. This figure far exceeds any other form of occupation listed, aside from the 16 per cent representing those in domestic service.

Working hours in factories were long and arduous and, although the pay was better than in agricultural labour overall, the quality of life was certainly not. By the mid-century a power loom weaver in a mill, depending upon how many looms he had responsibility for, could earn between 3s and 30s for a 69-hour week, approximately £6 to £60 in current terms. Introduced in 2013, the current minimum hourly basic wage for the over-21s is £6.31 which would give a basic income of £189.30 for a 30-hour week, three times the maximum nineteenth century wage for a third of the time. By 1875 the government had introduced an Act of Parliament limiting factory working hours to 56½ hours per week.

In order to survive, most members of a working class family, including older children, had to find work somewhere. Life was hard and a visit by a travelling circus or menagerie was always a welcome relief, but by now there were other entertainments on offer. During the latter half of the nineteenth century there was a rapid expansion of the rail network across Britain, and by the end of the century there were more than 70,000 miles of track covering the country. Workers in the industrial heartlands could now travel relatively quickly and cheaply to the coastal seaside resorts. Lancashire cotton workers visited resorts on the north-west coast, such as Blackpool and Morecombe. The woollen workers of Yorkshire favoured the east coast, and Scarborough, Whitby, Skegness and Bridlington.

In 1875 two things encouraged people to use the rail network even more. Firstly, the government introduced the Bank Holiday Act. Aimed initially at office workers and clerical staff, it fixed Boxing Day, Easter Monday, Whit Monday and the first Monday in August as official public holidays. Secondly, the Midland Railway Company abolished its second class rail tariff and lowered the price of the third class tariff, at the same time improving the standard of the carriages by covering the wooden seats with padding and material. Other railway companies soon followed suit and third class travel became very popular. With guaranteed holiday time and cheaper rail fares at peak holiday times, the coastal towns were filled with factory workers from the industrial centres.

In Blackpool, a business consortium bought a site on the Central Promenade, which had once housed Dr Crocker's Menagerie and Aquarium. In 1891, the foundation stone was laid for the new Blackpool Tower, modelled on the Eiffel Tower in Paris, and to be included in the complex was a purpose-built circus arena. The Blackpool Tower Circus opened for business on 14 May 1894 and became a huge success with visitors. Similarly, in 1898, a showman named George Gilbert moved to Great Yarmouth and built a wooden structure to present circus shows. Five years later this was replaced by a permanent stone structure named the Hippodrome.

Both the Blackpool Tower Circus and the Great Yarmouth Hippodrome are still popular venues today and are the only two surviving purpose built permanent circus buildings in full-time operation in the country. In a small way, the circus was responding to the competitive attractions of the seaside resorts. But, while the circuses in Blackpool and Great Yarmouth were permanent structures, the vast majority of circuses were still seasonal and itinerant. During the summer season and holiday times some circuses did set up along the coastal towns, but funfairs, end of pier amusements, donkey rides, the sand and the sea all competed for the attention of the visitors.

Also, with urban development often came a lack of suitable open space within a city to pitch their shows. The circus was now being moved to the fringe of society. For example, in the middle of the nineteenth century at least three sites in the heart of Leeds were used for visiting circuses. Yet by the end of the century those sites had been built upon or redeveloped and travelling circuses were forced to set up in open spaces such as Woodhouse Moor and Killingbeck Fields, on the edges of the city sprawl at that time.

The very nature of the circus audience, too, was beginning to change during this time. When Astley and Hughes first founded their circuses back in the eighteenth century their audience was predominantly, although

10,269. - BLACKPOOL. THE TOWER WITH BEACH

Crowds thronging the beach at Blackpool, with the Tower in the background, 1895. *(Library of Congress)*

not exclusively, adult. The circus was the fashionable place to be seen and was often frequented by the glitterati of society. As the circus developed, it became more democratic and returned to its roots as a popular form of entertainment appealing to all classes and all ages, especially in the provinces. In London the circus was also well supported by the nobility and continued to retain a more respectable image, but touring shows sometimes met with friction between the locals and the outsiders:

> *On Monday night an extraordinary occurrence took place at Motherwell. Lord George Sanger's Circus was performing there when an altercation took place between one of the natives of the place and a circus attendant ... and the latter, it is alleged, stabbed his opponent ... A riot ensued ... The police were completely overpowered for a time but the inhabitants of the town rendered valuable assistance ... About two o'clock yesterday morning a number of constables arrived from the surrounding districts ... about forty persons were apprehended.*
>
> (*The Aberdeen Weekly Journal,* 20 June 1888)

By the 1870s, several factors were to change the democratic nature of the circus audience. A new phenomenon had captured the interest of the largely working class male population – sport. Sporting competitions had always been popular but were hitherto quite 'genteel'. The first Football Association Cup season was held in 1871-1872, with 15 clubs competing. Each club developed its own partisan following of enthusiastic supporters, largely male and working class. The first Cup Final, between Wanderers and the Royal Engineers, was held at Kennington Oval before a crowd of 2,000. The admission price was one shilling.

The popularity of football grew tremendously, with more and more clubs attracting more spectators year by year. The Football League was formed in 1888 and it became increasingly common for the men of the household, fathers and older boys, to go to watch football matches leaving their wives, daughters and younger children at home. Similarly the game of Rugby Union Football was also developing at this time. In 1845 the rules of the game were formalised and, although initially supported by a more middle class following, the creation of Rugby League Football in 1895 made the sport more popular with the working class and Rugby League soon became established as a 'working man's game'.

Rugby and football were only two of the evolving sports of the time that added to the competition that the circus was now facing. Other popular sports such as athletics, tennis, cricket, rowing and cycling were all attracting spectators – the same potential audience for the circus.

In an age of enquiry, the aspiring Victorian middle classes sought their entertainments elsewhere. Whilst certain sports were well supported, it was the more artistic, scientific and philosophical pursuits that generally attracted the support of the middle classes. They went to the theatre or music recitals, they attended lectures or demonstrations. The appeal of the circus was lessening. Whereas previously it had had a democratic appeal across all ages, sexes and classes, the circus was moving towards becoming a holiday entertainment predominantly focused upon children. Whilst still having a popular appeal amongst the working classes, adults were now more inclined to take their children to the circus rather than attend by themselves. The circus was losing its status as a legitimate art form.

The arrival of the cinematograph in the 1890s also had a major effect upon the popularity of the circus. The invention of the moving image on film is commonly attributed to the Lumière brothers in Paris, with their first public screening in 1895. However, some years earlier in 1888, a Frenchman named Louis Le Prince produced some of the first short sequences of moving images at his workshop in Leeds. He first made a short film entitled *A Roundhay Garden Scene* and a short time later the more famous clip of *Leeds Bridge*. (The latter footage can be viewed on the Leodis website.)

Within a relatively short period of time many picture houses and picture palaces were established across the country. Hundreds of short films were now being made and shown. By the early part of the twentieth century a significant amount of money was being invested in this new industry. The National Council of Public Morals estimated that half the population of Britain went to the cinema at least once a week.

Circuses existed solely on the profits from their shows. Any money invested in the circus was due to the circus owners, and the profit margins could be quite slim, taking into consideration the total overheads of any one season – the performers, the circus workers, transport costs, animal fodder etc. Adverse weather, poor attendance or a calamity could be disastrous for any circus. In comparison, the profits of a picture house were far more secure. The overheads were lower and a different film could be shown every day. For the audience admission was cheap and there was the security of being in a warm building sheltered from any bad weather.

Photographic images had been around for several decades but to see a moving image was still a novelty. The circus relied very much upon tradition within its shows; the horse was still the mainstay of any performance,

The Empire Music Hall London by Joseph Pennell c.1890. *(Library of Congress)*

supported by displays of gymnastics and acrobatics, wire-walking and other aerial acts and clowning. It was difficult for the circus to be as innovative as the cinema. Film-makers even began using circus themes within their films. Buffalo Bill Cody died in January 1917 and by the April of that year the Essanay Film Company was preparing to make an autobiographical film of his life.

The circus was struggling to compete with this new technological invention, but perhaps the most significant competition was to come from the rise of Music Hall. The music halls were not only to attract the audiences away from the circus but they also poached many performers.

In the early part of the eighteenth century many inns and taverns had 'singing rooms' or 'glee rooms' on their upper floors, where gentlemen could relax with a drink and enjoy popular music and song. The singing room at the White Swan Inn, on Swan Street in the centre of Leeds, was very popular and in 1865 the landlord, Charles Thornton, built a new music theatre as an adjunct to the White Swan. It first went under the title of Thornton's New Music Hall and Fashionable Lounge, before it became The

Music Hall artists from the City Varieties Music Hall in Leeds. *(Reproduced with permission of the West Yorkshire Archive Service)*

White Swan Varieties and then Stansfield's Varieties, until eventually The City Palace of Varieties. Whilst not quite the oldest music hall in existence – that accolade goes to Wilton's Music Hall in London, which opened in 1859 – the City Varieties, as it is now commonly known, does stand by its reputation of being the oldest music hall in the country still in daily use. Unfortunately, and somewhat ironically, Wilton's Music Hall was converted to a Methodist chapel in 1888.

By 1865, in London alone there were 32 music halls and many other smaller venues. This had risen to 78 by 1878, with 300 smaller venues around the city. Most major towns and cities had at least one music hall at this time. Unlike the theatres of the day, with seats set out in rows, the main auditorium would have had tables and chairs set out so that the customers could eat, drink and smoke during the performances.

The Malt Cross Music Hall in Nottingham is a good example of this layout. Entering directly from the street, the customers would have been able to sit in a bar area with tables, chairs and banquettes to each side. It would not be until 1914 that drinking was finally barred from the auditorium and separate bar areas were created. The floor area is only about 45ft long by 30ft wide, and comparatively small. An iron balustrade balcony extends around three sides of the hall, with a simple high platform stage at one end. The basement of this particular hall was originally an ice skating rink as well.

In total the hall would have accommodated only around 200 people when full and, as a small establishment, it was often used as a proving ground for new and up-and-coming acts. On Wednesday afternoons the proprietors from the larger music halls in the city would visit the Malt Cross to view these new acts and then engage them if they were thought suitable.

Music hall admission prices were always kept at a reasonable rate. An early programme for the City Palace of Varieties dated 1902 shows that there were two performances nightly, with admission at: 2d Gallery; 4d Pit; 6d Circle; 1s Boxes. It provided a relatively cheap evening's entertainment for the working classes, whilst the provision of discreet curtained boxes allowed the upper classes to indulge. During the 1900s, King Edward VII would make clandestine visits to the music hall in Leeds – whilst visiting family at nearby Harewood House – and closet himself away in one of the boxes.

Aware of the closely packed audience with varied standards of personal hygiene, managers were keen to impress on how clean and safe their halls were. A 1914 programme for the City Palace of Varieties in Leeds carried this announcement: 'In the interests of Public Health this Hall is disinfected throughout with Jeyes Fluid'.

When one considers the obvious advantages of performing in a permanent theatre, away from the vagaries of the weather, away from the endless setting up and taking down and travelling, it is hardly surprising that many circus performers moved to working the halls. Most Music Hall artists enjoyed at least a one-week engagement, sometimes longer, and could command a reasonable fee of a few pounds, unlike the fee once paid to the great escapologist Harry Houdini. In an article in 2013, *The Yorkshire Evening Post* recorded in 1904, the manager's books showed that he received the equivalent of £7,500 for one performance.

At the rival Empire Theatre in Leeds, Houdini almost met his death on stage in 1911. One of his famous escape tricks was to be handcuffed and placed within a milk churn filled with water, from which he would manage to escape. An important part of this escape is that the lid of a milk churn is slightly domed, so that even when the churn is full of water there is always a small reservoir of air trapped above the water level. This allowed Houdini enough time to free himself from the handcuffs.

As Leeds was the home of Tetley beer it was decided to challenge him to escape from a cask of Tetley bitter instead. Accepting the challenge, Houdini was restrained and placed in the full cask. The lid was fitted, but instead of a layer of air being trapped above the surface, fumes from the beer filled the void. Houdini almost suffocated and drowned and the cask had to be broken open by men with axes. This was one of the very few times that Houdini failed a challenge.

Many other instantly recognisable famous names worked the music halls. Charlie Chaplin, long before he created his little tramp character, appeared on stage as an eight-year-old member of a clog-dancing troupe named 'The Eight Lancashire Lads'.

The Music Hall shows were always a mixture of popular song, music and dancing, interspersed with speciality or novelty acts. Many of these speciality acts could have easily been presented in a circus, as indeed some were, and included acrobats and gymnasts, jugglers, clowns, cycle acts, animal acts, wire walkers and aerialists. An 1880 poster for the City Palace of Varieties offers 'Taba – the lion tamer' and 'Zettini and son – the Great Parisian Acrobats'. A 1914 programme shows, in addition to song and dance acts on the bill, the 'Leotard Brothers – comical clowns, staircase performers, hand balancers, hat throwers and catchers', as well as two different films, one dramatic, *The Rival Musicians*, the other comedic, *Landladies Beware*.

In 1866 at the London Pavilion Music Hall several speciality acts appeared. A presentation of the 'Sphinx' illusion was given by a Mr Villiers,

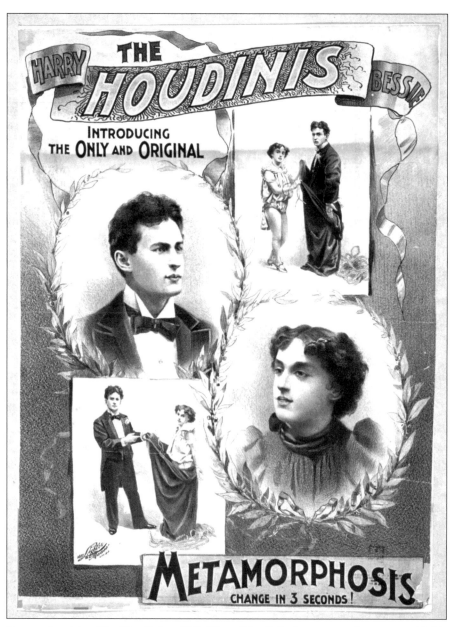

Poster advertising The Houdinis c.1895: Harry Houdini often appeared on stage with his wife Bess. *(Library of Congress)*

based upon the same illusion that was first given by a Colonel Stodare at the Egyptian Hall the previous year. *The Era*, 30 September 1866 reported that the performance: 'is given with wonderful spirit, and is evidently a novelty exactly to the taste of those who frequent this Music Hall'.

On the same programme was Daugwau, the 'Indian Juggler' who: 'Is an adept in his profession ... and ventures with unbounded success. Many balancing feats are executed by the juggler, and his entertainment is far from the least interesting in the nightly round'.

Also mentioned in the programme review by *The Era* were the 'Leopold Brothers', who performed upon the horizontal bar. The Leopolds were a troupe of comic acrobats and are examples of performers who worked both in the circus and in the music halls. In 1870 they appeared on the bill at the Agricultural Hall in Islington for the Christmas season entertainment, along with other acrobats, jugglers, clowns, vaulters and equestrians. They were joined by the renowned Frenchman Charles Blondin, famed for his tightrope walk across Niagara Falls in 1859. In this season he presented his latest and most astonishing feat:

The management of a bicycle on the long rope, stretched from end to end of the building, will induce thousands to visit the Agricultural Hall during the engagement of this acknowledged chief of funambulists. The ease with which M. Blondin preserves his balance, when mounted on the seemingly treacherous machine, dispels all apprehension of danger.

(*The Era*, 2 January 1870)

The following year the Leopolds were working at Bell's Hippodrome and Circus in Birmingham and in 1872 they appeared at Hengler's Cirque, on Argyll Street in London. They continued working with circuses, including performances at the Crystal Palace in 1876, until 1880 but by the August of that year *The Birmingham Daily Post* recording their appearance at the Birmingham Concert Hall. It would seem that around this time they began to develop into a troupe of acrobatic pantomimists rather than just performers on the high bar and they developed, in collaboration with a writer, Mark Melford, such a show entitled *Frivolity*.

In an open letter to the editor of *The Belfast News-Letter* (6 October 1883, quoting a previous review of 1881), an anonymous correspondent named Scaramucchio writes:

Time was when the Brothers Leopold contented themselves with the ordinary acrobatic business; then they added hat throwing and one or two other matters. Now they have developed into agile humorials [comedians], *worthy with comparison with such artists as the Hanlon Lees* [a well-known troupe of acrobatic pantomimists of the period who emigrated to America]. *To describe their grotesque antics, so as to convey to the mind of the reader an idea of even half the fun they provide, is simply impossible. We can only recommend that they should be seen. Their tumbling, their rock harmonicon playing – this is enchanting; their knock-about business, their wild quadrille in which they 'set to partners' by turning somersaults, and, indeed, everything they do, is replete with humour, and is characterised by finish and skill. It is not unlikely that this notice furnished the Leopolds with the first idea of making a debut in legitimate stage pantomime, which they did at Liverpool last August in Frivolity.*

Having created *Frivolity*, they toured this for a short time, before returning to their acrobatic roots and performing as comic acrobats. In 1887 they appeared in a mixed programme at the Paragon Theatre of Varieties on the Mile End Road and, by 1890, they were performing with Elphinstone's Circus at the Victoria Hall, with their 'clever acrobatic and boxing entertainments'.

By 1891 they were back in the pantomime business, appearing in *Beauty and the Beast* at the Drury Lane Theatre, alongside the famous clown, Whimsical Walker. Walker himself had begun life as a circus artist, having been apprenticed at eight years old to Pablo Fanque's circus for seven years in 1859. He worked with several circuses before going to America, where he worked with Barnum and Bailey's circus. On returning to England he worked with Hengler's before moving to the stage.

For some reason the Leopolds then revived *Frivolity* and began to tour again. The company was expanded, and by 1896 another comic acrobat, Fred Ingram, had joined the troupe. Also joining the company were the Trounsell Sisters, Lillie and Beatrice (distant relatives of the author of this book), who were both musical comedy actresses and dancers. Lillie went on to marry Fred Ingram, and Beatrice married another comedy actor named Herbert Dean. *Frivolity* went on to tour for many years, and although the original line up of the company changed several times, it continued until 1918.

Like the Leopold Brothers and Whimsical Walker, many other circus artists made the move from the ring to the stage during the latter part of the nineteenth century. To what extent these speciality acts became popular within the music halls can be seen in the December 1912 edition of *The Performers Annual*, a trade publication in which Music Hall artists advertised.

The popularity of the Music Hall was to reach its zenith during the First World War, but by this time the damage to the circus had been done.

Although it could be argued that by embracing circus acts the music halls were ensuring their continuation, Lord George Sanger's prediction was being realised; at the turn of the century the circus faced serious competition. The events of 1914 and beyond would be witness to a cataclysmic change in the circus industry.

Fred Ingram and fellow performers c.1900. *(Author's collection)*

Chapter Eight

The Circus Goes to War: 1900–1919

August 1914 saw Blackpool thronged with holidaymakers. The sun was shining and workers and their families from all over the north-west of England had rushed to the coast to take the sea air. There was a strongly held belief that a visit to the seaside during the summer months was good for the health. Many of the mill towns in Lancashire had agreed on a system of week-long local factory closures, commonly known as Wakes Weeks, and with the expansion of the rail and road network across the country it was now far easier for people to travel. Sometimes a whole community would descend upon the coastal towns at this time and seaside resorts such as Blackpool could be filled to capacity.

Men in straw boaters and flat caps strolled arm in arm with smartly dressed women in soft blouses, long skirts and 'Sunday best' hats. The jostling crowd drifted slowly along the promenade and the more adventurous could take a ride on one of the many steamers leaving from the end of the piers. Children played in the sand or at the water's edge, while adults indulged in hilarious donkey races along the beach. For a few pennies braver souls could hire roller skates and contemporary silent film footage. *Fun on the Sands 1914*, for example shows people clinging to each other to avoid falling over, much to the amusement of the onlooking crowd. There was open air dancing, and at the Pleasure Beach happy, smiling holidaymakers took rides on the bumper cars, the roller coaster or the water chute.

Towering above these festivities was Blackpool Tower. Completed only 20 years previously, the tower, modelled on the Eiffel Tower in Paris, stood on top of a building that housed a ballroom, a menagerie and a circus. The people watching George Lockhard, the circus ringmaster, resplendent in his pink hunting tailcoat, on that day were completely unaware that their world was about to change, but change it certainly did. With the recent assassination of Archduke Franz Ferdinand of Austria in Sarajevo, tensions had been rising across Europe and on 4 August 1914 Britain declared war on Germany.

For many people, especially those living in rural communities, the war in Europe may have seemed quite distant but the outbreak of hostilities did

Crowds in London on the outbreak of war in 1914. *(Library of Congress)*

have an immediate impact. On 3 August, sugar was priced at 2d per pound. By the time the shops closed on 4 August, the price had risen to 5d per pound, and by the end of the first week of the war sugar was being rationed by some grocers to 7lbs per person.

For some people the war brought new problems. Anti-German feelings ran high and in West Lothian a Canadian Indian circus performer was attacked in a wave of patriotic zeal, the crowd supposing that he was a German spy. *The Manchester Evening News* later reported that, 'sixteen German reservists employed in a travelling circus ... have been arrested; consequently the circus has been closed down'. Internment was to be the fate of many foreign circus performers, especially those from countries now at war with Britain. A report by Lord Kitchener to the House of Lords showed that by November 1914, 17,283 aliens had been interned. This number had grown to 18,670 by February 1915. Some of these internees were later released, but many were kept in internment camps throughout the war.

Because of this there was a consequent shortage of good acrobatic acts in both the circus and the music halls, as *The World's Fair* reported on 13 February 1915: 'There is a famine of acrobats. They are nearly all of them

Germans or Austrians … Many of them were interned, but have since been released, and have gone to America, which is the only place they are likely to earn a living just now'.

Many British and Colonial circus workers and performers volunteered for military service during the first few months of the war believing, like many, that it would 'all be over by Christmas'. On the outbreak of war, Bostock's Circus and Menagerie lost 41 of its workers who answered the call to arms, as well as its winter quarters in Glasgow, which were taken over for military purposes. Johnnie Quinn, a principal clown in some of the leading circuses such as Hanneford's, Duffy's and Buff Bill's (not to be confused with Buffalo Bill's circus) for over 20 years, volunteered for the Royal Munster Fusiliers on 8 August 1914. He spent over two years fighting, mainly in the Dardanelles, before being returned to England. *The World's Fair* newspaper gave weekly lists and photographs of those showmen who joined up; sadly as the war progressed these were joined by lists of names of those who had been killed in action.

Not all those performers wishing to join up were able to do so, some due to medical conditions, some because they were in a valuable reserved occupation and others were simply deemed too old. This last issue prompted Edward Charles Fanque, (commonly known as Ted) the son of the late Pablo Fanque, to write to *The World's Fair* on 28 November 1914:

I have no doubt there are many good showmen who would be proud to do their bit for the old country but are debarred on account of age limit. Well, sir, here's their chance, 45 years (upwards) is a good limit. You see in this case it's not the years that matter, "It's the man they want". I'm proud to say, I, myself, have passed the medical examination as being physically fit to go through a campaign, and hope there are many other showmen that will do the same.

As well as being a circus proprietor, Ted Fanque was a wrestler and extremely fit. Early in the war there was a movement to persuade Lord Kitchener to accept a battalion or more of picked men over the age of 45 and Fanque was lobbying for all those 'older' men who wished to serve in the military to put their names forward. By June 1915 he was: 'one of the 'decrepit' old men (of the '45 and over' battalion) who were refused by the War Office, although a thousand doctors said the men were fit to go through a campaign' (*The World's Fair*, 12 June).

In the opening years of the new century circus and variety acts were as popular as ever, as shown by these advertisements by artists. *(Images from* The Performer Annual, *December 1912, reproduced by permission of West Yorkshire Archive Service)*

'Lizzie Ward' – an elephant used to haul a cart in Sheffield during the First World War. *(Reproduced by permission of T. W. Ward CNC Machinery Ltd Sheffield)*

A shortage of manpower was not the only thing the circus had to face. In August 1914 three healthy elephants belonging to Bostock's Circus were requisitioned for military purposes, presumably haulage. Elephants belonging to Sanger's Circus were also taken for war work and there is Pathé Film footage from 1917 of his elephants tossing hay into a threshing machine and cranking a water pump. *The Western Daily Press* also reported on a circus expected at Porthcawl failing to appear, as its elephants had also been commandeered by the military authorities. Circuses across Europe were also affected in this way. In 1915 the German military requested all of Hagenbeck's circus elephants for transport purposes.

Not only elephants were requisitioned. In an age where motor vehicles were in their infancy, horses were still very much relied on for transport. Heavy draught horses, including those used for circus haulage, were commandeered to pull gun carriages and ambulance wagons. Trained performing horses were also seized for use as cavalry mounts, as they were already highly disciplined and considered ideal for that use. *The Lichfield Mercury* carried a small item in 1914 praising the Cossack cavalry in battle as they had, 'all the arts of the circus performer … with perfect command of his horse'.

A letter published in *The World's Fair*, 6 February 1915 also addresses this issue in response to a critical article on the treatment of circus animals:

if his wish that all animal training at circuses etc should be stopped were gratified, one of the chief sources of effective cavalry horses would be stopped also … In this country unfortunately, the public is quite ignorant of Haute Ecole [the classical art of riding] *… At the International Horse Show each year it is seen how the foreign officers … beat the men who ride on the stick-on principle. Now all these officers ride on the circus system … Instead of stopping circus riding, circuses should be encouraged as much as possible; a well broken circus horse is much more calm and confident in his rider.*

The circus horse on the battlefield had other attributes as well, as an account given in 2007 by Kate Wills on The Great War Forum website suggests. A badly wounded soldier was lying on the battlefield when he became aware of a nearby riderless horse quietly cropping the grass. He summoned up enough effort to call the horse and it came to him, nuzzling his outstretched hand. In a moment of inspiration the soldier pushed the horse's nose towards his leather belt and, to his surprise, the horse then seized the belt in its mouth and lifted the soldier from the ground carrying him safely back to his own lines. The soldier went on to recover and upon his discharge he adopted the horse. After extensive enquiries he discovered that the horse had once been part of a circus act in which it carried its trainer around the ring by his belt.

Circus and war intermingled in all kinds of strange situations. Performers turned soldiers on all sides, using their skills to both entertain and assist their comrades where necessary. The World War History and Art Museum

Horses being used as mounts for British cavalry in Boulogne, during the First World War. *(Library of Congress)*

in Ohio has a photograph of a fully-equipped German soldier, complete with steel helmet and rifle, parading along an improvised slack rope in front of his troop. Others performed to entertain the wounded. In 1917 at the Hospital Command Depot in Tipperary, Ireland, a performance was given by former circus stars. Included in the programme were Private Johnny Quinn, former clown, and Private Mark Crawley, contortionist. *The World's Fair* reported that: 'Those experiences [in battle] have failed to mar the pleasure that these artists took in entertaining their comrades at the depot'.

Serving soldiers were not the only ones to entertain the troops. Even retired performers did their bit for the war effort. An old English clown by the name of 'Footit', who had been with Lord George Sanger's Circus before retiring to live in France, spent a week in 1917 performing to British troops on the Somme. He gave two performances a day in tents and huts, or simply anywhere an audience could be gathered. One of his performances was given before 3,000 men who were returning to the trenches on the following day. He later told a reporter from the *The World's Fair*:

> *At the end of my show I called out to the boys, "Now give three cheers for your King and country". They cheered loudly, then I said, "Now give three cheers because you will all be in the front trenches tomorrow". One or two men laughed, but otherwise there was silence for a moment; then they all rose to their feet and cheered more lustily than ever. I cried, I couldn't help it; they are so wonderful.*

> (3 March 1917)

One of the more remarkable circus stories from the front line was reported by *The Manchester Evening News* in 1915. Allied troops were being heavily shelled by enemy gunfire and were unable to pinpoint exactly where the opposing forces were. The troops were sheltering in a number of farm buildings when a former clown noticed a tall chimney stack which would offer a vantage point over the enemy. Without waiting for orders, he slung his rifle across his back and raced across the open yard to the chimney, which he began to scale with all the agility acquired in his former circus life. His comrades cheered as he reached the top and, balancing precariously on the crumbling brickwork, 30ft above the ground, he was able to call down and direct fire on the enemy positions. Oblivious to the bullets buzzing around him, he even managed to un-sling his rifle and open fire himself.

The German forces were now directing their fire at the chimney and, as they began to find their range, chunks of masonry were being blown from the chimney and the soldier's position was perilous. His comrades called for him to climb down and finally his officer ordered him to the ground. Slinging his rifle once again, he stood tall before launching himself into the air. To the astonishment of all, he gracefully dived onto a low corrugated iron roof from which he rebounded 'like a rubber ball', neatly somersaulting to the ground. Turning to his comrades, he grandly bowed before announcing, 'My latest turn – the leap of death'.

It would be easy to form the opinion that the immediate impact of the war left the circus in Britain in a state of destitution. This was not so. It was true that many men had volunteered for service and that some, though not all, horses and draught animals had been commandeered by the military, but for many circuses, initially at least, life went on as normal. Towards the end of 1913, *The World's Fair* mentions nine different circuses touring Britain, and it is very likely that there were more.

So the outbreak of war saw little change in the number of circuses operating across the country. In the autumn of 1914, Hengler's Circus was in Glasgow, Sanger's Circus was touring the Midlands, Heckenberg's Circus was in Ireland, the American Circus was in Hull and the Royal Italian Circus was in the North West. The Blackpool Tower Circus was drawing crowds, as was the Olympic Circus in Liverpool. In London there was a circus at Olympia and a Wild West Show at the White City Stadium.

In December 1914, *The World's Fair* carried the following item: 'This season you can see more circus proprietors between O'Connell's Bridge and Nelson's Pillar, Dublin, than in all the rest of the United Kingdom put together … Seeing so many artists would make you think of 30 years ago when it was quite usual to see a lot like this in any city'. The article listed 11 different circuses then operating in Dublin, in addition to those mentioned above, so during the first few months of the war there were at least 20 circuses touring Great Britain and Ireland. In spite of the crisis, the circus was witnessing a resurgence in popularity. In fact, the entertainment industry in general was considered by the government to be of national importance because of its morale-boosting effect on the population.

The circus community responded to the war effort in any way possible; releasing men for active service and volunteering animals were just two of the ways in which it assisted. With the setting up of the Prince of Wales National Relief Fund, the circus was only too willing to contribute. There were regular donations made, with Sangers, Bostock's and Hengler's, amongst others, handing over box office takings to the 'War Fund'. In September 1914 the Royal Italian Circus gave a performance in Congleton to Belgian refugees. They marched to the circus arm in arm, men, women and children, waving the Belgian flag. Along the main street of the town the route was lined with local people, who cheered and waved hats and flags in support of the refugees. The performance was, 'one of the best seen in many years', according to *The World's Fair* (26 September 1914).

If the circus was to carry on as usual, then it still had to contend with all the trials and tribulations of being on the road. Fires were as always an ever-present danger. On 13 October 1914, Lord John Sanger's Circus marquee was completely destroyed by fire while it was in Leamington. The afternoon performance had been given and preparations had just been made for the evening show when the fire broke out. Although a call was made to the Borough Fire Brigade, the canvas structure had been reduced to ashes within a matter of minutes. One eyewitness described the rapid spread of the fire as, 'like an incandescent mantle being burnt for the first time'.

It was reported that the fire may have been caused accidentally by some small boys playing with some fireworks used for signalling purposes, known as Bengal lights, near the tent. Fortunately, the calm weather conditions saved the fire from spreading to the attached menagerie and there was no loss of life, human or animal. The evening performance had to be cancelled but it was not long before Sanger obtained a second marquee and the tour continued.

Unfortunately, circus fires did occasionally cause deaths. In 1915 a circus hand at Fossett's Circus Farm in Tiffield, near Towcester, was burned to death in his caravan. So intense was the fire that he could only be identified by a charred ring and the burned iron tips from his shoe heels. The coroner could only rule that he had been burned to death but that the cause of the fire was unknown.

Minor accidents, too were all a part of the daily routine of the circus worker, sometimes with more tragic results. One of the circus hands working with Lord John Sanger's Circus lost his life when he fell under the wheels of a heavy wagon. The man had been part of a team responsible for loading and transporting the marquee and in attempting to jump onto the moving wagon, he slipped and fell. At this time workers were not always insured against such accidents, and Sanger was ordered by the court to pay compensation to the man's mother. It was not only the manual workers and performers who suffered accidents. On a visit to Leeds in 1917, the Band Manager of Bostock's Circus arrived by train. Somehow, on leaving the carriage, he slipped and fell between the train and the platform. His arm was so severely injured that it had to be amputated.

Tragedy in the circus was not always related to physical accidents; sometimes personal feelings manifested themselves within the ring. In 1914, *The World's Fair* recounted a dramatic story about Tertjansky's Circus. While touring in Russia, a Romanian clown named Mirca was very quiet and sullen when not capering around in the ring. He had fallen madly in love with the circus's star equestrian performer, a young woman by the name of Fleurette, who rejected him, favouring the attentions of the handsome, young Cossack officers in the audience. All this was too much for Mirca to bear and one evening, as Fleurette was preparing her horses for her performance, he seized the opportunity and attempted to kiss her. Shocked by his sudden embrace, she broke loose from his grasp and lashed him across the face with her riding crop. Mirca ran off in shame but vowed that he would avenge this public humiliation, and his love for her began to turn to hatred.

Some evenings later, prior to Fleurette's performance, Mirca had been cavorting around the ring to the amusement of the crowd. As Fleurette's horse was led into the ring, Mirca began to pat it before moving to stand in the exit, watching carefully. The horse became restless but its groom took no notice. Fleurette brushed past Mirca as she entered, barely giving him a glance. Her face wreathed in smiles, she bowed lavishly to the audience and vaulted into the saddle. Only then was it clear that all was not well – the horse began to rear and buck. Fleurette desperately tried to control her mount but in spite of her efforts the horse collapsed to the ground, crushing her beneath. Many of the audience were terror-struck, others called for a doctor but by the time one was found, it was too late. The beautiful equestrienne was dead.

Suddenly, Mirca shouldered his way through the crowd and threw himself, distraught with grief, across the body of Fleurette. As he was dragged off, he made a dramatic confession that he was responsible for her death. Driven by his love for her and feelings of revenge for what she had done to him, he had placed an irritant in the ear of the horse as he had patted it. He was immediately arrested and taken to the local prison. However, this was to be a double tragedy, for that night Mirca committed suicide by hanging himself in his cell.

To add to the practical problems circuses had to deal with, an increasing amount of rules and regulations made life difficult for both performers and proprietors. During the early twentieth century, there was no national consistency with regards to the requirement to obtain a licence for the playing of music in a circus performance. Many different towns and cities operated different policies. In an important case in 1915 the band manager of Sanger's Circus was summoned before Birmingham Magistrates' Court for 'permitting music in a tent without a licence'.

The police had been called to the circus by local residents who complained of the show being a nuisance. A discussion was held over whether a music licence was required and, in the absence of one, the police suggested that the circus show continue without the six-piece band. In his defence the band manager stated that he had never been obliged to ask for a music licence in any other town or city the circus had visited. The summons was dismissed, but the band manager was advised to contact local councils in good time, so that any local requirements could be ascertained before a performance was given.

Contractual and letting arrangements with local councils could also cause difficulties for the circus, and also for the council on occasions. If a circus arrived in a town and set up on council land, then a letting agreement had to be sorted out in advance. However, if by arrangement it erected its tent on privately owned land, there was very little a council could do, even if the local inhabitants wished otherwise.

Such an event happened in Somerset in 1915, when a circus proposed to visit the town of Winsford on a Good Friday. The Winsford Urban Council explained to the protesters that it had no jurisdiction over privately owned land. The ratepayers then suggested that the council should cut the water supply to the land and make things as uncomfortable as possible, in order to deter the circus from visiting the town. When the council said it could not do that, the protesters requested it to do something in its official capacity to deprive the circus people from their revenue or prevent parades. Again, the council was powerless to act and the circus went on to visit the town, despite the protest.

But let it not be thought that the circus in Britain during this period was full of doom, gloom and despondency. There were also amusing incidents. At the Newry Quarter Sessions in 1915, Henry Hazenberg, circus proprietor, sued Francis Carvill over the ownership of a horse. In court, Hazenberg entered his name as Chadwick. When asked why he had changed his name, Hazenberg stated that before the war he had traded under the name of Hazenberg, as it had proved to be more profitable. Continental names were very common before the war and with such a name he always got good business but since the outbreak of the war, business had not been so good, so he had reverted to his own name of Chadwick.

When asked why he had taken the name of a 'brutal German', he replied, to much laughter from the court, that all shows are supposed to come from

Germany. The judge then said that he thought that there were a good many American names, to which Chadwick replied, 'Buff Bill's Circus and others'. The judge then turned to the court and, amidst gales of laughter, and suggested that any name would be good for a circus, except seemingly a British one.

In another incident in Ireland during October 1914, a circus worker with Buff Bill's Circus, Captain Albert Williams, was charged with 'disorderly conduct at the circus … and putting diverse persons at bodily fear'. It would seem that the producing of a toy pistol in a crowded area had caused some alarm and, in spite of conflicting evidence, Williams was bound to keep the peace for 12 months in the sum of £20.

Not all circus animals had been requisitioned for the war effort, and some provided light-hearted news stories. A young lady was visiting the circus at the Liverpool Olympia in January 1915. She had been shopping and had bought herself a new pair of shoes which were packaged in a box. Taking her seat at the circus she found the seat next to her conveniently unoccupied, so placed the box on it. During a varied programme including Walton's Musical Dogs, Captain Woodward's sea lions, clowns, bareback riding and Chinese equilibrists, there also appeared Captain Taylor's '4 Rascals' – a troupe of performing elephants.

During the performance, Captain Taylor would reward his elephants with a small piece of chocolate that he took from a box. One of the elephants, perhaps the chief 'rascal', seems to have quickly associated the tasty titbit with a box and while parading around the ring, spied a box on the seat next to the young woman. Without hesitation, it deftly reached over and plucked the box from the seat with its trunk. The woman squealed in alarm and the crowd roared with laughter as the elephant thrust the complete box into its gaping mouth and returned to the centre of the ring. Realising that shoes are not edible, the elephant shook its head and spat out the shredded cardboard box and then, one after the other, the saliva-laden shoes. The shoes were duly rescued by Captain Taylor and returned to the woman; it was reported that neither elephant nor shoes were adversely affected by this mishap.

Circus life during the early part of the war continued as usual, but as the war progressed the situation became more difficult. More money had to be found to finance the ever-escalating hostilities. In April 1916, Reginald McKenna, the Head of Customs and Excise, announced a new swathe of taxes designed to raise £5 million per year. The new taxes would affect the whole cross-section of society and he proposed a tax on consumables such as sugar, cocoa, coffee and chicory. He also recommended a tax on railway travel, with a surcharge being made for every ticket bought.

Most importantly for the circus, as well as the rest of the entertainment industry, McKenna proposed a new Amusement or Entertainment Tax. This was implemented in May 1916 and now meant that for every entrance ticket sold, circus proprietors had to add a surcharge, which was passed on to their audience. Proprietors had a choice: they could keep their prices as they were and ask the audience to pay more, or they could reduce their base price of admission to absorb the new tax and keep the entrance price the same. Every form of entertainment – from fairgrounds to theatres – which sold entrance tickets, now had the same dilemma. The initial tax levied was 1d on a ticket up to 6d, but by May 1917 this had been increased to a 1d tax on a 3d ticket.

This caused great hardship to the circus industry and prompted many letters to the Chancellor of the Exchequer, among them this letter published in *The World's Fair*, 23 June 1917:

Sir, As the proprietor of a travelling circus I wish to draw your attention to the considerable hardship which is inflicted on myself and other showmen by the Entertainment Tax. For a 3d and 6d circus the prices have now been reduced to 2½d for adults and 1½d for children, including tax. This means that people have to pay in the case of adults 25 per cent and in the case of small children 50 per cent. The extra 50 per cent on the 1d admission and 25 per cent for adults (almost entirely the working classes) practically precludes them from seeing a good wholesome show which has been travelling in this country for over 50 years. Under these circumstances and having regard to the very considerable hardship involved both to the showmen and the working classes, I beg to ask you if you can see your way to consider the remission of the Entertainment Tax on admission up to say 6d, on this and similar classes of entertainment, which, I submit, is of great benefit to the country.

– I am, sir, your obedient servant
George Proctor [circus proprietor]

Proctor received only a simple acknowledgement to his letter but, by July 1917, the tax rates on entertainments had changed once again. There was now a 2d tax on a 5d ticket. For tickets costing between 7s 6d and 10s 6d there was a 1s 6d tax; tickets between 10s 6d and 15s, the tax was 2s; and tickets above 15s, the tax was 2s for the first 15s and then 6d for every increase of 5s, or part, thereafter. Many of these upper value admission prices did not concern the circus, but for other entertainments, such as the theatre, they were a heavy burden. It is hardly surprising that some smaller businesses closed down because they could no longer cope with the financial impositions.

Into the last year of the war, in June 1918, the rates changed again, with the tax on lower bracketed admission prices having a direct effect upon the circus. Admission prices up to 2½d now carried a ½d tax; prices from 2½d to 4d carried a 1d tax; tickets from 4d to 7d had a 2d tax and from 7d to 1s there was a 3d tax. This was at a time when bread cost 2¾d a pound, milk was 2¾d a pint, butcher's meat 15½d a pound and sugar 7d a pound (Gazeley and Newell, 2010). In effect this was a tax reduction, but it came too late for many.

There were instances where circus proprietors either neglected or chose not to levy the tax on their tickets sold. In September 1917 Thomas Fossett was charged with evading the tax by not over-stamping his tickets and reusing them. In this case he was given a caution, but in November of the same year he faced the same charge and this time he incurred the maximum fine of £50. Fossett was not the only one caught doing this and in 1918 G. Pinder was also charged with avoiding the tax.

If the imposition of the Entertainment Tax caused hardship for British circuses, then further government restrictions brought further difficulties.

Women and children queuing for bread in 1918. *(Library of Congress)*

In March 1917, the government restricted the size of advertising posters. As the Advertising Manager for the Hippodrome in Liverpool commented:

> *No circus, large or small, can make a living without advertising, which is the road to success. No matter what the show is like inside as long as you flood the town with attractive and startling posters the public will certainly flock to see it. The new restrictions which come into force on March 11th 1917 limit the size of posters to 600 superficial square inches which is exactly a double crown size* [approximate metric size A1]. *The only means of advertising the circus now is with day bills, window bills and fly posting on the road, and before very long even these will be restricted, for I am given to understand ... that all theatrical and amusement bills will have to be dispensed with altogether.*
>
> (*The World's Fair*, 10 March 1917)

In June 1917 the government placed a ban on all external illuminated advertising signs and then, under the Horses Order of 1918, it became impossible to buy horses except under a licence issued by the Controller of Horse Transport. With all these restrictions being foisted upon them it is not surprising that several circuses toured abroad during the war years. In 1915 Harmston's Circus toured India, while in 1916 Boswell's Circus travelled to Bulawayo in Rhodesia (now Zimbabwe). The year 1917 saw both the Royal Italian Circus and Purchase's Menagerie in India.

One of the major pieces of government legislation affecting the circus, and many other entertainments, was the introduction of conscription. As of 2 March 1916, every British male subject who on 15 August 1915 was ordinarily resident in Great Britain and was aged between 19 and 41, was unmarried or a widower without dependent children, was deemed to have enlisted. Men could claim exemption from military orders on various grounds, including ill health and, if they had a conscientious objection, they could apply to a local tribunal for a hearing. If their application was successful, they would be granted a certificate of exemption. If the appeal failed they had no other option but to join the forces or face imprisonment.

The advent of conscription led to a spate of claims for exemption from circus workers, all recorded in *The World's Fair* newspaper; some of them quite genuine and others rather more unlikely. Bostock claimed exemption for his two sons and two other workers on the grounds that, 'they could not be spared without serious detriment to work of national importance [circus work]' (3 February 1917). The claim was disallowed and they were ordered for call-up.

A music hall juggler claimed exemption on the grounds that he was not fit for any kind of service. The Chairman of the Tribunal believed otherwise and took the opinion that, 'If you can go about presenting sea lions you can be of some service to the army' (3 November 1917). When the young man explained that he had nothing to do with sea lions but was a juggler and wanted to appeal, the chairman replied in the same offhand manner, 'You won't get it. If you can juggle on the Music Hall stage, you can go into the army'.

A lion tamer, appropriately named Leo Stanley, was arrested in January 1917 in full uniform and charged with being an absentee under the Military Services Act. The 19-year-old claimed to have been a member of the Highland Light Infantry, but when questioned at the tribunal, admitted that he had bought the uniform in Petticoat Lane. The chairman asked him what he did for a living and he explained that he had been a lion tamer for two years since buying some lions from Bostock's. A fine of £2 was imposed and Stanley was handed over to the military.

A circus performer named Claude Powell made an application for exemption on the basis that, 'he was not ordinarily resident in this country' (30 June 1917). Although he had been born in Rochdale, he had travelled widely with various circuses before returning to England for an engagement at Blackpool. Powell claimed he was 'in this country against his will and that he could not get away'. His claim was denied and he was ordered for military service.

Another, even more bizarre, incident occurred in Eastbourne in 1917, when a military absentee was paraded through the streets to the tribunal. The absentee was 18 years old and stood only 27 inches tall, but why this caused so much amusement was that he was being escorted by an extremely tall Canadian soldier, an entertaining picture that would have made a circus act in itself. The youth was taken before the tribunal and was later formally discharged.

Conscription now took many more men away from the circus and life was becoming so difficult for some circuses that Lord John Sanger announced in February 1917 that his circus, with an unbroken record of activity since 1843, would close until after the war: 'It is chiefly the labour trouble that has made us come to this decision ... We have decided to heed Mr Neville Chamberlain's appeal, and not hold men employed with these show horses who can be utilised for work of national service. When the war is over we shall resume our tour' (*The World's Fair*, 17 February 1917).

When one of Britain's most prestigious and long-running circuses announced its closure, this was a clear sign of the times and of things to come. As popular as circus had been at the beginning of the war, the glory days of the Victorian circus were no more. Although the war would end within two years, it had already caused damage to the industry from which it would struggle to recover.

During the four years of brutal carnage in the fields of Europe the world seemed to have become more cynical – and it was changing fast. Gone was the hedonism and pleasure-seeking ethos of the previous generations. To rebuild and regenerate were now the key approaches to life. Pragmatism and utilitarianism were now core values in this new world. Business, industrialisation, expansion, emancipation and enfranchisement – these were all the new watchwords of a new society. But where would the circus be in all of this?

Social revolutions bring about artistic revolutions and as in all revolutions, the new ousts the old. A new society demanded new art forms and the circus of the pre-war era was now considered to be somewhat old-fashioned. Other entertainments were to emerge. The world was teetering on the edge of the mass media age and the circus would have to compete with this or die. The next 50 years would see rapid, tremendous social change, and the circus would change with it.

Chapter Nine

Decades of Depression:
The Circus Between the Wars

The band gave a flourish and the final glittering parade of The Great Victory Circus came to an end as the last of the circus performers left the ring. As the houselights came up, one of the directors of the Olympia Exhibition Hall turned to one of his guests and enquired whether he had enjoyed the show. After a few pleasantries had been exchanged, the guest, Bertram W. Mills, confessed that he had been rather bored by it all and that if he could not give people a better circus than that he would eat his hat. This statement would prove to be one of the major turning points in British circus in the twentieth century.

Bertram W. Mills had been a captain in the Royal Army Medical Corps during the First World War and after leaving the army he had returned to work in his father's coaching and funeral business. Whilst the funeral business was always in demand, the coach-building side of the business was soon in decline, due largely to the rapid growth in the motor industry. Mills was a man with many interests, including the breeding and showing of horses, which would bring him into contact with the circus world.

In November 1918 the nation breathed a collective sigh of relief as the war came to an end and people faced the future with optimism. The Prime Minister, David Lloyd George, had promised that Britain would become a 'land fit for heroes' and during the years immediately after the war this seemed to be so. The first wave of servicemen returning from the war were able to find work quite easily, if they were not sent to Ireland to deal with the troubles there.

Factories and industries increased their production to meet the demands of a new society. Families were better off than they had been for a long time. A skilled man could earn on average £5 per week, with an unskilled labourer a little less at £4. With consumer products now readily available and relatively cheap, life was looking comfortable for many. But this prosperity proved to be short-lived.

By 1920 domestic output was declining, as other world markets began to increase. Before the war, in the coal industry alone Britain had exported 73 million tons of coal annually; this had now declined to 25 million tons by the end of 1920. Across the country employers looked for ways to reduce costs and many men and women lost their jobs. Those servicemen demobilised as late as 1920 found themselves returning now to a land of dole queues. It was against this backdrop that Mills took up the challenge of creating a new breed of circus show.

Having signed a contract to produce a circus show for the 1920/1921 season at Olympia, Mills' first plan was to engage the Ringling, Barnum and Bailey Circus from America. This would have brought what was arguably the largest circus outfit in the world back to London. However, by June 1920, John Ringling had been unable to find adequate shipping space to bring such a large outfit across the Atlantic and requested that the contract be cancelled. This placed Mills in a difficult position. He had a contract with Olympia to produce a Christmas show, but was unable to engage a ready-made circus. Undaunted, he decided that the only way forward was to create his own circus and so he and his son Cyril set about visiting the major circuses across Europe to engage quality acts.

It was this insistence upon quality that proved to be a success. The Great International Circus opened at Olympia on 17 December 1920 to high acclaim. Popular newspapers hailed its success with headlines such as 'Great Circus Revival' and 'Best show in London for many years'. Even *The Times* proclaimed, 'The Big Circus – Enraptured Audience!'

Much of the success of the circus was down to Mills approaching the project as a business enterprise. He sought to engage only quality artists who would give the most polished performances and he was not afraid to promote individual acts as 'stars'. In addition to this, he realised that the state of the circus industry was in decline and that something was needed to raise the social status of circus as a form of entertainment. He also recognised that an expensive show would need to attract an audience able to afford the most expensive seats. He did this by holding pre-show dinners to which he would invite as many influential people as he could, including entertainment critics. Some might argue that this was a rather cynical approach but Mills was a businessman and clearly aware of the power of public relations, and so his initiative paid off. Over the next 50 years these pre-show functions became a feature of the Christmas Olympia seasons and were patronised by the great and good of society, including members of the aristocracy, cabinet ministers and even royalty.

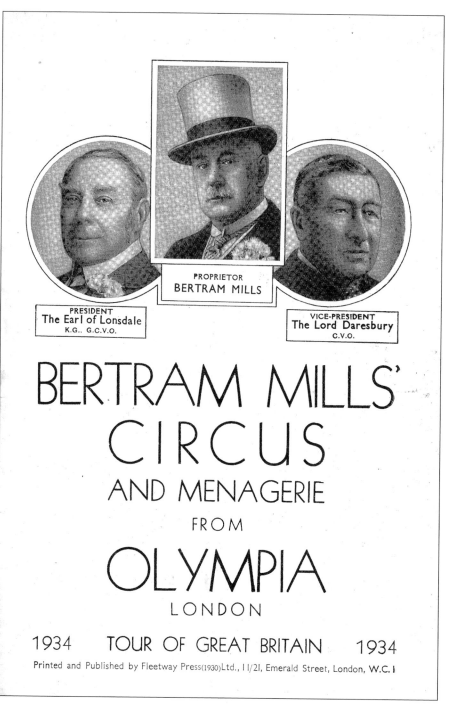

PROPRIETOR
BERTRAM MILLS

PRESIDENT
The Earl of Lonsdale
K.G., G.C.V.O.

VICE-PRESIDENT
The Lord Daresbury
C.V.O.

BERTRAM MILLS'
CIRCUS
AND MENAGERIE
FROM
OLYMPIA
LONDON

1934   TOUR OF GREAT BRITAIN   1934

Printed and Published by Fleetway Press(1930)Ltd., 11/21, Emerald Street, London, W.C.1

Bertram Mills and associates from the 1934 Olympia season programme. *(Author's collection)*

Whilst Bertram Mills' Circus achieved success in London during the early 1920s (it would be some years before he took to the road as a tenting circus), the rest of the circus world struggled on with varying degrees of proficiency. A letter to *The World's Fair* published in 1925 highlights the state of some provincial circuses:

During last summer I was spending a few days in a very pretty rural spot of dear old England. A circus was billed for the following day. Soon after breakfast I made my way to the camp expecting to find the tent half up, but found nothing doing, no sign of any circus. About 9.30am a man rode in on a pushbike, unfastened the gate, selected a sunny spot in the hedge, and lit up. In five minutes he was nodding, in ten he was sleeping. He was the advance guard!

At 10am the first wagon, with stable, etc came on, the other vans kept on coming at irregular times up to about 12.30, when I counted between 40 and 50 horses that looked fairly well fed, and some half a dozen were of class, but all looked dirty and unkempt … The wagons were dirty and in bad repair … The tent-men looked tired and weary. A man on his way to work stopped and said what a dirty lot … Some ladies and gents and those of the upper classes came to have a peep, but soon turned away …

The show opened at 2.30pm and was about a quarter filled, mostly women and children. Two of the men I had noticed earlier in the day building up were now dressed for the ring and were just finishing the ring fence and seating … At the evening performance the tent was about half filled, but none of the upper class in the carpet seats … I thought the show required turning inside out to be made presentable, profitable and appreciable. Again, the thought occurred to me, what is wrong with the circus?

The circus described above, fortunately not named, was a far cry from the opulence, glamour and success of the Olympia shows of Bertram Mills, but considering the challenges the circus industry was facing it is hardly surprising that many circuses found life difficult. In addition to the obvious loss of manpower, the Entertainment Tax was still in operation. In 1925, in a move to abolish the tax in parliament, a Member of Parliament, Mr A. Greenwood, stated in *The World's Fair* that: 'It was a war tax which it was understood would be abolished within a reasonable time of the conclusion of the war'.

The war had taken its toll and society was changing. Suffragettes were continuing to lobby for the right of all women in society to vote, something that was finally achieved in 1928. Esther Roper of the National Union of Women's Suffrage Societies and her lover Eva Gore-Booth, the Irish poet, campaigned for the rights of women in a variety of occupations, including circus performers.

Women had always worked in the circus. For female circus artistes it was a comparatively safe working environment. They had a degree of financial freedom and mobility, which allowed them to compete in a predominantly masculine world, and it was quite possible for a female star artiste to earn more than a male support performer. The female circus performer challenged the prevalent views of working women and crossed gender boundaries.

This was particularly so in America at this time, where the world's first Circus Suffrage Society was formed in 1912. Seventy-five female performers from Barnum and Bailey's Circus held a Suffrage Rally in Madison Square Gardens, in New York. Led by the equestrienne Josie DeMott Robinson, acrobat Zella Florence and strongwoman Katie Sandwina, they attracted much publicity and ended the rally by naming a baby giraffe 'Miss Suffrage'.

After the British Broadcasting Company (BBC) was formed in 1922 the number of people listening to radio programmes grew. In the same year the discovery of the tomb of the Pharaoh Tutankhamun captured many people's imagination and there was a craze for all things Egyptian. For many ordinary British people the cinema was another escape from the drudgery of everyday life and some went several times a week. For the price of a 6d ticket people could lose themselves in a newsreel, a feature film, maybe a second film and sometimes even a cartoon. Favourites such as Felix the Cat and Mickey Mouse made their first appearances during this decade.

This was also the age of the silver screen with glamorous stars, such as Greta Garbo, Ramon Novarro and Rudolph Valentino. But more was to come – in 1927 the first 'talkie' appeared in Britain. *The Jazz Singer* was the first film to have synchronised sound and picture and it changed the nature of the cinema forever. The new technology was here to stay and by 1929 even the newsreels had sound. It was now generally accepted that decay was slowly setting into the circus world and that there was a growing feeling: 'that a certain number of superior (and possibly well meaning) people cultivate the air of looking down upon any circus that does not happen to be in the first flight, as to size of tent and the number of artistes and animals engaged therein, and descrying it whenever it is possible to do so' (*The World's Fair*, 24 January 1925).

Even so, some well-known family names in the circus world were still touring in the middle of the decade. Bostock and Wombwell began their 1925 tour in Glasgow; that same year Sanger toured a 20-act show in which, according to *The World's Fair*, there was 'never a dull moment'; W. Pinder and Sons were in Aberdeen, and Duffy's Circus was touring Ireland. Other established circuses touring that year were the Rosaires, George Barrett's Canadian Circus (actually from Yorkshire), Broncho Bill, and Bailey's.

With reference to Tom Fossett's Diabolo Circus, the former variety artist Harry Wilding writes in *The World's Fair*: 'Yet despite the bitter cry of unemployment, which has been heard throughout it [current touring season], the high price of all commodities, the lessened purchasing power of money and the hundred and one other things, this show ... has enjoyed the most unqualified prosperity' (24 January 1925).

For all this apparent success, life was hard on the road for the circus artist. Some circuses operated in conjunction with fairgrounds. Renee Marshall (née Scott of the famous Scott family of circus performers) remembered life on the fairground circuits during the 1930s, in a radio interview over 70 years later:

The fairground was all right if you did one show a day or two shows a day, but we were doing four and five and we did 30 at Bolton New Year Fair and 20 the next day. When I tell you, my hands were peeling red with the skin coming off, that's with holding on the bar doing the trapeze and I was getting tired. The more tired you are the more you hold on and all the skin was coming off my hands. That was the worst part throwing a lot of shows on the fairground, you did all the shows and it nearly killed you.
(*Swings and Roundabouts*, BBC Radio 2, 2006).

Some provincial circuses, such as Fossett's, were still doing well in spite of the adverse social and economic conditions. In Nottingham, the Christmas season at the New Empress Rink was so popular that it had to be extended by one week, and in London at the Agricultural Hall the first ever all-female circus in Great Britain proved to be a great attraction. But for all the good circuses, it was the less reputable ones that attracted the most attention, especially from organisations involved in protecting animals from cruelty. The 1920s saw a hardening of attitude towards the use of animals in circuses.

Ninety-one-year-old Mrs Erica Parnell recalled her childhood years in 1920s Scotland and how her mother felt about circuses: 'She thought there was cruelty involved in training ... and she wasn't very sure about it ... it wasn't good for the animals ... My mother thought there must have been some cruelty to get them [the animals] to do some of the things they did, that's what she objected to'.

First World War poster advertising the Our Dumb Friends League. *(Library of Congress)*

This attitude was reinforced by incidents such as one which occurred in the village of Kippax in West Yorkshire. According to the memories of the late Harold Gummerson (preserved by the Kippax Local History Society), a small travelling menagerie was parading along the High Street, when one of the elephants made a dash for freedom and attempted to pass along a narrow passageway named Providence Place. In doing so, it became wedged firmly for some considerable time before being released. The event drew a large crowd, many of whom sympathised with the animal. Providence Place became locally known as 'Jumbo Nick' from that time on.

One of the more active animal protection societies at the time was Our Dumb Friends' League. For them, the sight of dirty, unkempt horses, as described by the letter published in *The World's Fair* quoted above, would have added fuel to their campaign against performing animals in circuses. Originally founded in 1897 as 'a society for the encouragement of kindness to animals', the league became known for its Blue Cross Fund to raise money for wounded horses during the war.

At the conclusion of the war, an element of the society extended its activities towards the use of animals in circuses and was instrumental in lobbying parliament for a Performing Animals Bill to be passed. In March 1925 the Bill passed the Committee stage. It would require the registration of all people who exhibited performing animals at public entertainments and those who trained animals for such a purpose. The Bill would also give power to the courts, acting upon complaints from the police or other local authorities, to impose restrictions or conditions on such training or performances.

The Bill was not universally popular, however, and Lord Raglan objected to it in the House of Lords on its second reading: 'Much of the evidence given before the select Committee … was most unconvincing. The Bill was the outcome of the visit of excitable women, who formed themselves into bands to visit circuses, where they howled at the trainers of performing animals' (*The World's Fair*, 8 April 1925).

Although the Bill was not passed until July 1925, and did not come into force until January 1926, many local authorities still imposed conditions or sought to ban circuses from their areas. A Rodeo Circus season was planned for Leeds in 1925, but a protest committee was set up to try and stop it. Unable to do so, the local authority then made it clear that if the circus was to come to the city that all steps would be taken to ensure that the conditions of lease would be strictly adhered to and that certain practices seen as especially cruel were forbidden. There should be no steer roping, where animals are wrestled to the ground and trussed with ropes. The use of a cinch rope, a particularly brutal form of slip-knot used around the neck of the animal, was also strictly forbidden.

However, the introduction of the Performing Animal Act was generally welcomed by the circus industry, including prominent figures such as Bertram Mills, John Sanger and Frank Ginnett. They all added their signatures to a letter of commendation in which they congratulated the passing of the Bill which: 'has received the unanimous support not only of all political parties, but also of those who, like ourselves, love animals, and have always been anxious to safeguard their welfare and protect them from cruelty' (*The World's Fair*, 4 July 1925).

It is interesting that in a recent interview with the renowned ringmaster and performer, Norman Barrett, he echoed the same sentiments almost 90 years on, reflecting that those involved in the circus industry support the welfare of their animals:

They [protesters] *will stand outside and say 'the horses are in the stables for 23 and ¾ hours a day.' They want to come in the morning when they are out in the pens, the paddocks. I do think that all circuses have improved their husbandry …*

If you've got animals, you've got them 24/7. And all people with animals have got them because they like them … and unfortunately, of course, there are bad apples in every sack but that doesn't mean that everybody is tarred with the same brush … Provided animals are successfully, properly looked after … and after all, animals that have a task to do live a better life.

The introduction of the Performing Animals Bill in January 1926 coincided with the new Theatrical Employers Registration Act, which also applied to circuses and menageries. Any proprietor employing three or more workers or artistes now had to register their business for a fee of two guineas. For smaller circuses these two requirements were an added expense, but the larger businesses, such as Bertram Mills, were able to absorb the costs quite easily.

In spite of new taxes and regulations, to quote the old cliché, the show had to go on. Perhaps the largest of the entertainment events during the 1920s was the government-organised British Empire Exhibition of 1924 and 1925. Costing over £12 million to produce and attracting over 27 million visitors, it was, at that point, the biggest such exhibition staged in Britain that century. It would have been remiss of the organisers to have omitted circus from the celebrations, and a Royal Victory Circus was opened at the Wembley Stadium on 24 June 1925 to run for six weeks.

Well-regarded circus proprietors Frank Ginnet and D.W. Robertson were given the task of producing the event. Advance advertising for the show announced that there would be a five-ring circus in the stadium and that throughout each 90-minute show all five rings would be in use simultaneously. The programme featured a mimed stag hunt, with trained stags racing around the arena; motor polo, Roman bareback riding, and a team of first class clowns to 'look after the children while their parents visited the Exhibition'. Clearly the organisers perceived the circus as more of a children's entertainment.

The Royal Victory Circus was in good hands with Frank Ginnett. Frank was a fourth generation circus proprietor; his great-grandfather, like Philip Astley before him, had also been a soldier, and had fought for the French at the Battle of Waterloo before being brought to England as a prisoner-of-war. The show was a great success and contained 17 different acts, including many varieties of horse acts, clowns, acrobats, gymnasts, cyclists, trampolinists, vaulters, elephants, apes, dogs, bears, aerial acts of various description, and high diving. The programme opened with a Grand Entry, where all performers, both human and animal, paraded around the arena in one huge procession and concluded with the Stag Hunt.

A visit to the circus was highly recommended by *The World's Fair* in July 1925, and not just for children:

> *I certainly advise all to pay a visit to the grand five-ring circus in the Wembley Stadium at their earliest convenience, for the show is a brave one and a very great improvement on most seen lately ... Perhaps the greatest favourite in the show is Poppy Ginnett* [later to marry into the Sanger family] *– who treats us to such daring riding and driving that should arouse the flame of love in the heart of the unbetrothed male onlooker.*

At the close of the Exhibition it was estimated that just over 500,000 people had seen the circus in Wembley Stadium.

Whilst all this was happening Bertram Mills continued to focus upon his Christmas Olympia shows and they became famous for their quality and slick presentation. To appear in a Bertram Mills Olympia spectacular soon became the pinnacle of a circus performer's career. Mills toured widely to bring the cream of the circus world to the British public and brought many famous names to his shows, including the legendary juggler Rastelli, the aerialists

The Lady Hercules · Katie Sandwina
A Combination of female Strength, Form & Beauty.

'The Lady Hercules', Katie Sandwina poses showing her more feminine side and holding three men in her arms. *(Library of Congress)*

The Lady Hercules
Katie Sandwina

The Flying Condonas, the Schaeffer midgets, for whom he built a complete miniature village in Olympia; Katie Sandwina, the world's strongest woman; and the inimitable Coco the Clown. He drew his companies together from both the world of circus and of variety, for many performers moved from one art form to the other as opportunities presented themselves.

Katie Sandwina was one such example. Born Katie Brumbach in Germany in 1884, she began performing in her father's circus at the age of two as a child acrobat. It soon became clear that she had a prodigious strength and Katie went on to develop an act of feats of strength. With her long golden tresses piled high on her head, and reputedly 6ft tall (although in reality nearer 5ft 9in), photographs of Katie depict a feminine giantess. Performing as a 16-year-old in 1900, with the family show, her father would challenge members of the audience to step up and try to wrestle with Katie. A young acrobat, Max Heymann, accepted the challenge. At 5ft 5in tall and weighing only 165lbs, he was much smaller than Katie and easily beaten. However, they fell in love and went on to get married two years later.

Max subsequently worked with Sandwina and became her 'top-mounter', being carried high around the ring in the hands of his formidable wife. As an adult she would juggle and catch iron cannon balls on her neck, or lie on a bed of nails whilst granite blocks were smashed with sledgehammers across her chest. She first appeared in America in 1903 and legend has it that she challenged the famous strongman Eugene Sandow to a weightlifting contest. She lifted 300lbs clean above her head, while he could only manage to lift that weight to his chest. After this contest she took the name 'Sandwina' to celebrate her victory.

Working now with her husband, under the name of the Sandwinas, they left America and came to London to appear at the Hippodrome. She then performed throughout Europe and America again before Mills engaged her for the 1926/1927 season at Olympia, billed as the 'Wonder Woman'. When touring in 1928 she was billed as 'Catherine the Great'.

During one of her performances she challenged members of the audience to test her strength. For all her strength Katie was a mild-mannered woman, although when roused she could be fearsome. According to J.S. Clark in *Circus Parade* (1936), when she was accosted by a lecherous man one day Katie responded by knocking her assailant clean across the street and through a plate glass window with one blow of her hand! Sandwina retired from touring at the end of the 1940s and opened up a café-bar with her husband in New York. Even in her advanced years she was still a force to be reckoned with.

Journalist Sidney Fields interviewed Katie for an article, entitled 'Hercules can be a Lady' in 1947 and recorded the following incident:

> *One afternoon a bruiser walked in and after berating everyone in sight, started for Papa [Max her husband]. That always ends Mama's quiet patience. She didn't bother to yell, "Papa open the door". She floored the bruiser with one punch for the whole count and gave him a thorough lesson as she tossed him out. And the two cops standing right outside the door, twirling their nightclubs, cautioned Katie as they always do – "Mama, don't hit him too hard".*
>
> (*New York Mirror,* 15 December 1947)

It was not long after Sandwina performed at Olympia that Bertram Mills' Circus took to the road as a tenting circus. His two sons, Cyril and Bernard, were tempted by the idea of touring a circus show. Unfortunately, they had no experience whatsoever in this side of the circus business but, having persuaded their father to finance a tour for 1930, they set off for Europe to study the logistics of the big German touring circuses like Sarrasani, Krone and Busch. These were highly efficient businesses and here the Mills brothers were able to study how seating could be arranged to allow for the health and safety of the public; something that had not yet been given much attention in England. They also observed the use of steel King Poles, the supporting poles of the big top, which were safer and stronger than the wooden ones still commonly used in England.

Their visit having proved a valuable exercise, they planned their touring circus along German lines, even ordering a tent from a German manufacturer. But fate again took a hand. In September 1928 it was announced that the Great Carmo would be bringing his circus to England the following year. Two large circuses touring at the same time might prove too much competition so it was proposed that both circuses should merge on a fifty-fifty basis for a 1929 tour. It was agreed that the circus should be known as The Great Carmo Circus, but the advertising would also show 'From Olympia London'. The Mills family also insisted that the acts presented met with their 'quality' epithet.

The Great Carmo Circus rolled out in May 1929 and was generally well received by both the press and the public. Carmo was responsible for booking the sites and producing the show and the Mills brothers were responsible for overseeing the transportation of the circus. Transport was a big problem and their inexperience in moving such a large outfit led them to consider alternatives in their future tours.

The whole experience of working with Carmo's circus during the 1929 season had been a learning curve, so when the Bertram Mills Circus took to the road in April 1930, the Mills brothers endeavoured to do things differently and more efficiently. Bertram Mills had insisted that if he was going to finance a touring show, then his circus company would perform like professionals and live like gentlemen. They produced a quality show for their first outing, despite losing their big top in a gale in September 1930. They continued to expand over the next few years, until they had reached most of the populated areas of England.

The touring circus outfit had grown so large that by 1934 a decision was made to move the entire Bertram Mills Circus by rail between towns. This was the first time a British circus had moved from site to site in this way and when the circus pulled up in the sidings, people would line the streets to watch the circus move from the railway to its pitch.

The Bertram Mills Circus took to the road during one of the most economically unstable decades of British history and it is surprising just how popular and well-attended it became. This was a time of mass unemployment and in 1932, 2.5 million people were unemployed. Many families relied upon the weekly 'dole' money to barely scrape by; the weekly payment for a married couple with three children was £1 9s 3d. This was at a time when, in 1931, *Good Housekeeping* magazine was suggesting an annual budget for a family of £410. In his memoir, Cyril Mills, one of Bertram Mills' sons, recalls the many occasions when he saw hundreds of penniless children waiting outside the circus tent in the hope of catching sight of exotic animals or brightly costumed performers. Often he would sneak some of the children in to see a show for free, especially if it was a matinee performance with smaller crowds. This altruistic attitude was a Mills trait, for Bertram Mills himself had entertained less fortunate children at dress rehearsals at Olympia.

Those not invited in for free often took matters into their own hands, however. An elderly resident of Leeds described how, as a child in the 1930s, she and her younger brother would visit the circus whenever it set up on open ground near the Leeds Market. Lacking pocket money, they would wander around the outside of the big top until they found a spot where the lacing on the side walls was loose. Checking that no one was watching, they would then squeeze through the gap and hide under the seating. 'We always managed to get a good view – and we never got caught', she recalled.

In spite of widespread poverty, the circus continued to be as popular as ever during the 1930s. In January, the Kelvin Hall Circus in Glasgow

8   BERTRAM MILLS' CIRCUS—SEASON, 1934

PROGRAMME

FROM WHICH ITEMS IN THE PERFORMANCE WILL BE
SELECTED AT THE DISCRETION OF THE MANAGEMENT

1.   **THE GREAT WALLENDAS**
A thrilling High Wire Act, consisting of three brothers and one sister;
is world-famous and created a sensation at Olympia, London, during our
1930/31 and 1931/32 seasons. This family has succeeded in achieving what
seemed to be the impossible.

2.   **BERTRAM MILLS' LIBERTY HORSES**
Reputed to be the finest in the world; they have been entirely trained in
this country. Some of this splendid constellation are descended from the
magnificent stud once the property of Francis Joseph, late Emperor of
Austria.

3.   **THE THREE AMBROSIS**
These three Italian artistes are brilliant, fearless and superbly accomplished.
As a Perch Act it is in a class by itself. Gualtero, the principal, performs
the astounding feat of carrying the other two members on a perch
balanced on his forehead.

4.   **MILLIMAR GOLDEN STATUES**
This charming posing act is unique and artistic. It was performed for the
first time in England during our last season at Olympia, London.

5.   **THE FOUR SLOANS**
Celebrated British stilt walkers and clowns are members of a famous
circus family. They have appeared in the United States as well as all the
European capitals.

6.   **GREEN, WOOD AND VIOLET**
An irresistibly funny trio in what is known as a Humpsti-Bumpsti Act. It
arouses the most hilarious laughter and spontaneous applause.

STABLES AND MENAGERIE — containing a
wonderful collection of Horses, Tigers, Elephants
and other animals can be visited during the mornings
and at the conclusion of each performance.

WHAT IS IT ? ? ? " THE ROSS MECHANICAL
MAN "—Is it Man, Monster, or Mechanism ? ? On
view daily.

A varied programme of entertainments. Centre page spread from the 1934 Bertram Mills
Olympia season programme. *(Author's collection)*

7.   **THE COURIER OF ST. PETERSBURG**

Delbosq, descended from an English equestrian family whose connection with the circus dates back to the days of Astley, presents, with his nine thoroughbred stallions, an extraordinary act of skill and beauty equal to that of the great horseman, Andrew Ducrow.

8.   **BERTRAM MILLS' MULES, ZEBRAS AND PONIES**

Gindl, born in Vienna, gained early experience by joining a small travelling circus when a boy. He has trained these animals in this country to a high standard of excellence.

9.   **YUNG DSAI CHINESE**

They come from the picturesque city of Tientsin, and were educated in acrobatic and stage art from early youth. In addition to acrobatics they give a thrilling display of Eastern sword fighting.

10.   **FIVE DRATSA**

This troupe of eccentric comedians has no wish to elevate your minds. Its members want only to make you laugh. If they have succeeded in this ambition they will be amply rewarded.

11.   **JEANNETTE'S CRICKETING ELEPHANTS**

The latest achievement of these huge creatures is a Cricket Test Match, which their trainer, George O'Brien, believes qualifies them to challenge an M.C.C. or Australian Cricket Team. They also perform a number of other amusing and original episodes.

12.   **THE SHETLAND PONIES**

Clever little artistes providing an exciting hunting scene. Aided by Joey and the beagles, they are as funny in their burlesque as Charlie Chaplin and the Marx Brothers combined.

13.   **BERTRAM MILLS' HIGH SCHOOL HORSES**

Trained in England, are performed by Alfred Whiteley and Cossmeyer whose superb horsemanship invests the Acts with brilliant moments and entitles the artistes to rank amongst the highest exponents of the art of haute d'ecole riding.

14.   **PIM'S NAVY**

A thrilling, remarkable and original Trampoline Act, contributed by four of the world's greatest acrobats, including Pim, the Silly Sailor, the most genuinely funny acrobatic clown.

[Programme continued on page 10

STABLES AND MENAGERIE — containing a wonderful collection of Horses, Tigers, Elephants and other animals can be visited during the mornings and at the conclusion of each performance.

WHAT IS IT ? ? ? "THE ROSS MECHANICAL MAN"—Is it Man, Monster, or Mechanism ? ? On view daily.

reported a record-breaking season, with over 300,000 visitors during its six week run – an increase of 26 per cent on the previous season. In Manchester, *The World's Fair* reported that:

> *The attendance at the Belle Vue Circus provided another proof of the public's eagerness to obtain relief from the routine of the cinema ... The Kings Hall ... has been packed all through the holidays, and a good deal of money was turned away at both performances on Saturday. On Boxing Day, with three performances the circus accommodated close on 20,000 people ... It will cause no surprise if the run of the circus is extended beyond the advertised closing date.*

Another boost to the circus and entertainment industry was the proposed abolition of the Entertainment Tax on 6d admissions. The Chancellor of the Exchequer's annual budget speech was applauded by many: 'The duty on the cheaper seats in cinema houses, and that on those entertainments in which living performers have been putting up a very gallant struggle for

The Four Kemmys acrobatic troupe, pictured in the Bertram Mills 1934 Olympia season programme. *(Author's collection)*

survival against the competition of mechanical performances … I think it is time they had some relief' (*The World's Fair*, 20 April 1935).

The new tax came into force on the first of July and levied a ½d tax on admissions between 6d and 8½d. Beyond that a 3d tax was placed on the first 1s 9d of admission with an additional 1d on every 5d paid, or part, thereof. This was a welcome relief for many smaller circuses, which relied heavily upon filling the cheaper seats, especially while visiting the more economically depressed areas of the country.

The Royal Silver Jubilee year created, if temporarily, a buoyant mood in the country. King George V and Queen Mary were popular figures and for a brief spell there was a holiday atmosphere across the nation and a renewed optimism. Circuses flourished, not only the 'big names' such as Mills and Sanger but others, like the Great Continental Circus at Portsmouth and Fossett and Bailey's, and the strangely-named Tarrazarney's United Empire

The Courier of St Petersburg, an equestrian act made famous by Andrew Ducrow over 100 years earlier, pictured in the Bertram Mills 1934 Olympia season programme. *(Author's collection)*

Circus. Duffy's Circus was still touring Ireland, and George Chapman increased his touring units to two. The Chipperfield family was still in evidence, with Dick Chipperfield presenting his Circus Ricardo. William Pinder, the Kayes and the Rosaires were also touring in this year.

During the Jubilee year there seemed to be a circus on every corner, so much so that a visitor to London from the backwood regions of Canada found himself in Piccadilly Circus and approached a policeman asking, 'What time does the show start?' In fairness to the visitor, there was a show in Canada at the time named the Piccadilly Circus. It is hardly surprising, with so much circus activity going on across the country, that an editorial in *The World's Fair* of 13 April claimed, 'This Silver Jubilee Year finds the circus quite healthy in Britain'.

And so it was; if ministers of state and even royalty were seen at the circus, then things must be looking up for the industry. The Duke and Duchess of York took their two young daughters, the Princesses Elizabeth and Margaret, to see the Bertram Mills Circus at Olympia in January 1935. This may have been the princesses' first ever visit to a circus and it caught the public's imagination.

Many foreign performers now thrilled the audiences in British circuses in the same way that British artists were welcomed abroad. There was a natural two-way flow of talent, and foreign circuses also appeared in England that year. The Miller Brothers Australian Circus was appearing in Great Yarmouth, and Madame Clara Paulo's Circus was in Skegness. Volpre's Circus was touring and Hackenberg's Berlin Tower Circus was in Ireland.

The consumer industry also embraced the circus with open arms. Dame Laura Knight, the famous artist, was commissioned to produce designs for a dinner service decorated with circus scenes for A. Wilkins, a ceramic ware company. The 12-place dinner service can be seen today at the Manchester Art Gallery. Shops also realised that circus was good for business, especially during the Christmas season. Gamages of London engaged the Pinder family to present a 45-minute Christmas Circus show for the five weeks before Christmas, including performing dogs, ponies, clowns, acrobats and even an elephant. It was not long before other stores realised the potential of circus and Wright's Emporium of Richmond (London) engaged Kaye's Circus, and Volpre's Circus appeared at the Barton Stores in Wood Green.

Meanwhile, the influx of foreign performers was causing concern in certain circles. All 'alien' performers had to be granted permits by the Ministry of Labour, which operated a system based upon reference to a standard minimum scale of salary. In addition, no performer would normally be allowed to take engagements in the country for more than 26 weeks a year. The Variety Artists' Federation felt that these regulations were unfair to home acts and lobbied that the Ministry's regulations should ensure that in any one programme, at least 60 per cent of performers should be British. This question of alien performers would arouse much stronger feelings a few years later, but with a much more sinister tone.

But for all its popularity, circus life was still beset with problems. Fires and 'blow downs' (storms) were ever present dangers. Mechanical breakdowns made life difficult on the road. Accidents still happened, as in the death of a circus hand with Sanger's Circus in 1935, when the brakes failed on a truck he was driving down a hill in Gloucestershire. Animals still occasionally attacked the attendants, as at the Agricultural Hall, where a ring boy was mauled by a leopard when he entered its pen to extinguish a smouldering cigarette end, thrown down by a careless visitor.

Sometimes even personal conflicts between performers led to tragedy. During the late 1920s, the two aerialist Sylvain brothers both fell in love with the same female colleague. The girl did nothing to encourage either of them and, although they still maintained a professional attitude in the ring their jealousy grew to the extent that they would not speak to each other or even share the same caravan. One of the brothers took to drinking and, in time, this affected his performance. He may not have lacked courage in the air but his judgement was impaired and one evening he failed to meet the outstretched hands of his brother. In a ghastly fall, he broke his back and became paralysed. Racked with guilt, his brother then committed suicide the following morning.

If all these internal dramas and accidents weren't enough, the anti-performing animal brigade was still a concern for many circuses. Rosaire's Circus was the victim of a propaganda demonstration organised by misguided animal lovers. During one particular performance a group of young men entered and sat in ringside seats. They created no problems at all until later in the performance when an elephant act was being presented. At this point, the men jumped up and started shouting abuse, shaking and throwing pamphlets around. The elephants were startled by the outburst and became very restless. Had it not been for the presence of mind of the trainer and the attendants, panic might have broken out, especially among the large number of children present. The trainer managed to calm the animals and lead them out of the ring, whilst the attendants attempted to remove the young men. A fight broke out and they fled, followed by booing and catcalls from the rest of the audience.

Even the famous Sanger's Circus had a cruelty complaint launched against it while visiting Wolverhampton. The police were informed of alleged cruelty to a horse. Sanger claimed this was the first such complaint ever made during the 133 years of the Sanger family circus and the case was dismissed due to insufficient evidence.

The celebrations of the Jubilee Year were soon to be swallowed up by the political and social unrest across Europe. King George V would die in early 1936 and be replaced by his son Edward VIII, only for him to abdicate within the year in favour of his younger brother. In Britain the depression bit deeper and hunger marches became a common sight. Oswald Mosley's black-shirted fascists paraded the streets of London and met with violent clashes in the East End, while in Europe, Spain had descended into civil war and in Germany, Adolf Hitler's Nazi party was beginning to flex its muscles. The entertainment industry was given warning of what was to come when three entertainment organisations were suddenly closed down in Germany because, according to a report in *The World's Fair* of 27 July 1935, their activities were perceived as 'inimical' to the state.

In April 1938, Bertram Mills died whilst the circus was in Luton. The show went on that night, although the performers felt a great loss. He had been a highly respected figure and many people wondered how the circus would survive, but his two sons took on the responsibility and continued with the tour into Scotland. By now Europe was sliding inevitably towards another conflict and ticket sales were down, so at the end of the tour they focused all their attentions on producing a Christmas Spectacular at Olympia, still using the trademark name of the Bertram Mills Circus. Given the circumstances of an imminent war, it was well supported and made a profit, although approximately 50 per cent less than the previous year.

But far worse was to come.

Chapter Ten

Fighting for Survival: The 1940s–1960s

In September 1939 Britain was once again at war. Preparations were made across the country in readiness for attack or invasion. Thousands of children were uprooted from their homes and families in the city heartlands and sent to rural areas. In October 1939 all men aged between 18 and 41, apart from those in reserved occupations, were advised that they could be called up for military service and all able-bodied men aged 20-23 had to register in one of the armed forces. Blackout regulations came into force and citizens were equipped with gas masks.

But in these first few months the war proved to be something of an anti-climax, as nothing happened. In fact by the end of the year, 4,000 people had been killed or injured in blackout accidents, whereas only three members of the British Expeditionary Force had been killed in action during the same time.

At the outbreak of the war the railway stock used by the Bertram Mills Circus was requisitioned by the military for tank transportation. The circus had little option but to return to its winter quarters in Ascot, but that too was requisitioned for use as an internment camp. Some of the workers, finding themselves now unemployed, took the opportunity of temporary work with the military to help construct the camp. Rationing, air raids and the ever-tightening grip on the mood of the nation forced the brothers into the decision that the circus should cease to operate for the rest of the war. Even the Olympia seasons were shut down, the building being required for military purposes as a government clothing store.

For security reasons many foreign nationals, including circus and variety artists, were interned at the beginning of the war. Even some of the Mills' circus employees found themselves interned in the very camp they had helped to construct. However, by 1941, those who were considered to pose no threat were released to return to their old work in variety and circus. This aroused much bad feeling in certain quarters:

A strong protest has been made by the VAF [Variety Artists Federation] *to the Ministry of Labour and the National Service against the granting of a working permit to fulfil engagements to the Cairoli Brothers, Italian musical clowns ... the VAF points out that, "Apart from the national question it is grossly unfair that these aliens should be engaged in view of the very many performers who have been called and are being called up for military service".*

(*The World's Fair,* 19 April 1941)

So controversial did this question become that it prompted many letters to *The World's Fair* during 1941, expressing views which were personal, or angry in tone, right through to the more extreme:

To me it seems grossly unfair that I should have to see two of my sons willingly give up their careers to serve their country, and their places taken by enemy aliens to enjoy the freedom, safety and rights that are temporarily denied to my sons.

(19 April)

I read with interest ... the various contributions ... on the Axis-artiste question, but refrain from passing comment now, once again being in that frame of mind which would encourage those opposed to my views to suggest I was writing from sheer anger. I have not yet fully recovered my usual composure after being on fire-watching duty in Central London throughout the night of April 16th. On duty within short-blast range of a bomb which destroyed a theatre and a block of dwellings wherein I am afraid the death roll was heavy. From the ruins of which, on Saturday morning, they were still collecting "bits and pieces" of what had once been human bodies. No – perhaps it would be as well if I gave the Axis-born artiste question a miss.

(26 April)

Sir – We don't want Axis artistes now – or ever. How any right thinking Britisher can suggest the inclusion of these men in our present or future programmes is beyond my comprehension ... We, the true friends of the Circus can, and must see that they [British performers] *get fair play by boycotting all shows with Axis artistes on the programme.*

(3 May)

Perhaps it was this feeling of national outrage that prompted the government to introduce measures later in the year for the registration for industry of all interned men between the ages of 16 and 65, and for women between 16 and 50, of Belgian, Czechoslovakian, Polish, French, Netherlands, Norwegian, Austrian, German and Italian nationalities. Some of the most well-loved figures of the British circus in modern times were among the foreign nationals then facing internment. Charlie Cairoli, of the Cairoli Brothers, spent over 40 years performing at the Blackpool Tower Circus, which remained open throughout the war. He is such an iconic figure that there is now a commemorative statue to him in the town.

Similarly, Coco the Clown was born in 1900 in what is now southern Latvia, then under the control of Russia. Born Nikolai Poliakoff, he began

Vistascreen 3D Viewer card showing Coco the clown making up at the Bertram Mills Circus, c.1960s. *(Author's collection)*

performing in theatres from a very early age but when he was nine years old he ran away to join a circus in Riga. Apprenticed for four years to the Rudolpho Truzi Circus, he learned a wide range of skills but found that clowning was his forte. Surviving wars, revolution and imprisonment over the years, he eventually found himself working for Circus Busch in Germany.

On one of his talent-spotting visits before the war, Cyril Mills spotted Coco and brought him to England. Coco was technically not a clown but an 'auguste'. With grossly exaggerated make-up and costume, the auguste was reminiscent of the physically deformed medieval jesters who were regarded with amusement. The modern auguste was a foil to the classic white-faced clown and would be on the receiving end of many practical jokes, with custard pies and buckets of water playing a large part. Coco was always known as Coco the Clown and became a household name, ever popular with the children. At the outbreak of the war he decided to remain in England and immediately offered his services to the Entertainment National Service Association (ENSA) and often entertained the troops or performed at functions, like many other performers, to raise money for the war effort:

> *Coco, the famous circus clown … recently appeared at the Odeon Exeter, where he regaled the Services Night's audience with some of his examples in the art of clowning, and as may be expected earned full marks … The manager of the Odeon … mentioned that profits from the sale of Coco's book, Coco, the Clown would go to the Mayoress of Exeter's Depot Fund.*
> (*The World's Fair,* 7 June 1941)

Whilst in England and Europe ENSA was providing variety entertainment for the troops, but it was in America that circus was being taken seriously as a troop entertainment. In 1941 *The World's Fair* reported that the American army presented its 'first ever' fully fledged circus, with some 2,000 soldiers taking part supported by local girls. The American forces seem to have had a penchant for claiming the 'first ever' circus or the 'only' circus. A few years later an item in *The Press and Journal* reported that:

> *The 102nd American Infantry Division claim to be the only Division in the world with their own private circus. It is complete with horses, elephants, clowns, jugglers, acrobats, lovely equestriennes, "big top" and all the other appurtenances. The circus is at present playing in this town [Gotha, Germany] and has been such a success that the Division Commander has decided to take it around if the division moves … The circus was originally*

liberated near Zwickau by the 76th Division and after they moved on it was promptly adopted by the 102nd … The circus tent holds 3,600 people and is packed nightly with applauding American soldiers.

(25 June 1945)

The Bertram Mills Circus was not the only circus to become a casualty of the war. Sanger's Circus also suffered. After a lifetime of touring the country, John Sanger announced that his circus was to be sold off. His famous show had been beaten by the blackout, food rationing and shortage of labour. As he told a reporter of *The World's Fair*:

If we could have been assured food for the animals we might have kept them till better times came along … As it is I don't see how anybody can provide for the elephants, the lionesses and the cubs. They might have to be destroyed … Even if we had the food, we lack the grooms and keepers to look after the animals. Circus workers have almost entirely been called up.

(30 August 1941)

In spite of all the physical hardships encountered during the war, government legislation also added to the troubles of the circus. London County Council decided to place a ban on the use of dangerous animals in venues under its licence. This was intended as a precaution in case wild animals should escape as a result of enemy action. In addition to this, new restrictions were put into place regarding the use of paper for advertising for all entertainment establishments, including circuses. No more than 10 posters could be used for any one show or programme and the size of each poster was now reduced by half.

In spite of all this, some smaller family circuses managed to keep going throughout the war by curtailing their programmes and touring to areas less likely to receive air raids. The Fossetts, the Poole Brothers, Madame Paulo and the Rosaires all managed to keep busy. Many smaller, 'get rich quick', circuses appeared during the war. However, these were of a very inferior quality and were looked down upon by the established circus world. Some had only a handful of artists or animals and one even charged three prices for admission but provided no seating. This kind of circus reflected badly on the legitimate circus industry and many disappeared as quickly as they had arrived. But the damage had been done and it left a stain on the public image of the circus.

There was one new circus at this time of an acceptable standard, pulling in good crowds with its slick presentation. The circus was supported by the Rosaire family but its only problem was its name – the Jean Mills' Circus. It had no connection at all with the Bertram Mills Circus but the name was so similar that the Mills brothers took out a court injunction to stop the name Mills being used. The circus continued under the new name of the Continental Circus.

Fuel shortages meant that, for many of the smaller circuses still on the road, a reversion to horse power was the only way to transport the circus around the country. This led to a feeling of nostalgia for the earlier days of the circus before the mechanical age, and in a more peaceful time.

This was reflected in a series of letters to *The World's Fair* in early 1941:

For some time to come, mechanical means of transport will be none too easy, so what an opportunity for the present generation to witness the return of the fine old circus pulling in with its horses, together with the magnificent mid-day parade ... All the present day generation has to remember is a lot of wretched mechanical transport, or perhaps just as bad, the circus arriving by train ... What a truly magnificent pageantry it all was ... Some of those parades must have been pretty well a mile long. Superb professional cars mirrored and richly gilded; prancing steeds with riders dressed in dazzling costumes; clowns who, mounted on stilts several feet high, delighted the onlookers by peeping into the top most windows of houses.

(25 January)

I would like to see the return of the Circus as it was in the late seventies and early eighties [nineteenth century], *when I believe it was at the apex of its popularity. Then we had real circuses and real circus proprietors.*

(1 February)

I have seen so many attempts at revival of old time successes turn into miserable failures, that I feel that when once the spell is broken and a halt is called, a renewal of success is highly improbable. We are living in a mechanical age. Horses today do not have the appeal to the public mind that they did forty or more years ago ... Even the children no longer "play at horses" ... That the circus will continue its success as an entertainment there is little or no doubt, but its form will continue to change according to public taste and demand.

(8 February)

The last letter would prove prophetic. The war in Europe was to continue for another four years, until May 1945. Throughout all the hardship and adversity, the circus did continue to survive and, with the coming of a post-war new order, it had to change to adapt to a new society. Servicemen, like the Mills brothers who had both been in the Royal Air Force, returned to pick up the traces of their old profession.

The circuses that had managed to keep operating during the war, such as the Rosaires', Fossett's, Madame Paulo's and Cody's welcomed the return of their workers, and were all up and running by the autumn of 1945. In the following year Lord John Sanger announced his return by presenting his circus at Tamworth. As the Bertram Mills Circus had retained a skeleton staff over the war years and it only took a short while to get organised for a new season.

By the summer of 1946, a tenting circus was back on the road, beginning its tour in Windsor Park. The trains were returned, although they could only be used at weekends, and this meant that a limited tour took place. In the first post-war season the circus visited only about half the number of venues it had before the war, yet it was a sell-out and popular wherever it went.

It was the first Olympia season, however, that really returned the Bertram Mills Circus to the fore. Released from its use as a government clothes store, Olympia became home to the first post-war Christmas spectacular of the 1946-1947 winter season. The box office opened on 2 December and, before long, a queue had formed that stretched all the way down Kensington High Street. The show was a huge success and *The Picture Post* newspaper of 11 January 1947 carried a somewhat effusive seven-page special celebrating the return of the circus:

THE CIRCUS AGAIN

The season of the circus comes round, and with it comes, for the first time since Christmas 1938, The Circus – clowns, augustes, acrobats, elephants and all. To the performers, Olympia is the one date they all want to make. To the audience of children of all ages, it is the one day they never intend to miss again. "What is it about the Circus?" you may well ask yourself as you plunge into the stream of British devotees winding down the incline from the Hammersmith Road to the main entrance of Olympia.

Down they go, the cloth-capped fathers of families – a brace of children swinging on each arm, or following, like a covey of partridges, at mother's heels – and the bowler-hatted fathers of the nation; statesmen with rolled umbrellas; gaitered prelates with wireless aerials on their heads; belted earls preparing to loosen their belts at the ringside. What is it that brings them all along? What is it that paints that private smile of anticipated enjoyment across their features, and unites them in this bond of reverence? What is it that would presumably impel them all to turn and rend anyone who dared to question the sanctity and supremacy of "The Circus".

In spite of this hugely successful return, the Bertram Mills Circus was no longer the only major force in the circus world. Serious rivals were appearing. The Chipperfields had managed to keep going throughout the war and, at the end, they were arguably the largest touring unit in the country. They would continue to develop their circus, until by the early 1950s they had a tent able to seat 6,000 people, which also and held a collection of 200 horses, 16 elephants and over 200 other animals. They were also the first of the large circuses to introduce heating for the comfort of its audience:

Crowds who visit Chipperfield's Circus – now the largest travelling circus in Britain ... will do so in comfort. The first of its kind, a heating system is being installed in the big top which has a total capacity of half a million cubic feet and the plant will blow 4,000 cubic feet of hot air per minute into it.

(The Lichfield Mercury, 26 October 1951)

But it was a newcomer to the circus scene that caused the greatest stir. Billy Smart had been a showman all his life and had also operated funfairs. In the pre-war Olympia seasons, the Mills had always had a funfair attached to their circus and Billy Smart had presented there. In 1946 he decided to buy a second-hand circus tent and equipment and gathered together a small troupe of performers to present the Billy Smart's New World Circus. The circus ran in conjunction with a funfair and proved very popular.

In the austere post-war era immediately after the war there was a demand for family entertainment, and the circus provided this. As Smart's circus gradually developed, it also expanded to a big top seating 6,000 and, by the early 1950s, it became a part of the 'big three' circuses, alongside those of the Mills and Chipperfields. Although other smaller circuses went back on the road, these three large circuses would dominate the circus industry for the years to come.

The beginning of the 1950s saw Britain still in the grip of post-war austerity. Food was still in short supply – at the end of 1950, bacon was still rationed to three ounces a week, and a pound of steak cost three ration books. It would not be until 1954 that all rationing of goods would come to an end.

However, the Festival of Britain in 1951 and the coming of a new monarch in 1952 gave the country a new optimism. The celebrations and pageantry allowed the nation to begin to free itself from the repression of the war years. Street parties and carnivals were held, parades were mounted and there was an air of festivity around the country. A photograph in *The Dundee Courier and Advertiser* of 28 July 1952 shows a huge crowd gathering to watch a long parade of elephants belonging to Chipperfield's Circus.

Parades of this kind were to become common for several years and as a child in the 1960s, my wife can remember being taken to see the circus moving through Leeds on the way to its pitch. Amongst all this celebration Lord George Sanger's circus made a reappearance. Billed as 'The Greatest name in Circus', it began its tour in Lichfield in June 1952. An interesting sign of the times was appeared in its advertising, which stated that there was, 'car parking on site'.

The Bertram Mills Circus on Woodhouse Moor, Leeds in the 1950s. *(Reproduced with permission from Leeds Civic Trust)*

Just as after the First World War, the circus again found itself on a wave of popularity. Many veteran and retired performers of today began their careers at this time. The British clown 'Vercoe', Arthur Pedlar, remembers his first routine in the ring with some other clowns at the Cirque Medrano in Paris in 1953:

At that moment I enter the ring as 'Hobo' with a couple of sweeping brushes and just walk straight across the ring as though I was going from A to B. I am just about to climb out the other side by which time Ken sorts himself out ... takes the brushes from me, puts them down, gets me by the scruff of the neck and the seat of the pants and marches me back to the other two who have got the ladder and the unicycle vertical again. Ken puts me on the ladder and shoves me up the ladder and Frankie puts the saddle underneath me.

So I'm on the eight-foot cycle, hugging the top of the ladder, shaking like the dickens, too nervous to move. Olli is holding the ladder, then Frankie and Ken go and pick up the two brushes I'd brought in. They hold the broom heads up for me to get hold of and very gingerly I let go ... and Olli takes the ladder away. Gingerly we move off with one on either side holding the broomsticks ... we just get halfway across the ring when the ringmaster comes in and blows his whistle. "Time's up!"

Well, the heads of the brushes were loose on the sticks so these two just lower the sticks and walk off behind me and I'm still going on with a broom head in each hand, unaware that all support has disappeared. That's when that photo was taken. I do a half circle of the ring, see them standing in the entrance leaning on the broomsticks. I realise that I'm alone, do a circle of the ring, jump off and then we all take a bow.

For all the glitz and the glamour of the ring there were still far too many 'incidents' providing ammunition for the critics of the circus. In early 1951, *The Dundee Courier and Advertiser* reported on an accident in a Birmingham circus when, during a shooting act by 'Big Chief Eagle Eye', the orchestra leader was hit in the leg. He had to be taken to hospital to have the bullet removed. Also in 1952 a tigress attacked one of the elephants at the end of the animal act. The elephant crashed into safety barriers and the audience of some 4,500 spectators, including many children, scrambled towards the exits. Fortunately, neither animals nor humans were seriously injured.

The most serious incident to take place at this time was reported in *The Dundee Courier and Advertiser* 13 July 1953:

Portrait of Arthur 'Vercoe' Pedlar, taken in the 1950s. *(Reproduced with permission of Arthur Pedlar)*

Vercoe takes to the ring on his giraffe unicycle. *(Reproduced with permission of Arthur Pedlar)*

Two thousand people saw a circus performer fall to his death at Blackpool Tower on Saturday night. The two Kanters ... had begun their pole perch act. Wilhelm had drawn thunderous applause by balancing on his head on top of a 16-foot pole held on Olof's shoulders, and was sliding down the pole when he appeared to slip ... and fell eight or ten feet to the ground.

Although it may have had many potential dangers, there was a lighter side to circus life as well. Ringmaster Norman Barrett remembers many amusing moments during his lifetime involvement in the circus:

When I was about 15, with my dad in Scotland [George Barrett's Circus] *... I used to drive a four wheel drive lorry with three trailers behind it. And I used to get up in the morning at about half past four, put on a hat, glasses and a false moustache and drive this lorry. And I was 15! How I ever got away with it I shall never know ...*

With Robert Brothers' circus I always remember a guy ... He used to drive this lorry with the trailer with all the dogs in the back. I remember we were driving to Spalding, so he gets to the ground and he hasn't got a trailer, so Uncle Bobby [Roberts] *said, "Where's the trailer?" He says, "Behind." "It's not." And he says, "Don't be silly, it's behind." And he gets out and there's no trailer there. And he'd lost the trailer about ten miles away …*

One time [at the Blackpool Tower Circus] *we had four girls on the aerial ropes … and one of these girls was sick and we always had a reserve girl. Now the girl who was sick was very small, five foot two and very flat-chested. The reserve girl was a lot taller and very … well endowed but she had to wear the same costume. So they were doing the act … and as she went into the flag* [a figure in which the performer is at 90 degrees to the vertical rope, with the upper foot fixed in a loop and the lower foot placed on the rope and the arms extended] *the costume went 'rip'.*

Now everything is exposed to the audience and she's hanging on to it. And then she realises and the audience realises she's got to let go with her hands to grab the rope to pull herself up to let herself down the rope. This went on and all of a sudden some wag from the back of the circus shouted, "Go for it gal!" so she did and slid down the rope. And as she hit the floor the orchestra began playing, 'For she's a jolly good fellow' – and that was a magical moment …

At Belle Vue [in Manchester] *I was doing the birthday spot and I'd got a real cheeky kid in the ring … marvellous … he's doing all the gags, everything I want him to. So at the end I always used to finish this piece by saying, "Who supports city?" … "Who supports united?", so I say, "Actually I support the best football team in England – Blackpool." And this little kid says, "Here," and I put the mic in front of him and he says, "You don't call that a ******* football team!" Well, I looked round and there are 6,000 people and they're bouncing … Now I am sitting on the ring and I am crying with laughter … it was a great line!*

The advent of the television age did much to raise the profile of the circus with the general public. Public broadcasting had begun in 1936, but it was suspended during the war years. In 1952 there were still only approximately two million television sets in British homes, most in London, Birmingham, Cardiff, Manchester and Glasgow – the only areas able to receive programmes at the time. However, the coronation of Queen Elizabeth II saw a boom in the sale of television sets and by the end of the decade most people began to see a television as a necessary piece of furniture.

Although the Bertram Mills Circus held the honour of being the first ever circus to be televised – in 1937 when part of the Olympia season was

Norman Barrett – ringmaster. *(Photograph: Piet-Hein Out, reproduced with permission of N. Barrett)*

broadcast on five consecutive days – by 1953 it was not uncommon for live circus to appear on the screen. On 4 January 1953, the Bertram Mills Circus was given a one-hour screening with coverage of the Royal visit. As television technology developed, the BBC also began to cover live tenting shows: 'Another visit to the circus will be made on November 13, this time to Billy Smart's Circus under their new big top … viewers can expect all the clowning and thrills that go to make up Billy Smart's successful show' (*The Lichfield Mercury*, 6 November 1953).

Billy Smart's Circus became a regular feature on television and his Christmas 'Spectaculars' were always popular. As well as the Bertram Mills Circus, shows from the Blackpool Tower Circus and several other circuses appeared on the television at this time. In one 12-month period during the

Images from Vistascreen 3D Viewer cards 1960s: *(Above)* Clarinda mounting 'Othello'; *(opposite)* The Mohawks troupe of acrobats. *(Author's collection)*

1950s, 17 different circus shows were televised. Although this raised the profile of circus, this inevitably became a case of over-exposure.

The 'entertainment in the corner' began to encourage people to stay at home, rather than go out, and with the introduction of commercial television in 1955, the public now had a choice of programmes to watch. Soap operas became popular; the BBC had *The Grove Family* and *Dixon of Dock Green*, and the newly launched ITV offered *Emergency Ward 10*. There was television for children, with *Watch with Mother*, and sports events began to be televised. Soon there would no need to leave the home as all kinds of entertainment could be found in this magic box.

The popularity of the television naturally caused the circus to suffer. Cyril Mills recalled how his box office received many telephone calls asking

Spuggy the clown at the Bertram Mills Circus. *(Reproduced with permission of Keith Wardell)*

when the circus was being broadcast, as the callers wanted to organise a large children's party on that day. He also noted a drop off in the sale of the cheaper seats and a similar drop off in the attendance at evening performances.

Times were changing rapidly. From the age of the silent movies, the film industry had grown into a multi-million dollar business and visits to the cinema were now more popular than ever. A whole new music industry developed, focused on the young. A new popular youth culture was born – the Teddy Boys of the 1950s, the Mods and Rockers and the Hippies of the 1960s. During the 1950s and 1960s, the nuclear family began to disintegrate and people began to stop doing things as a family. This had a major effect upon the circus as it was seen as less and less of a family entertainment and more as something just for children.

The wheel was turning and circus was losing favour with the public. The economic and social conditions of the late 1960s and early 1970s made the life of a large touring circus no longer viable. Public opinion now weighed heavily against the use of animals in circus and the circus industry was beginning to come under pressure once again.

The major circuses responded to this pressure in different ways. The Chipperfields branched out into creating wildlife safari parks at Longleat and Woburn Abbey and their circus moved to South Africa. Rising costs and the inability to increase audiences had created financial problems for the Bertram Mills Circus. By 1965 the business was facing voluntary liquidation and arrangements were made to sell out the company to the hotel and property dealer, Maxwell Joseph. The 1966/1967 Olympia season was a sell-out, but that was to be the last season of the renowned Bertram Mills Circus. Similar problems were facing Billy Smart and reluctantly his circus closed in 1971.

The three big circuses of Britain were no more and the golden age of the modern circus had ended.

Chapter Eleven

And So the Wheel Turns: The Circus from 1970 to the Present

During the late 1950s and early 1960s, Britain was emerging from post-war austerity into a new era. By the 1970s a new, more affluent consumer society was born; wages were significantly higher than they had been for many years, while an explosion in the building industry and the relaxation on mortgage provision led to an expansion in home ownership. With the rapid growth in car ownership at this time, people were now also far more mobile and able to take advantage of new work and leisure opportunities further away from home. The post-war generation growing up expected to own their own homes, cars, televisions and other modern appliances – the age of materialism had arrived.

There was, however, a downside to this rapid economic progress. Industrial disputes, strikes, power cuts, fuel shortages and the introduction of the three-day week plagued the 1970s. More significantly, this increased affluence brought about the beginning of a breakdown of the extended family. In previous decades, working class families had usually lived in relatively close proximity, in the same or neighbouring streets, or sometimes even next door to each other. They often socialised together and this created a distinct family and community cohesion.

However, by the late 1960s many cities across the country had implemented a policy of 'slum' clearances; the mass demolition of traditional back-to-back inner city terraced properties. Families were either re-housed in new purpose-built towns such as Milton Keynes and Telford New Town, or were moved to high-rise developments, where many were soon to complain of being socially isolated.

For all the increased opportunities that this new age presented, a visit to the circus was still a special event for the young children of this time. One woman interviewed by the author remembered being taken on an annual visit to the circus as a child in the 1950s. She recalled that it was a big event and that her parents had to make sacrifices to save enough money to take her and her brother. This memory of the circus being an expensive treat has cropped up in several interviews. Another interviewee remembered:

Because we lived so far out of town there were very few treats we had in life ... and one was going to the circus ... because it came so rarely. I suppose they saved up for it ... but all the memories of the circus coming to town was [sic] good for me. I don't really know how they managed ... they definitely had to save up.

The 'Big three' circuses were still in their heyday in the early post-war period, but with the eventual closure of both the Mills' and Smart's circuses, a noticeable decline set in. Large touring circuses were no longer financially viable and although some smaller circuses were still in business, the working classes were no longer drawn to the circus as an entertainment form and it was disappearing. Families had begun to socialise together far less and although some of the post-war 'babies' did take their children to the circus, interest was waning. There were far too many other distractions, as one interviewee commented:

I don't think the magic's the same nowadays ... I don't know what it is ... it's a different generation and their entertainment values are different. They [the interviewee's children] *enjoyed the circus but I don't think they had the same pleasure out of the kinds of things as we did.*

The circus was rapidly becoming regarded as a third-rate children's entertainment, visited only at holiday times or as a Christmas Spectacular on television.

Also during this era, animal welfare groups began to apply an increased pressure on circuses over the use of animals in performance. They lobbied local councils and the government and even picketed some circuses, in some cases causing distress to audiences, performers and animals through their actions. Childhood reminiscences of the circus among people of the post-war generation are frequently dominated by memories of the animals. Horses, elephants, dogs, lions, tigers and monkeys are often remembered with fondness, although on occasions this could also be comical:

When I first got to a circus ... it was the first time I had ever got a hot dog ... and I'm sitting at the front and my parents had actually saved up to sit at the front and then they brought the elephants out. And you know what that elephant took off me? My hot dog! I was devastated ... and I was crying and my mum and dad thought I'd eaten it. I didn't eat it! And I've never really liked elephants since.

However, for all his bad experience with the elephant as a six-year-old, the same man went on to comment: 'All the animals have gone now ... it's a tragedy ... there's no lion tamers any more, or very few ... They think all tigers are like Tigger ... no, they were well looked after, that was their livelihood'.

Anecdotal evidence of cruelty in the circus during the post-war era by those remembering their childhood days is rare, and only one person interviewed made any adverse comment about animals in circuses:

I remember as a child seeing performing elephants, which I enjoyed at the time but now ... I think it's cruel ... as things have progressed I really prefer circuses now that don't have animals in ... we are animal lovers now and can appreciate the fact that animals shouldn't be kept in confined spaces ... now we would prefer to see animals like that in the wild.

Sufficient pressure was brought to bear that many local authorities ceased to issue licences to travelling circuses, and as a means of survival, many circuses chose not to present animals in order to avoid trouble. Although the vast majority of circus animals were well cared for, the organisation Animal Defenders International carried out in-depth investigations into circus animal welfare throughout this period. In 1999 they brought a much publicised landmark case of proven animal cruelty against Mary Chipperfield. Mary Chipperfield Promotions Ltd was an animal training facility that provided animal acts for work in circuses, films and television etc. Under the Protection of Animals Act of 1911, Mary and her husband Roger Cawley were convicted of cruelty towards some of their animals and had heavy fines imposed.

The Chipperfield case was to have a major impact upon the circus industry. At the time of the trial the BBC reported that:

Public opinion over the use of animals in circuses has changed with the growing awareness of animal welfare. Elephants, tigers, lions, chimpanzees and other exotic animals were once considered integral to circus entertainment. Now there is growing distaste at seeing wild animals performing in the ring. This shift in opinion, likely to be accelerated by Mary Chipperfield's conviction on animal cruelty charges, has ensured the evolution of the circus away from animals and towards more performance-based shows.

The issue of the use of animals in circuses is a complex one and opinions are deeply divided. For many, the removal of exotic animals destroys the tradition of the circus. For others it is a natural and humane progression; but the dichotomy still exists, as voiced by the circus owner Gerry Cottle in the BBC report also quoted above: 'In London the public do not want to see circuses with animals. But in the country they do. Even with our radical Circus of Horrors we still get people saying it is not the same and asking where the elephants are'.

In the foreword to the draft Wild Animals in Circuses Bill, presented before the House of Commons Environment, Food and Rural Affairs Committee in April 2013, Lord de Mauley wrote:

The British circus industry has a rich heritage dating back over two centuries, and I hope it will continue to thrive long into the future. For many years wild animals were an integral part of the circus experience: the only chance that most people would have to glimpse exotic beasts from distant lands ... Today the overwhelming view of the public, as well as such respected bodies such as the RSPCA, is that travelling circuses are no place for wild animals. Members of Parliament have long voiced concerns around the issue in debates dating back a number of years ... This legislation will end the use of wild animals in travelling circuses in this country.

If successful, the Bill will ban the use of wild animals in circuses in England from December 2015. Currently, government regulations require circuses using wild animals to be licensed, of which there are only two at present in England, Circus Mondao and Jolly's Circus. These regulations will be superseded if the draft Bill becomes law. The Committee has recommended in paragraph 17 of the Report (July 2013) that the government proscribe a list of animals that should no longer be used in circuses. It has suggested that initially a ban be placed on all big cat species and elephants but not on snakes, camels, zebras or raccoons.

Of course, there are opponents to the proposed ban and the Director of the Association for the Promotion of Traditional Circus Arts is quoted in the Report as suggesting that, 'Circuses without animals are dull or little more than a variety show'.

Whatever one's personal opinions on the debate, the image of the circus industry in Britain was greatly affected by this issue during the last decades of the twentieth century. But out of this backlash towards the traditional circus grew a new phenomenon. Born out of a desire to create a genuine alternative form of physical human circus, this 'New Circus' as it became widely known, had its roots in the community. New Circus performers began appearing at festivals, carnivals and other community events. Acrobats, stilt-walkers, jugglers, aerialists and all those others with human physical circus skills reappeared, some as organised performance groups, others as itinerant individuals. 'Circus' was once again being seen on the streets and seemed to be returning to its medieval roots.

This New Circus sought to dispel the mystique of the traditional circus which many claimed was guarded closely by tight-knit circus families. It attempted to give ownership of the circus back to the people. New Circus was open to all, not solely the property of full time professionals, and performers were now drawn from every social group, from children on the street to university professors. Circus skills were learned for pleasure and were used to enhance self-confidence. Where performances were given, they were not always to a paying public but were very often community based and a shared experience built around a theme or a story.

New Circus embraced the traditional physical circus skills but also encouraged innovation and experimentation – and was strictly non-animal. Often other art forms were woven into the performance so that New Circus became a synthetic art form, drawing on many different sources of inspiration.

Community circus events have been organised since the 1970s and one of the earliest exponents was Reg Bolton, born in Margate in 1945. Reg was a clown, a teacher, an actor and a writer and he became, 'An enthusiast who was enthusiastic about the possibilities for using circus as education, self fulfillment and community development' (*The Guardian*, 26 July 2006). Reg's pioneering community work with children on the streets of the Craigmillar estate in Edinburgh during the 1970s was seminal and paved the way for the New Circus movement in Britain and abroad. He produced several books, of which perhaps *Circus in a Suitcase* (1982) and *New Circus: World Wide Survey of the Concept of Circus Without Animals* (1987) were the most influential for the movement. He later moved to Australia with his family, where he continued his work until his sudden death in 2006.

Out of Reg Bolton's work grew the interest in Youth Circus and during the 1980s all over Britain people were setting up circus skills groups for

Frequently youth circus performances have a theme: Here young people take part in the show *Zirkusvamps*: 'Mad' Max. *(Photographs; Yvonne Notzon)*

young people. Amongst these groups were Albert and Friends in London (1983) and the Belfast Community Circus (1985). In 1991 I brought together several of these groups for a conference in Leeds, and out of this was born the National Association of Youth Circus (NAYC), supported by Reg Bolton as the Honorary President. The mission statement of the NAYC was to promote circus for, with and by young people and at its peak in the mid-1990s there were over 100 member groups within the NAYC. It formulated a recommended Code of Practice for those working in the circus skills with young people.

Unfortunately, it has been argued that an element of the New Circus movement had become equated with the 'lunatic hippy fringe'. A small number of circus skills workers did not present themselves in a particularly positive light and in working with young people, a minority displayed some unprofessional working practices. This only reinforced the negative image attached to circus during the wilderness years of the 1970s and 80s.

The NAYC was active in encouraging a closer collaboration between the traditional circus industry and new circus groups, and in promoting a new acceptability and respectability for circus as an art form. Working with circus owners such as Gerry Cottle and Martin Burton, the emerging

Frequently youth circus performances have a theme: Here young people take part in the show *Zirkusvamps*. Chloe, the author's granddaughter, performs as a vampire (top centre). *(Photographs courtesy of Yvonne Notzon)*

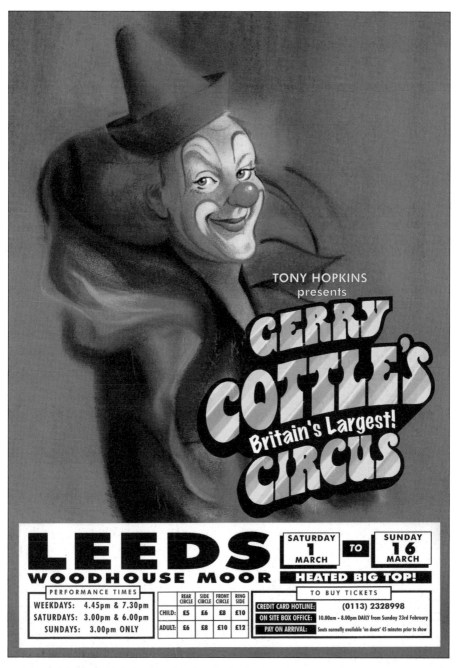

Poster for Gerry Cottle's Circus. *(Author's collection)*

A youth circus group from Latvia performing in the Leeds city centre. *(Author's collection)*

Circus Training Centres, among them Circomedia, the Circus Space and Skylight Circus, much positive and constructive work was done to raise the profile of the circus.

Many youth circuses worked with touring traditional circuses, visiting nearby towns and cities. Gerry Cottle, in particular, would make his big top and technical staff available for the Circus Zanni youth circus when he visited Leeds. In this way young people were able to present their skills in a traditional space. Youth circuses also provided a springboard for young people who wanted to go on to professional circus work. Many went on to train at the various Circus Training Centres. The Circus Space in London (now the National Centre for Circus Arts) offers a full time degree course in the Circus Arts.

Other young people developed their own professional expertise. The Rapide Brothers (also known as Izzo and Malteser the clowns) began as members of Circus Zanni youth circus and have developed their skills to the extent that in 2012 they were voted the 'Best Clowns in Britain' by the Clowns International group.

The 1990s saw a reinvention of the circus. Circus was slowly regaining a respectability and a new popularity. Alongside the existing traditional circuses, new circuses were emerging that would take the art form to a new level. The French based group Archaos exploded on to the scene in the early 1990s. Originally formed in the mid 70s, it had gone back to the roots of circus, travelling with horses and caravans. This experiment proved difficult to maintain in a modern world and so it reinvented itself into a contemporary show of live music, motorbikes and special effects. Labelled as a 'punk' circus by some, it was harsh and brutal in its presentation and caused great controversy. Its performances contained machinery, fire, explosions, chainsaw juggling, metal-clad clowns and, in some shows, an element of nudity. All of this was accompanied by ear-splitting live rock music. Themes and images were challenging to the senses and some people were offended by this. A few local authorities even went as far as to ban Archaos from performing in their areas.

Archaos is no more and its founder Pierrot Bidon has died, but this circus had an enormous impact on the contemporary circus world at this period and opened up a whole new audience to circus. Alongside Archaos, another group that has had a profound effect upon the circus industry in the last two decades is the Cirque du Soleil. Originally founded in 1980 in Montreal, Quebec, Canada as a touring performing troupe, the Cirque du Soleil has grown into a multi-million dollar industry, boasting over 20 shows

A new generation of clowns – the Rapide Brothers. *(Reproduced by permission of Ian & Gavin Radforth)*

in every continent except Antarctica. Their colourful performances are a synthesis of traditional human physical circus skills, physical theatre, music, choreography and visual imagery. It has been said that the Cirque du Soleil has revitalised the modern circus industry worldwide and it has brought a whole new generation of audience back to the circus.

However, whilst having raised the profile of circus worldwide, some now consider that the Cirque du Soleil industry has grown too large and is losing direction away from its circus roots. Now presenting more large scale 'arena' spectaculars, it no longer has the fundamental intimacy of the traditional circus.

Simon West, an acrobat from New Zealand, recently commented that he believes that the Cirque du Soleil might be in danger of over-reaching itself. In a time of global recession, audiences may be less inclined to spend an exorbitant amount of money on ticket prices and there could be a real possibility that we see such large-scale events becoming financially non-viable. Already a proposed Cirque du Soleil residency in Dubai has been 'put on ice' due to the current financial climate.

However, whether we like the Cirque du Soleil or not, it has to be acknowledged that it has rekindled an interest in circus globally. As Norman Barrett has stated:

> *The Cirque du Soleil isn't a normal circus going public ... we have had people come in here* [Zippo's Circus] *... last year there was a man, his wife and three kids. They asked to see us after the show. He said, "You might not believe what I've got to say but we've had a better time here for a third of the price because we felt part of what you're doing. We appreciated Cirque du Soleil but the children were bored after the first half".*
>
> *You can't knock their marketing ... I wouldn't start to knock Cirque du Soleil but we have our own niche. We have our own type of audience. We are doing it for the people, to create atmosphere. I have great admiration for what Cirque du Soleil do ... but I think we have gleaned from it.*

The current resurgence of interest in the circus in Britain can be measured by the number of tenting circuses seen around the country. The *2013 Circus Directory of the British Isles*, published in the *King Pole* magazine September 2013, lists 31 different touring circuses, including the names Chipperfield and Smart. In addition to this there were six resident circuses and six further circuses touring Ireland. If we add to this the Circus Training Schools, Youth Circuses and other events that have incorporated circus – an example of this

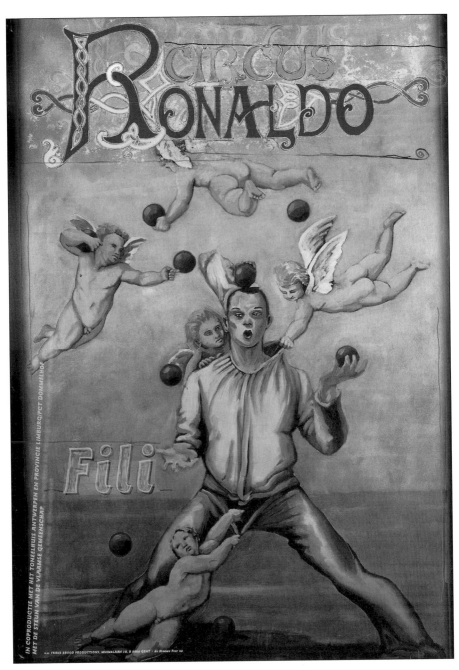

Poster advertising Circus Ronaldo. *(Author's collection)*

being the closing ceremony of the 2012 Olympic Games in London – then it can be seen that there is an enormous amount of circus activity going on. Circus continues to survive and, indeed, is thriving.

Across the country there is a move towards a return to a more traditional way of life; witness the growth in interests in the craft pursuits, such as knitting and baking. People are queuing up to take on allotments; farmers' markets are booming and television reality programmes offering the 'authentic' life of a previous era are as popular as ever. All of this indicates a desire to return to the more community-based values of bygone years.

The circus is experiencing the same effect. Families are returning to the circus and although the 'packaging' may be slightly different, the acts are intrinsically the same. Some circuses are adopting a retro style, seeking to recapture the experience of a small-scale village green circus. Gifford's Circus is an example of this, with its small white tent and brightly painted wagons touring the rural south-west of England. When the small Belgian circus, Circus Ronaldo, toured Britain it performed in a small tent with an ornately carved wooden stage. The circus wagons were drawn up in a ring around the tent, almost becoming part of the circus setting itself. Inside the tent the audience was so close to the performers that they felt almost part of the show. It created a virtually renaissance atmosphere.

The circus is alive. It has changed and adapted throughout the years. It has experienced wars, economic gloom and social upheavals but it has survived, and will continue to do so because it is an integral part of our culture. I leave the closing words to Norman Barrett:

My dad always used to say life is about a wheel. When he started his circus it was at a high, then the talkies came in and the wheel turned down. Then it came up again and then television came in and it went down again. Now we're on the way up because people want to be entertained ... Circus in general, it's starting to thrive again. People want to get up, they want to go out. Providing it's good it will survive. It's survived over 250 years and it will keep going.

Zippo's Circus at Brent Cross. *(Reproduced with permission of Martin Burton)*

Select Bibliography

Armin R., *Foole Upon Foole* (Ferbrand, London, 1605). Available online, at *www.physicalcomedy.blogspot.com*.

Bayley P., *Sketches from St George's Fields* (London, 1821).

Bolton R., *Circus in a Suitcase* (Butterfingers, 1985).

Bolton R., *New Circus: World Wide survey of the concept of Circus without animals* (Calouste Gulbenkian Foundation, 1987).

Chesterton G.K., *St Francis of Assisi* (Dover Books, 1923).

Clark J. S., *Circus Parade* (B.T. Batsford, 1936).

Cottle G., *Confessions of a Showman* (Satin Publications Ltd, 2006).

Coxe A., *A Seat at the Circus* (Evans Brothers Ltd, London, 1951).

Davis J.M., *The Circus Age, Culture and Society under the American Big Top* (University of North Carolina Press, 2002).

Dickens C., *The Old Curiosity Shop* (Wordsworth Classics, 1995).

Dickens C., *Sketches by Boz* (Penguin Classic, 1995).

Douce F., *Illustrations of Shakespeare and of Ancient Manners* (Tegg T., London, 1839).

Downing S.J., *The English Pleasure Garden 1660 - 1860* (Shire Publications, 2009).

Fields S., 'Hercules can be a Lady', *New York Mirror*, December 15 1947.

Findlater R., *Grimaldi, King of Clowns* (MacGibbon & Kee, London, 1955).

France A., *Le Jongleur de Notre Dame* (Ferroud A. & Ferroud F., Paris, 1924).

Frost T., *The Old Showmen and the Old London Fairs* (Classic reprint series, 2012).

Frost T., *Circus Life and Circus Celebrities* (Chatto & Windus, 1881).

Gazeley I. and Newell A., *First World War – working class food consumption* (University of Sussex, 2010).

Gollmar R.H., *My Father Owned a Circus* (Caxton Printers Ltd, Idaho, 1965).

Grimaldi, J.; Dickens, C. (ed.), *Memoirs of Joseph Grimaldi* (George Routledge & Sons, 1838).

Hemingway E., *The Circus* (Ringling Brother Souvenir Programme, 1954).

Hickman K., *Travels with a Circus* (Flamingo, 2001).

Holland C., *Strange Feats & Clever Turns* (Holland & Palmer, 1998).

Lewbel A., *Research in Juggling History* (Brandies University MA, 1995).

Lindsay J., *The Troubadors and their World* (Frederick Muller Ltd, 1976).

Lorenzo A., *Les fous du Cirque* (Ch. Massin, Paris, undated).

Loxton H., *The Golden Age of the Circus* (Grange Books Plc, 1997).

Macgregor-Morris P., *Spinners of the Big Top* (Chatto &Windus, 1960).

Mathys F.K., *Circus* (AT. Verlag Aarau, Stuttgart, 1986).

Mills C., *Bertram Mills Circus – Its Story* (Hutchinson, London, 1967).

Morley H., *Memoirs of Bartholomew Fair* (Chapman & Hall, London, 1859).

Neville G., *Incidents in the Life of Joseph Grimaldi* (Jonathan Cape, 1980).

Olsen K., *Daily Life in 18th-century England* (Greenwood Press, 1999).

Pepys S., Ed. Le Gallienne R., *The Diary of Samuel Pepys* (Modern Library, USA, 2001).

Petronius; trans. Thurston Peck H., *Dinner with Trimalchio* (J. Wilson & Co., Cambridge, USA 1898).

Picard L., *Victorian London; The Tale of a City 1840-1870* (Phoenix House, 2006).

Poliakoff N., *Coco the Clown by Himself* (Dent & Sons Ltd, 1941).

Queffelec H., *Francois d'Assisi; le jongleur de Dieu* (Calmann-Levy, 1994).

Sagne J., *Toulouse-Lautrec Au Cirque* (Flammarion, Paris, 1991).

Sanger G., *Seventy Years a Showman* (E.P. Dutton & Co. London, 1935).

Sergent A., *Barnum roi du bluff* (Pierre Horay, 1980).

Smollett T., *The Expedition of Humphrey Clinker* (Penguin Books, 1983).

Speaight G., *A History of the Circus* (Tantivy, 1980).

Steinmeyer J., *Hiding the Elephant* (Arrow Books, 2005).

Stevens Curl J., *Spas, Wells, & Pleasure Gardens of London* (Historical Publications Ltd., 2010).

Wade S., *Heroes, Villains and Victims of Leeds* (Breedon Books, 2007).

Walford E., *Old and New London* (Thornbury and Walford, 1878).

Willeford W., *The Fool and his Sceptre* (Northwestern University Press, 1969).

Willson Disher M., *Greatest Show on Earth* (G Bell & Sons Ltd, 1937).

Winkler D. and Winkler G., *Menschen zwischen Himmel und Erde* (Berlin, 1988).

Wroth W., *London Pleasure Gardens of the Eighteenth Century* (Macmillan & Co Ltd, 1896).

Interviews

Mr Arthur 'Vercoe' Pedlar, Clown (1 April 2013)
Mr Norman Barrett MBE, Ringmaster (2 May 2013)
The Rapide Brothers, Clowns (24 September 2013)
Mr Simon West, Acrobat (25 September 2013)
Mrs E. Parnell (26 December 2012)
Members of the public (1 October 2013)

Sources on the British Circus Industry

Archives, Museums and Libraries:

The National Fairground Archive at the University of Sheffield
This archive holds a variety of primary source documents, photographs and audio visual material relating to the history of fairs, circuses and travelling show people:

The National Fairground Archive
Western Bank Library
Sheffield S10 2TN
Tel: 0114 22 27231
Email: nfa@sheffield.ac.uk
Website: *www.nfa.dept.shef.ac.uk*

The National Archives
The major archive in Britain, providing unrivalled access to primary resource material for social historians:

The National Archives
Kew
Richmond
Surrey TW9 4DU
Tel: 0208 876 3444
Email: info@nationalarchives.gov.uk
Website: *www.nationalarchives.gov.uk*

West Yorkshire Archive Service - Leeds
As well as a source of material for local social historians, this archive holds primary source material relating to the Leeds City Varieties Music Hall:

West Yorkshire Archive Service
Nepshaw Lane
Morley
Leeds LS27 7JQ
Tel: 0113 393 9788
Email: leeds@wyjs.org.uk
Website: *www.wyjs.org.uk*

Leeds City Library
The Central Library has a Local and Family History Department which holds material relating to the Leeds City Varieties Music Hall. It also allows access to an online searchable database of nineteenth century newspapers and *The Times* digital archive:

Local and Family History Library
Central Library
Calverley Street
Leeds LS1 3AB
Tel: 0113 2478290
Email: localstudies@leedslearning.net
Website: *www.leeds.gov.uk/libraries*

The Leeds City Varieties
An original Music Hall, recently refurbished, still in everyday use as a theatre. Visits and tours by arrangements. The bar displays original posters and photographs of performers:

City Varieties Music Hall
Swan Street
Leeds LS1 6LW
Tel: 0113 243 0808 (Box Office)
Email: info@cityvarieties.co.uk
Website: *www.cityvarieties.co.uk*

Malt Cross Music Hall
Possibly one of the smallest and most unusual Music Halls in Britain. Now a café-bar, it still retains much of its original features. It also has a display about the history of the building and an archive of material, which is viewable on request:

Malt Cross Music Hall
16 St James Street
Nottingham NG1 6FG
Tel: 0115 941 1048
Email: info@maltcross.com
Website: *www.maltcross.com*

The Museum of London
The museum contains a wide range of displays concerning the history of London. Temporary exhibitions, such as the one in 2013 concerning the English Pleasure Gardens, are a valuable source of information:

The Museum of London
150 London Wall

London EC2 5HN
Tel: 0207 001 9844
Email: info@museumoflondon.org.uk
Website: *http://museumoflondon.org.uk*

The Victoria and Albert Museum
The V&A has a large collection relating to the performing arts and, in particular, to the early history of the circus:

The Victoria and Albert Museum
Cromwell Road
London SW7 2RL
Tel: 0207 942 2000
Email: info@vam.ac.uk
Website: *www.vam.ac.uk*

Websites:

Ancestry
(*www.ancestry.co.uk*)
A major genealogical and social history website providing a wide range of searchable records. A great resource for pinpointing circus workers through census records; birth, marriage and death indexes; apprenticeship records, convict transportation records and much more.

The British Library
(*http://bl.uk*)
A major repository for British newspapers as well as a range of source material relating to the circus. The British Library website and catalogue are searchable online.

The British Newspaper Archive
(*www.britishnewspaperarchive.co.uk*)
This website enables online access to a vast collection of historical newspapers held within the British Library collections. The newspapers are searchable by name and subject and provide a wealth of local and national coverage relating to circuses and menageries, as well as to individuals.

Circopedia
(*http://circopedia.org*)
A free online circus encyclopaedia, which contains information on various circuses, circus history, circus biographies and other circus-related topics.

The Circus Historical Society
(*www.circushistory.org*)
A major online resource for the history of the circus, although it mainly covers American Circus history. It has a search facility and holdings include digital copies of books and other interesting articles on the early circus.

The Circus Museum of the Netherlands
(*www.circusmuseum.nl*)
An online searchable website of circus posters, photographs and prints, which includes a collection of almost 8,000 posters dating from the late nineteenth century. The site can be searched by individual name, circus or act.

Findmypast.co.uk
(*www.findmypast.co.uk*)
A genealogical website also providing access to British newspapers from 1710–1953, searchable by name and subject. These include a range of contemporary information relating to circuses and individuals.

The Great War Forum
(*www.1914-1918.invisionzone.com*)
Although primarily a site for researching matters relating to the First World War, the Great War Forum can also provide interesting anecdotes and references to circus performers who served during the war.

The Institute of Historical Research
(*www.british-history.ac.uk*)
The Institute provides an online digital library containing some of the core printed primary and secondary sources for the medieval and modern history of Britain. The holdings are searchable by both name and subject. A very useful resource for matters relating to the circus and menageries in medieval and Tudor times, through exploration of the Close Court Rolls. The site also allows access to printed material relating to the nineteenth century London boroughs, where several of the early circus buildings were situated.

The Leodis Photographic Archive
(*www.leodis.net*)
A searchable digital archive of photographs of Leeds, Leodis contains some photographs relating to the circus in Leeds after the 1950s. The website also provides access to a collection of nineteenth century circus posters.

The Humour Foundation
(*www.humourfoundation.com.au*)
A website covering the history of clowning, types of clown, some famous clowns and hospital clowning, with links to other websites related to clowning.

Palace of Variety
(*www.palaceofvariety.co.uk*)
A website devoted to celebrating speciality acts on the Variety stage. It also has an interesting section on UK contemporary circus history.

The National Women's History Museum
(*www.nwhm.org*)
An American museum that researches, collects and exhibits the contribution of women to society in a context of world history. It has some interesting information of American women's suffrage and the circus.

The Scottish Music Hall and Variety Theatre Association
(*www.freewebs.com/scottishmusichallsociety*)
This website of an association dedicated to preserving the history of the Music Hall in Scotland, explores the connection between circus performers and the music halls.

World War History & Art Museum
(*www.wwham.com*)
A museum dedicated to the preservation and presentation of the First and Second World Wars, particularly through original artwork by men and women who served in these conflicts. The website has some interesting information and photographic images relating to the circus in the First World War.

Index

Albert and Friends (Circus) 195
Alien Performers 170, 173-175
American Museum (The) 102
Amphitheatre Anglais 44
Amusement Tax (see also Entertainment Tax) 146
Apollonicon, The 111, 112
Archaos (Circus) 199
Archee 13
Arlechinno (see also Harlequin) 28, 29, 30
Armin, Robert 12
Astley's Amphitheatre 73, 75, 76, 78, 79, 89, 90
Astley's Grand Amphitheatre 91
Astley, John 39, 42, 45, 49, 75
Astley's New Amphitheatre of the Arts 45
Astley's New Royal Amphitheatre 91
Astley, Patty 39
Astley, Philip (ix), 32, 34-52, 73, 122, 160
Astley's Riding House 39
Astley's Royal Circus 33
Atkin's Menagerie 57, 61, 62, 65
Atkins, Thomas 57
Auguste 176
Australian Olympic Theatre 72

Bagnigge Wells Garden 21
Ballard's Grand Collection of Wild Beasts 58
Balmat, Monsieur 43
Bannister's (Circus) 53
Barnum & Bailey (Circus) 109, 110, 111, 115, 132

Barnum, P.T. 95, 102, 103, 108, 109
Barrett, Norman 159, 183, 184, 185, 201, 203
Bartholomew Fair 14, 17, 18, 19, 55, 61
Batty, William (Circus) 79, 80, 90
Belfast Community Circus 195
Bell's (Circus) 114
Bertram Mills' Circus (ix), 160, 164-170, 172, 173, 177-180, 184, 186, 189, 191
Bidon, Pierre 199
Blackpool Tower Circus 122, 134, 141, 175, 184, 186
Blondin, Charles (xiii), 24, 109, 131
Bolton, Reg 194-195
Bostock's (Circus) 116, 136, 138, 141, 142
Bostock and Wombwell (Circus) 155
Boucicault, Dion 118
Brighella 29
British Empire Exhibition 159
Broncho Bill's (Circus) 156
Brookes, John 63
Brooke's Menagerie 61
Brumbach, Katie (see also Sandwina) 163
Buffalo Bill (see also W F Cody) 94-96, 109, 115, 127, 136
Buff Bill's (Circus) 136, 145
Bull Leaping 2
Burton, Martin 195
Byron, Lord 60

Cadman 17
Cairoli, Charlie 175
Capitano, Il 28
Castello, Dan 102, 109
Cawley, Roger 192

Cavendish, William 35
Chaplin, Charlie (x), 129
Chapman, George 170
Chapman, Nellie (see also Lion Queen) 91
Charini, Signor 43
Chipperfield's (Circus) 170, 180, 181, 189
Chipperfield, Dick 1670
Chipperfield, James 55
Chipperfield, Mary 192
Chunee the elephant 63-65
Cinematograph 125, 127
Circomedia 199
Circus Busch 164, 176
Circus Krone 164
Circus Maximus, The 3, 4
Circus Mondao 193
Circus Pinder 116
Circus Ronaldo 202, 203
Circus Space, The (see also National
    Centre for Circus Arts) 199
Circus, The 44
Circus, The Royal Edinburgh 44
Circus and sport 124-125
Circus and television 184, 186, 187
Circus and Women's Suffrage 155
Circus in Australia 72
Circus Zanni 199
Cirque Franconi 75
Cirque du Solei 199, 201
Cirque Olympique 75
Clarke's (Circus) 53
Clini-Clowns 12
Clowns without Borders 12
Coco the Clown (see also Nikolai
    Poliakoff) (ix), 163, 175-176
Cody, W.F. 95, 96
Colpi 39
Columbina (see also Columbine) 29
Columbine 30
Commedia dell'Arte 28-29
Cook's Amphitheatre 88
Cooke's (Circus) 53
Cooke, Thomas 52

Cooper & Bailey's (Circus) 109
Copperin 9
Corde Volante 75
Cottle, Gerry 193, 195, 197, 199
Coup, William 102, 109
Crawley, Mark 140
Cross, Edward 57, 63-65
Cross Menagerie 57, 61

Darby, William (see also Pablo Fanque)
    80, 85
Davenport brothers 117-118
Davis, William 73, 75, 76
Davis' Royal Amphitheatre 75
Day, John 60
Day's Menagerie 60, 61
Dibdin, Charles 42, 44
Dobney's Place 35, 36
Doctore, Il 28
Ducrow, Andrew 65, 73-79, 90
Ducrow, Peter 73
Duffy's (Circus) 116, 136, 156, 170

Eqyptian Hall, The 117, 119, 130
Elphintsone's (Circus) 132
Entertainment National Service
    Association (ENSA) 176
Entertainment Tax 146, 147, 154, 168
Evans, Sir Arthur 2
Evelyn, John 18, 21
Exeter Exchange, The 56-58, 60, 63-65

Fanque, Edward (Ted) 136
Fanque, Pablo (see also William Darby)
    53, 80-90, 105, 132, 136
Fawkes, Isaac 17
Fay, William 117-118
Flemish Hercules, The (see also Peter
    Ducrow) 73
Flying Condonas, The 163
Footit the Clown 140
Forepaugh, Adam 109, 110
Fortunelly 39

Fosset's (Circus) 116, 142, 177, 179
Fossett and Bailey's (Circus) 169
Fossett, Thomas 147
Franconi, Antonio 44
Frost Fairs 54, 55

General Tom Thumb (see also Charles
    Stratton) 102
George Barrett's Canadian (Circus) 156,
    183
Gifford's (Circus) 203
Gilbert, George 122
Ginnet 114
Ginnet, Frank 160
Gleemen 6
Great Carmo, The 164
Great Continental Circus 169
Great International Circus 152
Great Victory Circus 151
Great Yarmouth Hippodrome Circus 122
Greene, Alexander 72
Grimaldi, Joseph 26-27, 30-32, 39
Grimaldi, Joseph Giuseppe 26
Goldoni, Carlo 28
Guild of Royal Minstrels 6

Half Penny Hatch 36-37, 39, 49
Hall, Jacob 14, 18
Hanneford's (Circus) 136
Harlequinade 27, 29, 30, 43
Harlequin (see also Arlechinno) 27, 28,
    30
Harper, Richard 14
Hengler, Charles 86, 114
Hengler's (Circus) 79, 87, 131, 141
Hengler, Signor 43
Hercules House 73
Hernandez & Stone (Circus) 113, 114
Hogarth, William 18
Holloway's (Circus) 53
Holloway, George 105
Houdini, Harry 129-130
Howe & Cushing's (Circus) 111, 113, 115

Howes, Nathan 100
Hughes, Charles 40-45, 50, 73, 122
Hughes, John 35
Hughes' Riding School 40
Hutchinson's (Circus) 114

Izzo the clown (see also The Rapide
    Brothers) 199

Jamrach, Charles 57
Jamrach's Menagerie 57
Jean Mills' Circus 178
Jester 8, 9
Jestress 9
Joey (see also Joseph Grimaldi) 32
Jolly's (Circus) 193
Jongleur 4-6, 15
Jones' Equestrian Amphitheatre 43
Jones, Patty (see also Patty Astley) 35, 38

Kaye's (Circus) 170
Keeley & Hogin's American Circus 114
Kempe, Will 12
Kendrick's Menagerie 57
King Poles 103, 164
Kraul, Henry 61

Lautrec, Toulouse (x)
Leopold Brothers 131-132
Leotard, Jules (xii)
Lewis Lent (Circus) 111
Lion King, The (see also Isaac Van
    Amburgh) 66, 71
Lion Queen, The (see also Nellie
    Chapman) 91
Little Billy 37, 38
Lockhard, George 134

Macarte's Monster Circus 111
Malteser the clown (see also The Rapide
    Brothers) 199
Mander's Menagerie 61
Marshall, Renee 156

Marylebone Gardens 24
Mazeppa 76
Menage 35
Menageries 53-56
Mills, Bernard 164
Mills, Bertram W. 151-154, 159, 160
Mills, Cyril 164, 165, 176, 187
Milton's (Circus) 53
Minstrel 4, 6
Music Halls 127-133
Muller, Maximillian 17

National Association of Youth Circus 195
National Centre for Circus Arts (see also
    Circus Space) 199
New Circus 195-195
New Spring Gardens 21, 22, 35

Old Hats Public House 35
Olympia (Exhibition Hall) 141, 151-153,
    160, 163-167, 170, 172, 179, 184, 189
Olympic Pavillion, The 49

Pantalone (see also Pantaloon) 28, 29
Pantaloon (see also Pantalone) 30
Parker, John 44
Pawe's American Circus 113
Paulo's (Circus) 170, 177, 179
Pedlar, Arthur Vercoe 182-183
Pepys, Samuel 14, 18, 21, 22
Petronius 4
Pidcock 55
Pidcock's Menagerie 55
Pierrot 30
Pinder G. 147
Pinder W. (and sons) 156, 170
Placido 24
Pleasure Gardens 19-26
Polcinello 29
Poliakoff, Nikolai (see also Coco the
    Clown) 175
Polito's Menagerie 53, 56, 57, 60, 61
Polito, Stephanus 55, 56, 57, 60, 62

Poses Plastique 73
Powell's (Circus) 79
Price, Mr 35, 36
Purchase's Menagerie 148
Purdy Brown, Joshua 100

Quinn, Johnie 136, 140

Rahere 14
Ranelagh Gardens 22, 23
Rapide Brothers, The (see also Izzo &
    Malteser) 199-200
Rastelli 160
Redige, Paul 24
Rickett's Art Pantheon and Amphitheatre
    44
Ricketts, John Bill 44, 45, 100
Ringling Barnum and Bailey (Circus) 152
Ringling Brothers 71, 110, 116
Risley Act 39
Robert Brothers (Circus) 183
Robertson, D. W. 160
Rosaires (Circus) 156, 170, 171, 177, 179
Royal Agricultural Hall, The 91, 92, 95,
    109, 156, 171
Royal Circus, The 43, 44, 45, 75
Royal Grove, The 26, 42, 43, 45
Royal Italian Circus, The 141, 148
Royal Menagerie, The 55, 56, 57, 60
Royal Victory Circus, The 160
Rudolph Truzi Circus, The 176

Sadler's Wells 24
Sampson, Mr 35
Samwell's Circus 53
Sandow, Eugene 163
Sands, Richard 111
Sandwina, Katie (see also Katie
    Brumbach) 155, 161-164
Sanger (Circus) 89, 90, 91, 93, 97, 124,
    138, 140, 141, 144, 169, 171, 172, 177,
    181
Sanger, George 90-99, 109, 114, 133

Sanger, John (Jnr) 142, 149, 159, 179
Sanger, John (Snr) 90
Saqui, Madame 23-26
Sarrasani (Circus) 164
Saunders' (Circus) 53
Sells 'Brothers (Circus) 107, 109, 110
Skelton, Thomas 12
Skylight Circus Arts 199
Smart, Billy 180, 186, 189, 191
Smith & Gibbs Circus 114
Sommers, Will 12
Southwark Fair 14, 16, 18, 19
Spinacutti 24
Sprake's (Circus) 79
Stone & Murray (Circus) 109
Stratton, Charles (see also General Tom
    Thumb) 102
Sylvain Brothers, The 171

Tarleton, Richard 12
Taudivin, Mr 68
Tarrazarney's United Empire Circus 169
Tayleure's Circus 114
Tom Fossett's Diabolo Circus 156
Tourniaire's Royal Amphitheatre 88
Transfield (Circus) 114

Trimalchio 4
Troubadours 4, 6
Tyers, Jonathan 22

Van Amburgh, Isaac (see also The Lion
    King) 65-69, 71
Vauxhall Gardens 22, 26
Vercoe the Clown (see also Arthur Vercoe
    Pedlar) 182-183
Victoria, Queen 68, 89, 92, 95, 97, 102
Violante 17
Volpres Circus 170

Wallett, William 53, 80, 85
Washington Myer, James 114
West, James 76
Whimsical Walker 132
Wild Animals in Circus Bill 193
Wild's (Circus) 53
Wombwell, George 57, 62
Wombwell's Menagerie and Circus 57,
    58, 59, 61, 91

Youth Circus 194-196

Zippo's Circus 201, 204